Edith Wharton's
Brave New Politics

Dale M. Bauer

The University of Wisconsin Press

The University of Wisconsin Press
114 North Murray Street
Madison, Wisconsin 53715

3 Henrietta Street
London WC2E 8LU, England

5   4   3   2   1

Printed in the United States of America

Library of Congress Cataloging-in-Publication Data
Bauer, Dale M., 1956–
    Edith Wharton's brave new politics / Dale M. Bauer.
    244 p.   cm.
    Includes bibliographical references and index.
    ISBN 0-299-14420-8.   ISBN 0-299-14424-0 (pbk.)
    1. Wharton, Edith, 1862–1937—Political and social views.
  2. Political fiction. American—History and criticism.
  3. Politics, and literature—United States—History.
  4. Feminism and literature—United States—History.
  5. Women and literature—United States—History.
  6. Sex role in literature. 7. Women in literature.
  I. Title.
  PS3545.H16Z58   1995
  813'.52—dc20   94-13432

To my mother and father,
Dorothy and Daniel Bauer

Love me, love my Pekinese,
'Spite of your antipathies,
If you want to cultivate me,
Gotta love Cheeky.
> —Cole Porter, 1936,
> "Love Me, Love My Pekinese"

Contents

Preface

This is a book about the second half of Edith Wharton's career and a method of reading I describe as "cultural dialogics." I take my title for this study of Wharton's late fictions from the 1932 dystopian classic, *Brave New World,* recognizing her pride in the fact that Aldous Huxley acknowledged her anti-eugenics novel *Twilight Sleep* (1927) as a precursor to his most famous work. My title suggests a number of cultural references, but, most important, it signifies how the second half of Wharton's career differed from the first in its self-conscious attention to the politics of culture. In establishing the primacy of this concern, I also want to link Wharton to a group of popular writers in the twenties and thirties who actively debated the future of the world, including the future of fiction. As Sinclair Lewis wrote to her in June of 1931, the "three new young Americans"—Ernest Hemingway, Thomas Wolfe, and William Faulkner—represented a new force: "This last, Faulkner, is a new hurdle which every professional intellectual has to jump. . . . Mostly, I don't know what he is talking about, and his rapes and seductions are a little, for me, too much like medical manuals" (Lilly Library). Although Wharton often denied any involvement in politics and propaganda, she nevertheless debated—as what Lewis called a "professional intellectual"—their status in literature with authors like Lewis, Anita Loos, and even, indirectly, Carl Van Vechten. In the end, her own politics, loosely associated with a set of social values she aligned with the possibilities for what Wharton called cultivating the "inner life" in an alienated culture, were fully articulated by the time she wrote *The Buccaneers.* As she writes in a 2 November 1936 letter to Edward Sheldon: "I am still pottering along with the Buccaneers . . . and I hope to finish it within the next few months. I also want to write one or two more short stories, but the world is so changed, and readers and reviewers belong to such a new breed, that I feel in despair at the lack of any interest or understanding in the inner life, which was the material of novelists in my day. I can think of lots of things I want to write about, but who will read me?" (Lilly Library).

Wharton entered the 1920s seeing herself, as one might expect, as a major figure in American and European letters. How could she have imagined that a generation of critics would see the Pulitzer Prize for *Age of Innocence* as a kiss of death rather than a validation of her new artistic

aspirations? How could she have predicted that her critics would generally dismiss the last seventeen years of her career as the weakest phase of
her achievement? For Wharton was seen by such diverse critics as Percy
Lubbock—in the first book devoted to her work, *Portrait of Edith Wharton* (1947)—and R. W. B. Lewis, in his groundbreaking biography, as
working with diminished powers and scattered attentions. Regardless of
how the novelist herself came to feel about the Pulitzer Prize (her caricature of Mrs. Jet Pulsifer, the literary matron of young male writers in the
1929 *Hudson River Bracketed,* gives us a clue of how she mocked it),
the recognition accompanying the prize marks a shift in her career and
the critical assessment of it.

The first half of Wharton's career may be described as generating a
certain way of reading her, one first developed out of the New Critical
model largely appropriated from reading Henry James (and thus made to
seem natural and fitting for Edith Wharton, too) and then later unwit-
tingly reconstructed by many feminist critics. The chapters that follow
offer both a reading of Wharton's late fiction and my own "use" of
Wharton (see Introduction). To that end, this study begins with her 1917
Summer and ends with her death in 1937, a twenty-year range which
brings Wharton to a brave new politics. This second half of her career
has been the less intensely studied one precisely because of the way that
Edith Wharton has been used by conservative and feminist critics arguing
specific agendas. I have developed a paradigm of reading that moves
away from the earlier emphasis on aesthetics, just as Wharton's focus
itself moved away from a strict preoccupation with form to her more
variable, but no less brilliantly achieved, immersion in mass culture.
Wharton was seldom interested in dedicating her fiction to social problems or in reflecting a specific reality, since she distrusted the ability of
"the big 'intelligent public'" to recognize the complexity of the relation
between political reform and narrative resolution (see Gribben 13). By
presenting these problems—of reproductive choice, personal affiliations,
and political allegiance—in dialogue with each other and through internal and social debates, Wharton offered her own reconstructed social
scene, relying much more than before on the mass culture around her to
explore the intricacy of her own antimodernism. While the first stage of
her career has given rise to formalist readings of Wharton's concerns, the
second half, which I explore here, calls for a different way of reading her
more elaborate understanding of culture. Therefore, the changes in Wharton's style and in our own different literary concerns prompted my analysis of Wharton's "cultural dialogics," a theory of her late fictions that
suggests how her writing configured the mass culture around her as

another "voice" in the representation of an orchestrated, and carefully controlled, dialogue.

Many critics have found the first half of Wharton's career, from *House of Mirth* (1905) through *The Age of Innocence* (1920), as her defining era, with the second half falling short by comparison to her brilliant critical successes in *The House of Mirth, Ethan Frome* (1911), and *The Custom of the Country* (1913). The thematic pointedness of those books disappears in the late fictions. Even her earlier novel devoted to social ills, *The Fruit of the Tree* (1907), fails to weave together the complicated issues of reform, scientific engineering, and medicine and the effects of these on the inner lives of the main characters. That novel focuses on the binary opposites of labor and leisure, devolving into what Sinclair Lewis generally describes as "undigested chunks of theorizing" in the letter to Wharton quoted above. When her aesthetic of concentrating public meaning in the private search for intimate fulfillment does not falter, as it does in *The Fruit of the Tree,* Wharton's books can be thematized as triumphant "feast[s] of words," Cynthia Griffin Wolff's fine phrase for Wharton's delight in aesthetic form and beauty. Yet the second half of the novelist's career cannot be summarized as neatly, for the novels of this period offer a vision of the interrelation of intimate and inner life with the political ambiguities of mass culture.

The chapters of the present volume are not apologies for the "lesser works" that supposedly resulted from Wharton's benighted effort to write popular fiction after 1920, novels interesting only because Wharton wrote them and useful only because they show the superiority of her earlier achievement. As I will argue here, Wharton's late fictions reveal an author hungrier than ever for fame and critical acclaim, as well as for a wider audience than she had even imagined during the advent of her career. Wharton celebrated both her marketability and her controversiality insofar as both of these traits seemed so removed from the label of "lady novelist" that critics associated with her then and even now (see Showalter 145–46). It seems to come as a surprise that, as one critic recently argued, "Wharton was a fiend for advertising and promotion. . . . Between her demands and her demurs, Wharton became the very model of a market-wise, talented 'problem author'" (Aronson, *NY Times Book Review,* 2 January 1994, p. 7). While these remarks primarily concern the first half of Wharton's career, they are even truer about the later novels addressing contemporary issues in mass culture, topics that Wharton believed would assure her a wider readership if her novels were advertised more accurately. My aim is to show how her challenge to the narcissism of the "new America" which she found in the twenties and to her fears of an authoritarian culture in the thirties signal a brave new politics: her new purposes emerged in the teens, especially in *Summer* (1917), and were most clearly visible in *The Mother's Recompense* (1925) and *Twilight Sleep* (1927), culminating in her last novel, *The Buccaneers* (published posthumously and unfinished in 1938). In these works, Wharton envisioned a series of social crises that foreclosed the possibilities of fulfilling the "inner life," by which she meant the critical analysis of the social conditions that make intimacy possible in an overregulated, even Taylorized society. My study foregrounds those social or political anxieties Wharton addresses in 1917 and after, and in doing so I focus on how Wharton's narratives arrange and attempt to resolve her own cultural fears and ambivalence.

Part of the critical problem, I came to see, is that Wharton's late novels examine the interrelation of political and historical issues and their effect on intimate experience. No longer centered so much on creating imaginary characters, as in *House of Mirth* or *Custom of the Country,* these novels suggest that the "inner life" is best understood within a wider scope, a deeper consciousness of the dialogics of culture as well as character. One may, as Elizabeth Ammons and Candace Waid do, try to thematize this move away from characters by calling attention to an organizing anxiety like the challenge of motherhood, but any such theme is likely to ignore some other topic Wharton sees in relation to it. I have avoided this temptation to read Wharton as political allegorist, despite the fact that her ironical self-rendering as "Edith Agonistes" lends credence to her own tendency to do so. I argue, instead, for the prominence in Wharton's late career of the rhetorical context of the debates into which Wharton entered in the twenties and thirties. Her novels conduct cultural conversations, what Steven Mailloux calls "rhetorical exchanges," in addressing eugenics, the "revolt of modern youth," the rising tide of individualism, and the emerging Italian fascism and German nationalism. Even within these new contexts of debate, Wharton does not rely on her old style of authorial engagement. While *The House of Mirth* presents internal dialogues and multiple voices of social positions, especially about gender and class, as I argued in *Feminist Dialogics* (1988), her late novels no longer rely on internal dialogue, ventriloquism, or multivocality as the marks of authorial style. Rather, Wharton's late style exhibits more ambivalence than irony because her plots develop unresolved ideological conflicts rather than tragic conclusions. In short, the readings that follow show how Wharton's late fictions were engaged with the most heated and fractious arguments concerning the rise of social scientific discourse, the power of mass culture, and the replacement of the cult of personality over "character," that nineteenth-century locus of hereditary qualities that Wharton had once assumed was immutable.

In this book, I move away from the Bakhtinian terms I used in *Feminist Dialogics* to describe Wharton's style, in large part because I see this phase of Wharton's career as so markedly different from the first half. Bakhtin's explanatory terms do not adequately describe Wharton's immersion in the contemporaneous rhetoric of politics and ethics, along with her engagement with the ascendant rhetoric of intimacy as the end result of the drive for personality. Although I do not claim Wharton as an early feminist, I see in her new politics an intense, sometimes painful, confrontation with her own presuppositions and expectations. As I explain in Chapter Two, the Wharton who declares a preference for Anita Loos's *Gentlemen Prefer Blondes* over Carl Van Vechten's *Nigger Heaven*, and satire over propaganda, comes to realize that such inclinations carry with them definite social consequences. Thus, "Edith Agonistes" emerges in the thirties as a writer who planned to lead her readers to a more contested cultural territory.

Perhaps Wharton would be alternately pleased with and uncertain about her current cachet: I have recently seen her name in *Vogue*, in a *New Yorker* cartoon, even a *New York Times* article about women's power lunches (17 November 1993). These references at least suggest that she has become part of the mass culture whose emergence she had so vigorously resisted in the twenties. Whatever Wharton has been accused of—elitism, anti-Midwestern prejudice, anti-radicalism, and nostalgic utopianism—her name carries with it the kind of cultural capital associated with a stable social order, like Osric Dane's in the Lunch and Culture Club Wharton lampoons in "Xingu." In the middle of the new enthusiasm for Wharton, when her popularity comes from her status as an icon of a by-gone era rather than as a writer devoted to the most pressing problems of her day, it is important to recognize how Wharton's confrontation with the difficulties and responsibilities of political choices—in eugenics, narcissism, even fascism and totalitarianism— makes her late fictions as exhilarating and contemporary as they are.

Permission has been granted to reprint material that first appeared, in somewhat different versions, in other places: Chapter Three appeared in *Arizona Quarterly* 45.1 (Spring 1989): 49–71. Copyright © 1989 by the Arizona Board of Regents. Chapter Five appeared in *College English* 50.6 (October 1988). Copyright © 1988 by the National Council of Teachers of English. Reprinted with permission. The cover photograph and the previously unpublished letters by Wharton are reprinted by permission of the author and the Watkins/Loomis Agency. I am also grateful to the staff at The Beinecke Rare Book and Manuscript Collection at Yale University, especially Patricia Willis and Ellen Cordes, and the Lilly Library at Indiana University, where Heather Munroe generously gave her time and attention. I also want to thank Miami University for a faculty leave in the Fall of 1989 and the University of Wisconsin–Madison for a leave in the Fall of 1991, two semesters which allowed me time to work at the Beinecke Library, Yale University, and the Lilly Library, Indiana University. A University of Wisconsin Vilas Research Fellowship generously supported me during 1992–1994. I also owe a debt of gratitude to my first-rate research assistant, Richard Schur.

While many friends and colleagues have offered invaluable help throughout, no acknowledgement of their generosity can begin to account for these debts. At Holy Cross, I had two unselfish colleagues in Pat Bizzell and Steve Vineberg, who guided me through earlier versions and plans for this book. Tom Byers and Susan Griffin at the University of Louisville; Susan Jarratt and Kris Straub, during the years when we were all at Miami University; and, at various conferences and through correspondence, Diane Price Herndl, Carol Holly, Colleen Kennedy, Susan Jaret McKinstry, Judith Roof, Pat Sharpe, Annette Zilversmit, and Lynda Zwinger have all offered insightful criticism and encouragement. Andy Lakritz continues to influence my work in surprising and thoughtful ways. Robin Grey, Elaine Orr, and particularly Priscilla Wald were sympathetic readers of many chapters and influenced my thinking about the way to write American literary history. At Wisconsin, I am grateful to my American literature classes, English 619 (on Henry James, Edith Wharton, and Charlotte Perkins Gilman) and English 217, with Phil Gould. My colleagues Tom Schaub and Sargent Bush, two exemplary readers, provided me with direction at crucial periods in my writing. Three colleagues and friends in Madison, Sarah Zimmerman, Judy Berman, and especially Susan Bernstein, gave me their careful critical attention. Susan read every chapter, sometimes two or three times, and the revisions were made all the easier by her playful and pointed critiques. Ann Ardis and Mary Pinard have always provided great advice about academic writing and criticism; they gave me the kind of intellectual and emotional support truly good friends offer.

I also want to thank Barbara Hanrahan for introducing me to the joys of working with the University of Wisconsin Press, and to Allen Fitchen and Rosalie Robertson, Betty Steinberg, and Mary Elizabeth Braun, for their dedication and zeal. Sylvan Esh guided me through the last stages of the process with patience and intelligence.

Jane Marcus gave helpful comments on the *Twilight Sleep* chapter, and Bill Cain read the manuscript with his usual enthusiasm and care. They both exemplify the spirit of professional unselfishness. To my teachers—Wolfgang Iser and Eric Solomon—I owe my thanks for inspiring my excitement in the intersections of narrative and culture.

To Gordon Hutner, I give my love and gratitude for bringing his indefatigable energy and intelligence to my work. No friend or partner could provide more love or more joy.

Edith Wharton's
Brave New Politics

Introduction

One of the dominant questions which informs my work, both here and in feminist theory, concerns what motivates women to align themselves in various communities, whether as feminists, liberals, right-wingers, essentialists, or otherwise. This question arises out of the hotly debated theoretical issue of identification, or the ways in which vicarious alignment with cultural figures or characters seems to fulfill psychological needs and provide pleasures, usually through fantasy. In studying culture, we need to understand why people identify as they do and why they align themselves with different cultural movements as well as with various representations. Recent studies, such as Kathleen Blee's *Women of the Klan* and Claudia Koonz's *Mothers in the Fatherland,* have sought to explain why some women have identified their aspirations with reactionary or totalitarian organizations. Cultural theorists today—from Constance Penley on starzine fans, to Paul Smith on Clint Eastwood, to John Guillory on cultural capital—all discuss a similar process of identification, by which readers or viewers are induced to align themselves imaginatively with characters, with movements, with icons. To that end, I ask: Why does Wharton identify herself ambivalently as a social analyst, sometimes as an antimodernist, and, just as often, as a liberal cultural critic?

Divided as they were between her desire to preserve the vitality of the "inner life" and her agonistic stance toward fascistic and authoritarian culture of the thirties, Wharton's own allegiances to culture were variously split. Rather than call Wharton a feminist reader or writer whose politics were consistently progressive, I would say that her ambivalence in reading and writing culture is crucial to understanding why and how she is compelled to reorient her fiction in post-World War I culture. Her ambivalence emerges from her clear-sighted acknowledgment that the past was not utopian and her recognition that the present and the future are, for her, mired in incredible political and social follies such as the eugenics movement, fascism, and Nazism.

Throughout this book I use Wharton's politics to illuminate the last twenty years of her life, a move some might see as consistent with the aims of New Historicism. Yet, following Carolyn Porter, I also ask how we can know when we are being "historical enough": Is there any historical context that would completely illuminate the twists and turns of Wharton's late career? In response, I would suggest that this book is an extension of what I term cultural dialogics, the varying intensity of a writer's engagement with material history as revealed through the layers of cultural references with which a writer deepens her work; moreover, cultural dialogics reveals how internalized the cultural voices are even as the writer interprets and evaluates their directives in orchestrating among cultures a "dialogic encounter" (see Bakhtin 7). Like Ammons in her influential study *Edith Wharton's Argument With America,* I too see Wharton engaged in an argument with a "new America." This argument includes international and sexual politics, but it is not merely two-sided. It includes a myriad of positions, a shifting ground of claims about culture and narrative.

One way to see the argument of this logic is to explore the implications of Wharton's narrative strategy in intertwining the politics of countries with the politics of intimacy, as well as with her self-consciousness about authorship. As Amy Kaplan posits about Wharton's "profession of authorship," the novelist labored to "write herself out of the private domestic sphere and to inscribe a public identity in the marketplace" (67). Kaplan aims to "contest both the traditional view of Wharton as an antimodernist and the recent feminist criticism which too often equates the dilemma of her women characters, entrapped in the domestic realm, with that of the writer herself." She sees this as a "dynamic and often unresolved conflict," which fueled Wharton's career from amateur into professional writer (68).

Even this innovative reading of Wharton's career—devoted to undermining what Kaplan calls the dyadic boundaries between private and public, feminine and masculine, home and business—does not take into account Wharton's comprehension of the cultural work fiction performs. Kaplan's view of Wharton is limited by its reliance on reading Wharton in opposition to traditional *literary* history: the "gentlemen of letters" (68); "the sentimental or domestic novelists" (70); "female precursors such as George Sand, George Eliot, and Anna de Noailles" (74); or the "aggressive advertising of a growing publishing industry" which created literary "celebrities" (82). Despite her oppositional stance, Wharton's fiction was not restricted to literary precursors, but comprehended the ramifications of politics and mass culture arising within modern life.

Merely dismissing Wharton as antimodernist, a label suggesting uninterest in politics, wrongly erases Wharton's profound concern for changing her culture, which may even surpass her concern with authorship. The larger questions Wharton addressed were inherently theoretical ones, ones which targeted the source of her greatest ambivalence: what made people evade ethics and responsibility in order to embrace the easy solutions of scapegoating, evasion, cynicism, and denial of large social contradictions. Some of Wharton's critics frame the issue of antimodernism as her growing anxiety over a declining audience and her defiance of the ever-increasing tendency to replace elite culture with popular taste, an opposition she saw as destructive to the culture she wanted to promote. "Edith Agonistes," as my conclusion suggests, is her self-designed epithet for her ironically self-appointed role as the embattled savior of the "inner life."

The question of Wharton's profession of authorship, then, should account for the transition she undergoes in the twenty years from 1917 to 1937, the year of her death. Although she worried whether she could still sell her fiction, her concerns were no less than the matter of individual and mass identification of subjects with the various particular affiliations, ideologies, contradictions that mass culture had to offer. At first reluctantly and then cautiously, Wharton refused to imagine that the American self and culture were already inflexible or standardized. Her great hope for American culture was that it was *exactly* too independent, or "breezy," as she has it in *The Buccaneers,* to remain attached to any particulars, although its cultural *fixations,* such as the flapper, troubled her (355). In her late fiction especially, Wharton became increasingly keen on instructing her audience to remain malleable, since she seemed to imagine the culture rigidifying into dangerous postures.

Yet that is only one of her visions. The other was that fiction could change a reader's identifications with cultural icons. If mass culture could not be changed, then what could be improved was the process by which people learned how to respond to mass culture and to adopt alternative values. By depicting characters who struggle to adopt new values for new cultural situations, particularly the increasing speed of cultural production, Wharton provides models to challenge the trend to quick cultural adaptation or what was coined "assimilation." Pauline Manford of *Twilight Sleep* (1927), a woman who adapts to all of the options available to her, as contradictory as they are, is her countermodel. Kate Clephane of *The Mother's Recompense* (1925) cannot adapt, but Wharton is no less sympathetic with that "failure" than she is to Pauline Manford's "success." Aldous Huxley's praise of Wharton's stand against the galvanizing issue of the teens and twenties, eugenics, is one mark of her new attitude toward history (see Chapter Three, below); another is her identification with women who are confronting the demands of modernity to motherhood, erotic companionship, and the "new narcissism" of flapperhood. And in this suppleness and intensity I find Wharton's new politics brave.

The courage of her politics is not just to be found in Wharton's rejection of the eugenics movement and other fascistic means of social control or engineering. Nor is it her reevaluation of the advertising culture and its pervasive reshaping of values, the subject of Chapter Four, which could just as easily be interpreted (and has been) as reactionary. What is brave is that, in her late works, she advocates a position that amounts to a new theoretical model of readerly identification; Wharton invents new ways of investing sympathetically in characters who are bewildered about and struggling to find niches in modernity. Her protest is lodged in her challenge to modern, post-war culture's ways of incorporating selves—Althusser's interpellation—into the vast hegemony of commodities and mass culture. Wharton realized that this cooptation could only be altered, not rejected. Hence, she was not merely an oppositional critic or a reactionary one, but one who understood that an absorption in culture was one sole way to engage its processes. I want to show how Wharton indeed immersed herself in her times, anticipating as she did Adorno's insistence in *Minima Moralia* that "one must have tradition in oneself to hate it properly," rather than simply retreating into nostalgia as so many of her interpreters have supposed. Her argument with American culture may be targeted at topics now too specific to her time to make immediate sense, but her intervention into that culture's process of identification was precisely the issue at stake during her late career when she created characters who challenged the personal and psychological politics of the American century.

One distinction is necessary: the new objects and status of culture in and of themselves—film, psychoanalysis, drugs like twilight sleep, even celebrityhood, among others—symptomized how culture operated upon the individual to erase the "inner life." Substituted in its place was the outer life, the life of standardized and commodified beauty, taste, culture. Her "uses" of cultural references to eugenics, to Fordism, Taylorism, Billy Sunday, Mary Baker Eddy, New Thought—all indicate that these were ways to integrate the subject into the new symbolic, indeed specular, order of culture. This specular order manipulated the outer life, but ignored the inner life which her fiction sought to preserve. "Edith Agonistes" took on the new temples and new Pharisees of modern life.

In her autobiography, *A Backward Glance* (1933), Wharton describes her worries about modernity even before World War I, in reaction to Henry James's late phase. We can see Wharton's preoccupation with "atmosphere" as the grounds for developing subjectivity, but it takes a turn different from the serious encounter of master and pupil. At least five times in *A Backward Glance* she repeats that James's great virtue was his "quality of fun—often of sheer abstract 'fooling'—" (179). In James, she found someone to share her sense of irony: a "common sense of fun . . . first brought about our understanding. The real marriage of true minds is for any two people to possess a sense of humour or irony pitched in exactly the same key" (173). She also found in James one who could give her "a huge laugh," at his "silver-footed ironies, veiled jokes, tiptoe malices" (178). Their shared ironies lead her to some disappointment in his major phase: "And one result of the application of his theories puzzled and troubled me. His latest novels, for all their profound moral beauty, seemed to me more and more lacking in atmosphere, more and more severed from that thick nourishing human air in which we all live and move" (190). Just as Henry James bid Wharton to profit early in her career from his negative example when he urged her to "do" New York, so she found the memory of his later example equally instructive. This criticism suggests Wharton's theory of her own late—and her own major—phase: the artist cannot isolate "in a Crookes tube for our inspection" characters that must engage in the world (190). The atmosphere alone, the "thick nourishing air," is less important than the "living and moving" in it; the writer must develop the irony and sympathy necessary to provide an alternative to the alienation James would take as his subject in his major phase. "I can only say that the process [of story-telling], though it takes place in some secret region on the sheer edge of consciousness, is always illuminated by the full light of my critical attention" (205). For Wharton, the secret to successful writing was the fun—both humor and irony, satire and parody—injected into the conscious and unconscious processes of critical attention.

Since Wharton could keep that atmosphere nourishing, rather than stultifying, she accomplished what even the Master could not do. Far from the aestheticization of life that constituted James's experiment, Wharton's attempt is something altogether different: the immersion in cultural experience, even alien experience, paradoxically to avoid alienation. Finally, from James, Wharton learns the dangers of a detached vision, one that perpetuated the habits of acquisitive and enterprising Americans divorced from the modern world. In contrast to what Wharton perceives as James's centrifugality, she articulates a "very different" motive energizing her first attempts: "My idea of a novel was . . . something far more compact and centripetal . . ." (205). This force is first found in The *House of Mirth* (1905), when she connects private and public domains, but can most fully be seen at work in her last, unfinished novel, *The Buccaneers*, which I examine at the end of this study. I trace the direction of Wharton's "centripetal" force as she turns her attention to the social world around her.

Wharton's Late Career

A daughter's "dark inheritance" from her mother is a recurring theme in Wharton's fiction, in short stories like "The Other Two," "Roman Fever," and "Autres Temps . . ."—from which the phrase comes—and in novels like *The Reef* (1912). Almost all of her fiction from the 1920s involves the effects of the mother's inheritance and the mother's culpability for her daughter's pain, an inheritance that is not simply financial, psychological, or social. What Wharton calls in *The Reef* (1912) "the blundering alchemy of Nature" in relation to inherited qualities, was also more popularly studied in eugenics, the social science of controlling birth patterns (96). In their own way, Wharton's novels grappled with such new social sciences as biological racism and scientific sexism, which proliferated in Reconstruction-era social discourse. By focusing on the psychological and social heredity between generations of women, Wharton entered into the heated controversies of the period about the meanings of the categories of race and gender, as well as the new social designations of eugenic and dysgenic societies. Later works, like *The Children* (1928), are also preoccupied with the transmission of genes, with breeding, and with taste, but Wharton's larger concern about totalitarian politics overshadowed such fears about degenerating cultural values. These late novels address post-World War I cultural politics, while showing how her earlier obsession with kinship structures is gradually transformed into a focus on the alienation of the individual. The growing legislation of private life, under the aegis of progressivism, troubled Wharton. Her work becomes increasingly critical of mass culture and its evasion of the emotional, moral, and spiritual concatenation of feelings that she referred to as the "inner life," a pattern in Wharton's novels Carol Wershoven described in 1982. Irritated by the new technology, Wharton yearned for something beyond the titillations of mass culture. The Emersonian motto of Lily Bart's stationery in *The House of Mirth* (1905)—"Beyond!"—becomes Wharton's unspoken, perhaps unacknowledged search for authenticity, for what Jackson Lears defines as the "unproblematic immediacy in personal as well as artistic expression."[1]

When I began writing about Edith Wharton's politics, in her "Roman Fever" (1934) and in *Twilight Sleep*, I wanted to reclaim Wharton's status as a woman of the world, someone deeply knowledgable about and involved in the political scene around her. I had in mind a reading of Wharton's gender politics in the context of international politics of her time, namely fascism and Nazism. Subsequent research in Wharton's late novels, from *Summer* through *The Buccaneers,* confirmed my sense of her significant interest in such totalitarian anxieties as reproductive politics in general, and eugenics regulations in particular. The symbolic incest about which she writes and her concern, in fiction like *The Old Maid* and "Roman Fever," about the legitimacy of children attest to her attraction for taboo subjects.[2] Less a biographical study than a cultural one, the chapters that follow demonstrate Wharton's side-taking in debates about social and sexual license. Ultimately, she feared the latter far less than she did the social repressions and control which were the focus of her earlier fictions like *The House of Mirth* (1905) and *Ethan Frome* (1911). This social control was taken to its extreme in the eugenics movement, which she likened to the Inquisition.

This book explores Wharton's engagement with the cultural meanings and purposes of the early twentieth-century eugenics movements and the new social sciences, many of which rationalized racialist thinking under the guise of late nineteenth-century expansionism and early twentieth-century social reform. Moreover, I take the new value for mapping culture, rather than simply critiquing it, as the premise of Wharton's late style. Cultural dialogics is a way of reading fiction as a stratification of dialogues with the authoritative notions, ideas, values of the day. Bakhtin's notion of cultural dialogism is also suggested by what Matei Calinescu calls "inner dialogy" or the "strange ability . . . of thinking against oneself" (90), of interrogating one's own values by imagining real alternatives to one's own. By thinking against herself, Wharton is able to expose the limitations of her culture, instead of carping at or arguing with it. So I want here to suspend traditional notions of Wharton's career and show the complex, ambivalent status of her fiction and its engagements: this often contradictory and perplexing involvement reveals a deepening response to the new cultural atmosphere of modernity which this genteel American writer is often accused of ignoring. Traditionally, Wharton's critics have been invested in her focus on manners and morals and have tended to dismiss her late fiction as sloppy, cranky, or uninteresting. Wharton has been characterized as the arbiter of an older generation's taste and undervalued for her treatment of the narcissistic and dangerous habits of a newer generation.

Consider how Wharton's late work has been dismissed or trivialized in literary histories. Frederick Hoffman, in *The Twenties* (1949), claims

Wharton was "insulted by history" (85). He repeats a common critical dismissal of her late novels as the norm: "Mrs. Wharton did return, many times, to the present—no aspect of the 1920s failed to get her attention—but the results did not remotely equal her earlier work" (Hoffman 51); "Her recent books, since *The Age of Innocence,* have been of rather inferior interest" (Wilson 326). Wharton's writings about the war were referred to as "ladylike but cogent magazine pieces" (Furnas 232). One of her harshest critics, the popular writer and twenties social critic, Carl Van Vechten, contrasts the California writer Gertrude Atherton to Wharton in reviewing Atherton's popular 1923 novel *Black Oxen:* "Between writers of natural temperament and genius, however exaggeratedly they may express themselves, and careful artisans who know how to give their work at least the appearance of art, I cast my vote in favor of the former. . . . Usually (not always, to be sure) the work of Mrs. Wharton seems to me to be scrupulous, clever, and uninspired, while that of Mrs. Atherton is often careless, sprawling, but inspired. Mrs. Wharton, with some difficulty, it would appear, has learned to write; Mrs. Atherton was born with a facility for telling stories" (Van Vechten 1923, 194). Van Vechten's point is that Wharton, in their own day, is "mistakenly" heralded as a finer, more cultivated writer than Atherton, whose less artful tales, he submits, are "likely to outlive any of the works of Mrs. Wharton, aside from 'Ethan Frome'" (196).

Carl Van Vechten's attack on Wharton, which he repeats in his 1926 *Nigger Heaven,* resonates with the general trend in mid-century Wharton criticism: that Wharton's novels of the twenties and thirties did not equal her novels of the teens. Mary Papke's *Verging on the Abyss* (1990) also charts Wharton's literary reputation, contending that Percy Lubbock's assessment in 1947 of Wharton's career held sway for years, along with Millicent Bell's study in 1965. As Papke argues, "Many 1960s critics . . . upheld to some degree the Jamesian domination theory, and it is only with the clearly Whartonian studies of the 1970s" that Wharton's literary stock rose (96). Another evaluation, in 1975, suggests the traditional limits by which she is now read: "Some of her late novels of manners, such as *Glimpses of the Moon* and *Twilight Sleep,* are simply not good books" (Lindberg 11). This aesthetic disregard misses Wharton's shift in focus during and after World War I, when she takes up explicit issues of cultural politics. More recently, James Tuttleton near-sightedly complains about "the feminist takeover of Edith Wharton," asserting that Wharton's principles "constitute a deliberate affirmation of conservative values" and that her belief in "received tradition . . . answered deep human needs" (13). A much more compelling, but still traditional, picture of Wharton emerges in Shari Benstock's imaginative study, *Women of the Left Bank*. Benstock describes Wharton's Paris salon life, where Wharton frequented "strongholds of 'bourgeois severity'" and practiced high bourgeois "decorum and *politesse*" (1986, 60–62). Benstock suggests that, by 1906, Wharton was seen in Paris by "a younger generation" as a "symbol of outmoded gentility"—a reputation she needed to live down in order to play up her marketability in mass-consumer culture. Benstock claims that salon life had no prestige in post-war culture, but does that mean it had no relation to cultural politics? I ask the question because Wharton critics have typically divorced her work from larger ideological issues implicit in the act of writing fiction. More recently, Benstock argues that Wharton's European and American lives cannot be easily separated and that "the emergence of the 'Modern,'" along with the tragedy of World War I, galvanized her critical and social energies (1993, 29). Wharton critics have denied her politics, in part because her views are often conflicting and in part because her work has not been read in light of the relevant intellectual debates of her day. Here, I want to argue for Wharton's connection to the political world around her, a connection her critics have often fervently denied or misrepresented.

Wharton's fictions debate individualism and familialism, among other public policies of the twenties and thirties; at the same time, they are self-reflexive about the compatibility of private life with an inconsistent public morality. She firmly believed that good or bad politics did not make great art, but that does not mean that she strove, as her heroine in *The Buccaneers* says, for the "beyondness of things." Like the motto of Lily Bart's stationery, the "beyondness of things" looks past the surface of culture, sometimes to history, sometimes to utopian possibilities for change. In this sense, Wharton is something of a critical utopian ethnographer, decoding New York society for her public, placing the unquestioned norms of her culture under scrutiny. Given her remarks in *The Custom of the Country* and *The Age of Innocence* about anthropology and the "tribes" of old New York, we can hear how Wharton drew on popular discussions of universalist and relativist claims for culture. Her fictions after *The Age of Innocence* produce a map of American society, particularly women's culture, which has been depreciated as Wharton's defense of elitism and conservatism, or a nostalgia for "old New York" social rituals. Her fictions are not studies of "primitive" society; Wharton had, in *The Age of Innocence,* only a few years before Margaret Mead's *Coming of Age in Samoa* and Bronislaw Malinowski's *Sex and Repression in Savage Society,* already dismantled the binary opposition between primitive and civilized cultures, by showing that civilized New York is as dependent upon rituals of exclusion and scape-goating as any other pattern of culture, and by portraying the "cultural elite" in much the same way as was typical of studies of family degeneracy popular from the 1880s to the 1920s (see Chapter One). One of the most quoted sentences in *The Age of Innocence* reveals part of her cultural perspective: "They all lived in a kind of hieroglyphic world, where the real thing was never said or done or even thought, but only represented by a set of arbitrary signs" (45). Wharton shows this "set of arbitrary signs," her social set, to be interpretable and thus open to demystification. She interprets the New York culture from within, opening up its often unarticulated norms to social, readerly inspection. Wharton makes a significant rhetorical move in her late fiction by backgrounding her critiques of repressive cultural norms and by foregrounding, instead, the consequences of mass culture and the anxieties it generates. After *The Age of Innocence,* Wharton is not so quick to dismiss the arbitrary signs of culture, but to adapt those signs to her own purposes.

In short, Wharton was sensitive to issues of interpretive power. What previous readers of Wharton's political fiction miss is that the "other" for her is not primarily the middle or lower class, but her own class. She implicates herself in that otherness, documenting her own alienation from the new post-war America which is her subject in the late novels. While in her earlier fiction she attacked the repressive constraints of American society, she now contends with a "new America" which is tolerant of everything, discriminating about nothing. I turn to Edith Wharton's late fictions in order to show how she faced history and, in particular, to address how her rhetorical stance has been misprised in American literary studies.[3]

In doing so, this book is neither a new historical study of Wharton's fiction nor a Bakhtinian reading of those fictions, although Bakhtin's work influences me here and elsewhere. Instead, this project demonstrates Wharton's immersion in a complexity of struggles that calls for a new method of reading her. I believe Wharton's fiction has been too narrowly circumscribed, her interests, often, too shallowly recounted. My investment here is in making an argument for Wharton's changing sense of culture and her many sources of discontents, but also for her many sources of fun, jokes, malices, and ironies. Reading Wharton's cultural dialogics is a way of analyzing her "thinking against herself" as repository of the ethics of the "old America," while simultaneously challenging what she calls in the 1925 novel, *The Mother's Recompense,* the "new America."

The Use and Abuse of Edith Wharton

Why does Wharton provide such a rich source for theoretical and historical interpretation? My answer to that question can be broached by looking at two recent social critics—one a psychoanalytic-feminist, the other
a Marxist—who have employed Wharton to their own ends. In writing
their own cultural texts, both Jane Gallop in *Reading Lacan* and Richard
Ohmann in *Politics of Letters* appropriate Edith Wharton and, specifically, *The Age of Innocence* as a touchstone for certain kinds of critical
experiences. First, Gallop recalls the end of the 1920 novel as a reflection
of her personal drama in going to meet Lacan. She claims that "reading
Lacan" compels her to read beyond the text and to learn to read as a way
of situating herself in the world (34). Reading Wharton exerts the same
sort of pull on her. Gallop has gone to Paris to meet Lacan; he is dying,
and she is dejected:

> I read the last chapter of Edith Wharton's *Age of Innocence.*
> An American is in Paris, outside the apartment building
> wherein dwells the woman he has long loved in his mind but
> not seen for thirty years. He is supposed to go up to see her,
> but he sits on a bench outside. . . . *The Age of Innocence* ends
> thus: he "got up slowly and walked back alone to his hotel." I
> thought I understood. He chose not to see her, understanding
> that in any case he could not really see her whom he had loved
> for so long. I felt a little better. (1987, 35)

What interests me here is Gallop's intense identification with Newland
Archer, with Wharton's renunciation of the "real" encounter for the
imaginary one with the lover. Wharton's novel, then, becomes the paradigm for Gallop's experience in (not) meeting Lacan. The imaginary
identification becomes "more real" than the encounter could be, given all
the anticipation of it. In reading her experience *through* Wharton, Gallop sees her romanticized yearning for Lacan as a necessary renunciation—like Newland Archer's or like Kate Clephane's in *The Mother's
Recompense.* She uses Wharton to show how desire outstrips attainment,
exceeding the satisfactions of the real. She demonstrates the Lacanian
principles of desire and lack, the imaginary and the symbolic, through
Wharton's fiction.

Richard Ohmann employs Wharton's *Age of Innocence* as the basis for
his lectures on incorporating theory into the literature classroom. In offering a historical materialist analysis to counter the capitalist mentality stu-

dents inherit from their culture, Ohmann presents Wharton as an ironic social critic. *The Age of Innocence,* he contends, is marked by social exclusions among the leisure class. Ohmann provides his class plan and lecture notes over five and a half pages, documenting his way of teaching the ideology Wharton explores and suggesting its sociological meaning:

> But we can't take this satire as the novel's main perspective. If we did, the novel would have only the slightest interest for most of us: OK, so these are trivial, self-important people with quaint mores; is that enough to keep us reading for 350 pages? (Not me.) Wharton's gentle mockery isn't the final word, because the novel's main characters are more generous and intelligent than what the satire mocks, and because the ethos of "New York" causes them pain and deprivation. One can mock the "system" (8), but one can't dismiss it, because it damages human beings. (119)

Ohmann goes on to describe his approach to the constricted values suggested by Wharton's fictive anthropology, which he employs to teach historical and theoretical consciousness to his students. Like Gallop, Ohmann reads through his personal experience of identification with Newland Archer in order to suggest the values beyond individualism, free market economics, and capitalist ideology. Thus, Ohmann advocates an *ethos* through reading Wharton.

I am not setting up these "uses" to contrast them or to show how limited they are next to a reading of Wharton's cultural dialogism. Rather, they show, I think, the range of approaches to Wharton that has replaced the view of her as nonpolitical aesthete and social elitist. In the following chapters, I also put Wharton to my own use, expounding Wharton's reactions to the debates about reproductive rights and technology she inherited from Victorian American culture and its legacy to American modernism—and to the larger fascist movement in both European and American culture. Wharton's late novels—from 1917 to 1937—offer a cultural dialogics which, I hope, does "justice" again to Wharton as intellectual historian and critic (see Ozick 17).

Unlike Gallop or Ohmann, my interest in Wharton is less psychoanalytic or pedagogical and more cultural. I demonstrate how disquieted she was by culture and by her unresolved debates with it. Perhaps the 1913 novel *Custom of the Country* offers the best case for a dialogical reading of Wharton's attitude toward culture. The novel is most famous for its savage irony about the "customs" of marriage in the United States as the only way for young women to rise. Wharton repeatedly invokes American culture and its sign systems: the Masonic lodge and emblems of Abner Spragg (77, 136, 178, 188); the Christian Science that the hotel women at Skog Harbour, Maine, discuss, along with the Subliminal (35); the "aboriginal" and middle-class New York of Ralph Marvell's youth and the primitive Elmer Moffatt of Undine's youth (45, 133); and Bowen, the sociologist manqué of American customs (161). Wharton intertwines all of these concerns about "modern" culture in the great category of "anthropophagi," her project being to decipher the text of American customs (303). Until 1920, Wharton's greatest concern is the family as the "fetish" of modern life (289), a fetish that has its roots in the contemporaneous discussions of race and race suicide, since Wharton's world was just beginning to see race as a biologically specific category and not, as Wharton had more loosely used the term, as a line of descent. Undine is confronted with Raymond de Chelles's family and their desire to "continue the race" (272). Undine, however, refuses to take the racial argument into account, another example of her penchant for temporizing.

As Christopher Herbert posits in *Culture and Anomie* (1991), the "anthropological idea of culture" emerged in the nineteenth century (1). The emphasis on "customs of a country" provides just such an example of this new consciousness: marriage and divorce rites are assumed to represent the signs of a cultural reality just as much created and enforced as any fiction. Fiction, like culture itself, is a set of symbols, ostensibly leading to a "complex whole" (19). But if poststructuralism has taught us anything, it is that these "complex wholes" are of a deliberate critical construction. Herbert claims that the "myth of a state of ungoverned human desire" (29) with which cultures are juxtaposed is an equally compelling myth. Hence, the "primitive" (and the anthropological interest in savage cultures) is a way to stave off the fear that civilized culture is, after all, just another fiction. Such demythologizing, Herbert suggests, leads to ideological double-thinking, along with incredible ambivalence about the repression that sustains culture. Making a fetish of familial culture, as Wharton's old New York families do, allows their terror of ungoverned passions to be contained. The rhetoric of "continuing the race" and suppressing the "primitive" are parallels to the emerging psychoanalytic, sexological, and eugenic discourses circulating in pre-war culture. By the time of the publication of *Age of Innocence*, however, the kinship structures of modern life no longer preoccupy Wharton; her interest in this particular fetish plays itself out, but she turns from this approach to culture to one that is much more complex, because dialogical.

Wharton is deeply ambivalent both about the unchecked desires and

about the renunciation of desire (or "willfully purging one's self of desire") that high culture demands (Herbert 33). Herbert's insight in this
context is important: "The intense cultivation of desire and the vigilant
repression of it cannot merely have alternated as disjunctive phases in
nineteenth-century life, but must have been inseparably locked together
in a culture that in fact fostered desire as powerfully as it did puritanical
repression, and must have generated as a result no small quotient of
tension and ambivalence" (35). In the nineteenth-century anthropological model, culture functions as an imposed restraint upon the primitive
and unlimited impulses and desires. Wharton had a genius for separating
out these intertwined cultural imperatives: in one character, Undine, she
represents untrammeled desire; in another, Moffatt, "primitive" unchecked self-aggrandizement; in a third, Marvell, the unstable contest
between desire and repression. Undine herself is attracted to the primitive in Elmer Moffatt and marries him several times. She exemplifies the
Victorian's fixation with unchecked desires; only fungible commodities
and serial intimacies can temporarily satisfy these new desires.

Beth Kowaleski-Wallace has argued that the typical identificatory
reading sides with the son Paul Marvell, whose birthday party Undine
forgets. We read by our identification with the child and the husband,
who mirror for us the tension between desire and renunciation so embedded in modernist culture. Kowaleski-Wallace's essay rightly questions the
internalization of this binary structure, since it is precisely the one that
Wharton's fictions explode. Wharton shows the "primitive" to be lodged
in highbrow culture, even if she cannot—because of her own ideological
blindness—show the "civilized" in lowbrow life. Wharton speculates on
the cultural machinery that keeps these forces in operation. One could
argue, according to the degenerationalist anthropology common in the
teens and twenties and linked to fears of "race suicide," that Moffatt's
introjection into New York society, like Undine's, causes its infelicitous
genetic permutations. Degenerationalist anthropology took as its mission
the exposition of how cultural decline was initiated with the influx of
rural, immigrant, and African-American genes into the "native" American stock. Moffatt, as the primitive in society, mocks New York custom—
as he had once mocked Apex's Temperance Society by becoming drunk at
one of its meetings—by becoming the exemplar of opposing excess.
Wharton enjoys puncturing the culture's hypocrisies along class as well
as gender lines, and this is one of the greatest sources of pleasure in her
satire. On the Riviera, amid another instance of those hypocritical pretensions of hotel life, Undine vaguely contemplates the race consciousness thrust upon her by her new society:

> The inmates of the hotel were of different nationalities, but
> their racial differences were levelled by the stamp of a com-
> mon mediocrity. All differences of tongue, of custom, of phys-
> iognomy, disappeared in this deep community of insignifi-
> cance, which was like some secret bond, with the manifold
> signs and passwords of its ignorances and its imperceptions.
> It was not the heterogeneous mediocrity of the American
> summer hotel, where the lack of any standard is the nearest
> approach to a tie, but an organized codified dullness, in con-
> scious possession of its rights, and strong in the voluntary
> ignorance of any others. (205–6)

Wharton's scorn is saved for the "codified dullness" (in *The Children,* for
the "standardized beauty") of the Riviera set. Yet she herself is everywhere conscious of race—of the "coloured help" (178), of the popularity
of Negro music and Creole dishes (273), and of the "swarthy London
Merchant" (299–300)—and of the racial differences of the service class.
As we will see in the conclusion, the Negro minstrel show is a significant
detail in *The Buccaneers,* revealing Wharton's racial unconscious and the
limits of her bravery.

Race prejudices are very much the subject of Chapter Two, but I want
only to say here that they point to Wharton's larger problems with the
way class and gender inform private consciousness. Wharton grasped the
national craving for intimacy that consumed bourgeois realist fiction.
Relations with others took the place of cultivating one's self insofar as
the way to rise was by exploitation and manipulation of others. Undine
refuses to distinguish anyone by race or custom in their general "community of insignificance," but that is not because of some deep-seated egali-
tarianism. Rather, since there is no one with whom an intimate relation
might benefit her in her days after her divorce from Marvell, she instead
broods and fears associating with "the wrong people" (205). Undine's
search for authentic experience is not the unproblematic immediacy
Wharton was trying to invent for herself, say, with Morton Fullerton and
later with a number of other friends. Rather, Wharton sought to identify
a "community of significance" that was neither ignorant nor dull nor
homogeneous. That Wharton saw mass culture as all of these alerted her
to the necessity of creating a culture for her fiction and its values.

Wharton's Uses of Culture

Given Wharton's vested interests in portraying American culture from an anthropological perspective and in reinvigorating the culture of authenticity, of an "inner life," this book's focus is intricately tied to Wharton's cultural community. Wharton's fiction was deeply committed to shaping culture, by arguing with it—as Ammons has led the way in showing—and by challenging it. Because culture is a construct, Wharton sees it as open to change, with fiction a motivating agent of social transformation.

Even Wharton's pronouncements about the primitive, the savage, and the lowbrow were not simply personal, but part of a more general response to waning Victorian values. I have resisted looking for a consistent logic in Wharton's reactions to social issues and in the political interests of her fictions since her ambivalence makes her difficult, if not impossible, to pin down. The following chapters trace the patterns of culture that interested Wharton in her late career, patterns that repeatedly show she could no longer criticize American culture with the absolute certainty of her early fiction, in which her convictions were clearer because the patterns of culture were fully crystallized to her. By the war, she had clearly become too embroiled with and indebted to that society.

To demonstrate the earlier origins of such patterns, it is worth looking back to *The Reef* (1912), where Wharton explores the complications of an affair between a governess, Sophy Viner, and George Darrow, the 37-year-old diplomat about to be married to Sophy's employer, the widowed Anna Leath, with whom Darrow had been in love years ago. After the affair ends, Sophy becomes engaged to her employer's stepson, Owen Leath. Anna discovers Darrow's and Sophy's past connection and cannot overcome her reluctance to marry Darrow. As autobiographical as the novel is in its treatment of sexual involvements, their compromises and aftermath, *The Reef* is also filled with portentous comments about the state of international politics. Although the book is set in Britain, it deals head-on with the state of American foreign diplomacy at the time Wharton was writing the novel. The parochial American Adelaide Painter speaks of an impending international crisis in the same train of thought as her denunciation of the "enormities" of French servants (211). Darrow's profession as a diplomat is crucial for Wharton's purposes since it recalls the political stand of her beloved Morton Fullerton, the American journalist with whom Wharton had a passionate affair beginning in 1908 and sputtering to a close in 1911. In addition, Darrow so ineptly handles his affair with Sophy Viner and his impending marriage to Anna Leath that it again bears comparison with the brutish bumbling of Fullerton.

The pretext of the marriage plot is fixed on Darrow's assignment to South America from his present London diplomatic post. But why is he being sent to South America? And what is Wharton's interest in the "primitive" setting? Later she will return to this topos in *The Children* (1928), a novel in which Martin Boyne banishes himself for three years to Brazil, after his failed intimacies with Rose Sellars and Judith Wheater at the end of that novel. South America, Wharton suggests, and diplomatic history seems to corroborate, beckons to men of failed relationships. Darrow had requested the assignment as a means to study and publish about "certain economic and social problems" (117); he uses the diplomatic service as a means of distraction and a way of forcing the question of marriage to Anna.

Some of Wharton's most rigorous critics have read *The Reef* as an autobiographical meditation about Fullerton's influence on her sense of passion and fulfillment. Colquitt, Erlich, Keyser, Ammons, and Tuttleton are all persuasive on the connections and the exchange of letters and manuscripts between Fullerton and Wharton as a paradigm for the exchange between Anna and Darrow in the novel.[4] Gloria Erlich has argued that "Carnal knowledge crisscrossing these generational boundaries would make family life too claustrophobic for comfort. The drama that Darrow had selected for Sophy's introduction to Paris theater was *Oedipe*" (109). Seeing Anna and Sophy as "defining complementarities," Erlich contends that the novel works through Wharton's relation with Fullerton and the passionate knowledge she had gained (110). In the same vein, Cynthia Griffin Wolff's judgment of the novel is apt in this context of reading Wharton's novel as personal, not political: "What is central both in Wharton's life and in this novel is the *problem*: the immensely convoluted, many-sided problem of sexuality. . . . Yet there is a simultaneous sense that sexuality and aggression have their darker sides, even, at their roots, some hidden horror. . . . Individual 'right' is balanced inconclusively against social 'need'" (1977, 219). Seeing sexuality as an individual right—and not a larger force in culture—leads Wolff to suggest the fear of some "hidden horror" at the base of intimacy. I would argue, however, that Wharton raises instead the problem of victimization at the heart of casual affairs like Darrow's with Sophy and of international affairs like the Monroe Doctrine. Politics and sexuality were topics that Wharton could rarely, if ever, separate: both "theories of life" fail to account for the wreckage that political and sexual conquest leave in their wake.

Elizabeth Ammons also writes that this novel "deepen[s] the argument" Wharton has with America and, more important, that Wharton's affair with Fullerton "little changed" (57) Wharton's stance regarding politics. As Ammons argues, "Wharton's object of attack is the culture that represses women and encourages them to believe that love and marriage will someday release them into 'reality'" (88). Setting the repressed woman against the New Woman, Wharton ostensibly shows the failure of love to redeem self-abnegation. But reading Wharton in tandem with Fullerton on international politics tells a different story, one that is less a merging of two fairytales (Ammons 1980, 79) and more a version of two international plots: French marriage and sexual customs and South American politics, both converging on the notion of power.

Yet *The Reef* is no roman à clef. The difficulty in reading Wharton, as many critics before have pointed out, is the tricky conflation of her personal and political metaphorizing. This translation of international into private politics is not easy to theorize for Wharton's method in *The Reef,* as elsewhere, calls up a series of theoretical arguments about reading fiction in the context of material history. While she insists on the absolute separation of politics and fiction, propaganda and art, her autobiographical impulse, especially under Fullerton's influence, appears almost everywhere in her fiction. Still, no simple autobiographical correlation emerges. Wharton's art is distinguished by the fine integration of discourses of social and political phenomena and their imbrication with intimate lives—by its cultural dialogics. Wharton weaves together a political and private vision, which makes her dismissal of propaganda all the more understandable. She does it imperceptively, maybe unconsciously, but no less sharply than her socialist friends like Upton Sinclair.

I want to turn instead to the exchange of manuscripts, not love letters, between Morton Fullerton and Edith Wharton. I see in them another version of the means by which Wharton mixed erotics and politics, seeing them as interconnected since the binaries of the private and the political, and of the self and culture, no longer held for her. Rather than analyzing *The Reef* as only a veiled commentary on her sexual relations with Fullerton, we can see encoded in the novel the lovers' ongoing debate about international politics, an exchange which began with her intellectual responses to Fullerton and developed into her tireless work for World War I charities and, eventually, into a new attitude toward writing fiction. Wharton offers no critique of Fullerton's politics (as she does his prose), but her own work offers a glimpse of the private dimensions paralleling international policy. Wharton was reading Fullerton's second book on politics, while also showing sections of *The Reef* to him during its composition (Erlich 108). At the same time, Fullerton showed Wharton drafts of his *Problems of Power* (1913). In an October 1912 letter to Fullerton, she admonishes him to clean up his prose, banish his "Latinisms," and return "to English" (Lewis and Lewis 281). She urges him to distance himself from "all the scientific-politico-economic charabia" influencing him and to "vivify" his work. Yet what about his effect on her novel? How has Wharton vivified her own concerns by a more detailed knowledge of politics?

Her early exchanges with Fullerton on America's "problems of power" provide one of her main contexts for understanding American politics, specifically the Monroe Doctrine and the Open Door policy by which America, in 1823, had affirmed its own sense of exceptionalism and worked to keep the European presence out of America and the territories south of the US. While Fullerton writes about the Open Door policy in South America and the Panama Canal, Wharton, too, has her Open Door. It is the metaphor for the casual affair—the open door between connecting hotel rooms—and the crisis of passion in *The Reef*: "The room was getting on his nerves. . . . It was extraordinary with what a microscopic minuteness of loathing he hated it all: the grimy carpet and wallpaper, the black marble mantelpiece, the clock with a gilt allegory under a dusty bell, the high-bolstered brown-counterpaned bed, the framed card of printed rules under the electric light switch, and the door of communication with the next room. He hated the door most of all . . ." (75–76, Wharton's closing ellipsis). The "Open Door" policy Fullerton describes looks much like Darrow's sexual policy writ large: Darrow, like the US, controls the pace of both relations, although Anna Leath tries to delay Darrow in her first forestalling of his visit. He retaliates with Sophy Viner, with whom he has an affair because of the convenience of the connecting door between their hotel suites. The door represents the dangers of succumbing to desire and will to power in both personal and global politics. "The Open Door" policy, and the immigrationist sentiments surrounding it, is a topic Wharton takes up later when discussing eugenics, nativism, and sexuality. In 1912, in *The Reef*, she focuses on the negotiations of the United States as a world-power and uses these as the backdrop for a drama of repression and passion.[5]

US relations with Latin America from 1890 through 1920 were, as one diplomatic historian has put it, "ideologically confusing" (94).[6] The rationalizations for expansion into Latin America ranged from the Manifest Destiny claims for American imperialism to newer ones for the "racial uplift"—under the banner of progressivism—of Latin American peoples. Latin America could be "Americanized," keeping its "weaker races" safely below the border while the profits of such Americanization would flow north (Jules R. Benjamin 95). As Fullerton would write in his 1913 analysis, the growing naval strength of the US led to this ideological confusion, since it linked patriotism or nationalism—discussed in terms of American defense—with industrial imperialism, or American imperialism.

Fullerton's 1913 *Problems of Power* explains the international debate about the Panama Canal and Germany's desire for expansion and emigration into South America, at a time when the US wanted to maintain its rights to intervene in the southern hemisphere. In Fullerton's view, the Monroe Doctrine is at stake since the US should be defending its own rights to influence and expansion in South America. Yet Fullerton's perspective on the US as world power is guarded: "It is by the force of things that the United States has evolved two cardinal policies: a hitherto practically effective 'Monroe Doctrine,' and also a less successful principle, that of 'The Open Door'. . . . [I]n becoming members of a World-Power the Americans have been so astonishingly transformed that even one who has been absent from their shores for a period of only twenty years must inevitably, upon his return, find his compatriots almost unrecognizable" (14–15). The last five pages of Fullerton's study are devoted to the potential problems of the US in negotiating with Europe and with Latin America the territory opened up by the Panama Canal in 1914. He argues that a new alliance must be formed in order to solidify the Monroe Doctrine. Fullerton warns of the "new Power" of the "Revolution of Panama" in the "American Mediterranean, between Venezuela and the Gulf of Mexico" (316). Its imperialism has made the US vulnerable to suspicion in the world (318). He also admonishes, "It is probable that the Americans, absorbed . . . in their 'national ignorant self-sufficiency,' preoccupied by the pressing problem of organizing democracy on the vastest scale on which that operation has ever been attempted, engaged in the gigantic task of constructive nationalism, to which they have been impelled by the energy and intelligence of Mr. Roosevelt, may not yet be alive to all the consequences of their Martian enterprise" (316). Fullerton's argument with America is with its ignorant and arrogant exceptionalism, its contradictory sense of democratic and expansionist ideals. This American absorption in domestic affairs—to the exclusion of political consequences—is the very subject of Wharton's novels.

As Fullerton writes, "The opening of the Canal will not diminish, but aggravate that distrust of the United States which marks the rapidly growing nationalism of the South American States. Pan-Americanism will become more than ever a Utopia" (322–23). Proselytizing for a strong

American navy to protect its interests, a navy devoted to defense rather than colonialism, Fullerton claims that the navy will prevent American "dismemberment." Since the US can no longer afford to be isolationist, Fullerton argues, it must be willing to take responsibility for its grand affairs, an irony that Wharton was sure not to miss, given her complicated break-up with Fullerton. Wharton's George Darrow—qua diplomat—would face this same situation in South America, so it is no accident that Wharton sends him there on his diplomatic mission. Wharton's plot about Darrow's responsibility in his affair with Viner parallels Fullerton's concern about the plotting of international relations. Both were concerned with the "blundering alchemy" which resulted in applying social engineering (or Manifest Destiny) to intimate or international affairs. Granted, Fullerton's call for a greater diplomacy with South America is not the same as Wharton's call for sexual integrity in *The Reef,* but the two situations share a similar imperative: an argument against self-absorbed and egotistical affairs, international or sexual.

As in many of Wharton's other fictions, particularly after the beginning of World War I, she returns to and disparages her usual targets: Bohemianism, a "cheaper convention" of life than the theories of fatalism or pragmatism usually associated with Anna's son's, Owen Leath's, class (26); anarchist-free love-revolutionary life in Paris (39–40); Anarchist waiters in Unions, who "[slap] down the dishes" (136); the "nasty foreigners"—aka French governesses—who disrupt the domestic sphere of Givré (159); and the "new theories" of free love—the "stuff that awful women rave about on platforms" (290). All of these smaller annoyances will galvanize in Wharton's larger political vision after World War I, in her contempt for uncontrollable passions manifesting themselves in public lives. For this novel, they provide the political subtext, set against the girlhood of Anna Summers Leath, when "people with emotions were not visited" (86), and repression was the key to social intercourse. Twice Wharton refers to the "police" as a central metaphor for the control of passions and sensations in Anna's world: once when Anna imagines her father calling the police to ward off unwanted passions; and again when contemplating Anna's old life "as a kind of well-lit and well-policed suburb to dark places one need never know about" (353). In both cases, repression must be accomplished by surveillance and discipline.

Curiously, Wharton's notion of the police-state over desire corresponds with Fullerton's version of the US as a world power, a necessary force in South America, especially around the Panama Canal. Fullerton calls for greater continuity in the defense of American international power; he rightly notes the increased antagonism on the part of South

American patriots that will be fostered by the opening of the Canal. Hence, he makes a case for greater "defensive precautions" since "the United States is now out in the open" (324). Wharton's insistence on South America as Darrow's destination prefigures her fear of a growing international unrest, usually located in Wharton's fiction by the inability of Wharton's male characters to commit unambivalently. Fullerton's study alerts her to the consequences of America's unchecked Monroe Doctrine—and the dangers of unreflecting conquest.

Selden's "republic of the spirit" in The *House of Mirth* is a corollary to George Darrow's imperialism of the soul in *The Reef.* Fullerton's emphasis is on American vulnerability springing from its unguarded expansionism, while Wharton's is on Sophy's naive vulnerability in the face of Darrow's reckless and arrogant disregard of her feelings. In *The Reef,* Darrow's and Anna's ideas of diplomatic sexual behavior conflict, and the disjunction between these private negotiations remain the focus of Wharton's erotic plot. Anna clearly underestimates the difficulty of managing positions. She wants Darrow to be pure and absolutely committed to her; the idea of his affair with Sophy Viner—while she had put him off for a month—prevents her reconciliation and leads to her renunciation. Darrow, on the other hand, underestimates Anna's inflexibility and sees his own temporizing as a convenient strategic maneuver. That maneuver may fall below his ideal, yet he maintains a ready balance between commitment and expedience.

Free Love politics, associated in *The Reef* with anarchy and anti-democratic leanings, inform the marriage plot of the novel. Those politics are also related to what Fullerton calls "the pressing problem of organizing democracy on the vastest scale" and, more generally, for Wharton, with sexual politics. Darrow and Anna explore the grounds of sexual intimacy, and their discussions cover the same territory regarding female autonomy in sexual issues that the New Women debates did in the 1890s. Insofar as Wharton invokes the anarchists and the Free love theories, she does so to raise the specter of uncontrolled passions against which she plays out Anna's and Darrow's drama of unregulated passions and repression. It is precisely the challenge to patriarchal control represented in the Free Love proponents that Anna internalizes and with which she struggles. Free Lovers—along with suffragists, moral reform society activists, and anarchists—were one of the groups promoting "voluntary Motherhood" in late nineteenth-century society, as Linda Gordon documents in her study of the politics of the birth-control movement (93). As Gordon points out, "Clinging to the cult of motherhood was part of a broader conservatism shared by Free Lovers and suffragists—acceptance of traditional sex roles. Even the Free Lovers rejected only one factor—legal marriage—of the many that defined woman's place in the family. They did not challenge conventional conceptions of woman's passivity and limited sphere of concern" (1982, 67). Did Wharton subscribe to the popular prejudice against Free Lovers, or did she embrace the ambivalence of their position, using it to highlight Anna's own split between passion and principle? In asking Darrow whether sexual affairs are "what men do," Anna is trying to make sense of his act, and trying also to consider the effects of her passionlessness upon her first, now dead husband, Fraser Leath. Darrow's diplomatic tact upsets her in that he seems to be able to smooth out any difficulty. Her suffering is predicated on her ignorance of affairs themselves, about whether such things "happen to men often" (339).[7] Wharton's female characters remain generally ignorant of the political scene, with their ignorance shored up through their inarticulateness. In contemplating the affairs of men, Anna Leath moves beyond the repression of her girlhood and glimpses the relation of sexual politics to the world at large.

Wharton deploys social debates as transitional or pivotal occasions for speculating on the merging of her characters' political and private lives. For instance, Darrow's professional and personal diplomacy annoys Anna, who sees that his self-possession prevents their real intimacy. "The idea that his tact was a kind of professional expertness filled her with repugnance, and insensibly she drew away from him" (321). She cannot stand the smoothing over of rough or intense passions, and she retaliates with the same in kind—a withdrawal. It is exactly the professional intrusion into personal life against which she guards herself, but that protection destroys her passion. Anna's retreat is a pretense, as is Sophy Viner's removal to India at the end of the novel. Similarly, in *Twilight Sleep* (1927) and *The Children* (1928), Wharton's characters will also scatter themselves to the ends of the earth in order to avoid each other.

Sophy Viner embodies Wharton's distrust of the New Woman, a source of considerable ambivalence for the writer. As a working woman, Sophy Viner displays all of the instability of status of the governess position, what Jeanne Peterson calls "status incongruence." Peterson remarks that the governess was always in a liminal position because "the possibility of real upward mobility was a chimera. Indeed, employment as a governess was only of very limited use even in maintaining gentle status" (7). By the same logic to which Wharton subscribes, Sophy's engagement to Owen Leath must be broken off, preventing her upward mobility. Sophy's decision to end the engagement and to head for India may alleviate her passion for Darrow, but it also shows how working women are forbidden middle-class respectability. Peterson also argues that sexual relations with servants would have been taboo, their working-class status prohibiting any "social obligations, while sexual relations with a woman so nearly of one's own class could not be isolated from a whole complex of responsibilities" (210*n*46). This disparity in status may explain Darrow's attraction to Sophy while she is a free agent in Paris, and his change of heart towards her at Givré, the place of her employment as governess. Owen violates Darrow's class assessment of sexually available women by seeing only Anna as a viable possibility. Sophy's sister Laura is a "kept woman," a singer—perhaps, as Ammons suggests, a prostitute. Sophy's decision to leave for India itself suggests an equation of her with the exotic and the unknown, and associates the third world (the "primitive") with sexual possibility. Darrow's diplomatic mission in South America puts each of Wharton's characters on a different continent, with the world thus conveniently divided into civilized and uncivilized. But the cost of those evasions is the end of passion.

Wharton highlights the uncanny relation between power in US imperialism and power in male-female relations, here played out as the sexual tension between Darrow and his two conquests: the discarded Sophy and the naive, repressed Anna. Wharton sees sexual romance as a relation of power, leading to her career-long fascination with the politics of intimacy. Darrow had thought of his affair with Sophy as a "transient intimacy" (75), but Wharton shows how no affair—international or sexual—is transient because of its inextricability from power. Once the doors are open, in hotel rooms or across US borders, Wharton sees an inevitable struggle for domination. Darrow's imperialistic foreign policies are related both to his South American assignment and his affair with the "other" woman, Sophy—a woman who represents for him a world alien to Anna's familiar and sheltered one. The class differences between the characters are really a "cover story" for Fullerton's warnings about US imperialism toward third-world, "weaker" races. Reading Wharton's novel this way aligns various tensions in the story: the sexual plot, the class inequities, and the failed diplomacy of intimate relations.

The Reef anticipates Wharton's new engagement—her cultural dialogics—that is completely articulated in *Summer,* the subject of the next chapter. Wharton's focus on social purity—from the eugenics debates and family studies to larger political issues of bolshevism and fascism—takes its lead from *The Reef.* After her involvement in World War I relief agencies and volunteer work, her cultural criticism has a sharper edge to it. "Evasion" is Wharton's key word in her late novels: the "new America" is filled with ways to evade the responsibilities of

intimate and international relations—of both public and private kinds—
that Wharton came more and more to advocate in her late works
(*Mother's Recompense*, 96). Her heroes and heroines in the novels of the
next decades fight sexual intolerance and refuse American repression. In
Summer, Charity Royall bridges ostensibly eugenic and dysgenic communities and becomes a hybrid of both cultures. Chapter One contextualizes
Wharton's awareness of the class connotations of eugenics debates about
good and bad mothering and explains Wharton's implicit argument
against social engineering. Chapter Two adumbrates issues of social purity by addressing Wharton's disturbing racial politics; *The Mother's
Recompense* is Wharton's struggle to write a new ethical fiction without
revealing her own ethics too fully, since those values ran counter to the
prevailing spirit of individualism and narcissism of the 1920s. Moreover,
Wharton did not want to advocate the tenets of social control that she
strongly questioned in *Summer*.

By the end of the decade, however, in *Twilight Sleep* and *The Children*,
Wharton abandons part of that old conservatism and attacks the eugenics movements which have violated her sense of family life, particularly the ethical and social meanings of motherhood. Chapter Three
thus treats Wharton's distrust of legislating reproduction. In Chapter
Four, on the Vance Weston novels, we see Wharton's interest in the
companionate marriage debate and in evangelism of both preachers like
Billy Sunday and advertising pleas for mass culture, an immersion that
challenges her conservative views about the link between aesthetics and
politics. By the thirties, however, Wharton's fictions can be read as
troubled commentary on questions of incest, illegitimacy, and creativity.
Chapter Five deals with these topics and their important political ramifications for the rise of totalitarianism in Europe. "Fasciste Italy is
evidently to differ in no important respect from the other. . . . What
a country to live in!" Wharton writes to Minnie Cadwalader Jones
(11 December 1922, Beinecke Library). Whether in Italy, France, or America, Wharton feared the tyranny of fascist legislation of private life. As
intellectual historian and social critic of "a world populated by . . .
fiends," as Wharton wrote to Minnie on 21 March 1932 (Beinecke Library), she used her rhetorical power as an "India-rubber optimist" to
counteract the "world-woe" she inherited after World War I (letter to
Elisina Tyler, 19 September 1936, Lilly Library). All this was her goal,
while maintaining the sense of humor she feared Henry James lost in his
major phase. From "India-rubber optimist" to "Edith Agonistes": Wharton's at once optimistic and agonistic strategies create the "brave new
world" of her late fictions.

1

Summer and the
Rhetoric of Reproduction

Wharton's brave new politics may be said to begin with the national anxiety over the need for social engineering and population control, an uneasiness especially about the value of motherhood. For Wharton's taste, America was too invested in finding social scapegoats for its problems, whether in eugenic and dysgenic families, immigration patterns, women's sexuality, or even banking and bankers. Wharton saw the eugenics craze of the teens and twenties—the pseudo-scientific study of heredity and human breeding—as both the symbol and symptom of America's search to localize and totalize its new social problems. Perhaps her most concentrated work on the dynamics of the family and the significance of heredity before winning the Pulitzer Prize in 1921 for *The Age of Innocence* (1920) is *Summer*. Indeed, Wharton's fictions of the teens, especially *The Reef* (1912) and *The Custom of the Country* (1913), generally reflect her emerging interest in anthropology and, more specifically, in family studies, an offshoot of the eugenics movement, and in the hereditarianism that Wharton addressed head-on in the late twenties.

Summer witnesses the origin of Wharton's interest in nativist arguments, family system studies, and reproductive politics. The call for reproductive rights—in Margaret Sanger's early work in 1914 and 1915 and in Henry H. Goddard's *The Kallikak Family* in 1912—came with the more conservative call for eugenic programs. These programs had the improvement of the human race as their objective, but they were undergirded by the nativist claims that the "lower orders" were reproducing at a faster rate than even the fittest of the so-called 100% Americans. Not coincidentally, Wharton's novel about abortion also concerns Charity's origin in a mountain community that, by late nineteenth- and early twentieth-century standards, would have been considered dysgenic: Charity comes from a lawless, inbreeding, "uncivilized" culture engaged in unregulated reproduction of the "lower" orders, precisely the kind of community eugenicists feared.

Wharton's novel coincides with studies of purportedly degenerate clans, several of which have been considered in Nicole Hahn Rafter's *White Trash: The Eugenic Family Studies:* of the Jukes in New York, studied by Dugdale in 1877; of the tribe of Ishmael in Indiana, by Mc-Culloch in 1888; and of the Kallikaks in New Jersey, by Kite and Goddard in 1912. Such family studies considered heredity to be the source of alcoholism, crime, poverty, sexual licentiousness, and polygamy. The early eugenics movement presented a "graphic rhetorical gesture, an affirmation of class position and entitlement" (Rafter 16). Wharton's novel is a critique of hereditary family studies and their assumptions about sexuality, especially that "mothers are more responsible than fathers in generating bad offspring" (Rafter 66). "Maternal culpability" became the dominant cry in these 1880 debates; and, finally, in 1913, the Eugenics Record Office published its Bulletin Number 13, entitled "How to Make a Eugenical Family Study," so that people could track down the degeneration in their own communities. In this light, *Summer* is Wharton's backward glance to the nineteenth century and its legacy of sexual intolerance.

With the failure of what was generally called the maternal instinct, it was feared, would come the decline of Western civilization. Charity Royall, however, serves as Wharton's counterexample. *Summer* sets the scene for Wharton's later arguments by having the heroine, Charity Royall, emerge from one of those communities to exemplify the independence and assertiveness of the New Woman. Charity's conduct is complex enough to be beyond the conventional codes of "decent" women, but by 1917, she is still not the flapper Wharton despised. The novel's concern with the mother and her instinct is related to the putative decline of good American stock. Wharton concentrates her energies on the question of the daughter's inheritance, a topos to which she returns in both her shorter and longer late fictions. The question of *Summer* is whether Charity Royall inherits her birth mother's penchant for the lawless "herd" from the Mountain towering nearby the town of North Dormer. Or does she acquire characteristics from her adoptive mother, Mrs. Royall, whose maternal instinct Charity measures as "sad and timid and weak" (24)? Or is she moved by Miss Hatchard's offer of maternal advice, contained within her cryptic offer of help "in case" of Mr. Royall's untoward sexual advances (27)? Finally, Wharton considers the last mother figure of Dr. Merkle, a woman doctor who offers Charity an abortion—for a price. The impossibility of identifying the "good mother" in the novel leads to Wharton's drama of cultural scapegoating of "bad mothers," whose laxity and degenerate behavior were all considered signs of greater dysgenic decline. All of these images of "bad mothers" came at a time when the burden of good breeding fell upon what was called "maternal culpability." "If you smile at that now," one eugenicist cautioned, "some day you may bitterly rue your smile when you see in your child some weakness or waywardness that you can trace to your wife's relations with the fatality of cause and effect" (Holmes 199).

Wharton's lover, Morton Fullerton, engaged her interest in the American context of eugenics debates in that his criticism challenged American nativism and its assumption of unquestioned cultural superiority. As early as 1893 in *Patriotism and Science: Some Studies in Historic Psychology* and later in *Problems of Power,* an analysis of international politics (1913), Fullerton wrote about the problems of modernity, particularly America's obsession with imperial power (see Lewis and Lewis 282). In the former, in a chapter entitled "On a Certain Danger in Patriotism," Fullerton argues that American writers need to act as critics rather than as patriots (21). These writers, Fullerton contends, must address a host of social ills facing America, indeed all the Western nations, and he denounces "a loud-mouthed patriotism" (24) and a nationalism that leads to xenophobia and barbarism. "Any demand made upon us, therefore, in restriction of our individual liberty to think freely as citizens of the planet first, with our thoughts and visions on larger notions than those of nation, or even of race, must, in general, be resisted" (48). Fullerton worries that an unchecked patriotism encourages the imperialism which he distrusted and limits a greater vision of human nature, beyond race or nationality. He concludes that "the modern America of the States is entering upon certain social problems absolutely new to it" (83). Central to Fullerton's criticism is his attack on the notion of "a chosen people, and . . . the notion of a chosen race" whose vulgar gods are money and power (49, 79–80), invoking the racial stereotype that his antagonists despised most. By telling the Americans First crowd that they were acting like usurers and greedy capitalists (i.e., like the stereotypical Jew), he assails their inauthenticity and their pretensions. Arguing for an international community, he pleads for tolerance (82).

In a 22 September 1911 letter to Morton Fullerton, Wharton suggests an early interest in "Gobinisme," a eugenics trend named for Joseph-Arthur de Gobineau who advocated racial aristocracy (Lewis and Lewis 257–58). Wharton writes to Fullerton about her recent reading in "a rather good book of E. Seilliere's, 'Les Mystiques du Neo-romantisme,'" which documents Gobineau's and Vacher de Laponge's (a student of the Aryan race) Pan-German idea (Lewis and Lewis 257). In fact, by 1908, Wharton had already been aware of Vernon Kellogg's *Darwinism Today: A Discussion of Present Day Scientific Criticism of the Darwinian Selection Theories* (1907), to which she refers in letters to Charles Eliot Norton and to Sara Norton and also in two letters to Fullerton (Lewis and Lewis 131, 146, 148, 151). Kellogg's study documented the challenge to Darwinianism and the anti-Darwinian temper of the first decade of the twentieth century. Since no critic of Darwin has invented a "substitutionary theory . . . to replace that which they are attempting to dethrone" (28), Kellogg argues, "the theory of descent was, and is, invulnerable" (25). At the same time, Wharton's reading in sociology and anthropology coincided with her husband Teddy's rest cures and her own, which these "new sciences" prescribed. Before the Great War, Wharton might have endorsed these theories. Afterwards, she comes to question Kellogg's once-popular ideas about the hereditary nature of feeblemindedness—along with the advisability of eugenic engineering—as a result of the staggering jolt of the war and of her sympathy for what R. W. B. Lewis tellingly describes as "the wretched of the earth— . . . for the victimized, the uprooted, the sick and the shattered" (R. W. B. Lewis 1993, 373). Wharton's own thinking on eugenics, from *Summer* in 1917 to *The Old Maid* in 1924, is a response to the pervasive belief in the teens and early twenties that America's new social anxieties required genetic engineering and policing. Fears of racial degeneracy—expressed in old cultural catchphrases like "good stock" and "racial purity"—led Wharton to ponder legitimacy and illegitimacy in the American scene as she remembered it.

Summer is an ambivalent mixture of her reaction to studies of family heredity and her rejection of the doctrine of maternal culpability, which accompanied theories of racial and cultural degeneration. Wharton's comments about *Summer* in her 1934 autobiography, *A Backward Glance,* lend an ominous tone to the cultural debate over eugenics: "I had wanted to draw life as it really was in the derelict mountain villages of New England . . . utterly unlike that seen through the rose-coloured spectacle of my predecessors. . . . In those days the snow-bound villages of Western Massachusetts were still grim places, morally and physically: insanity, incest and slow mental and moral starvation were hidden away behind the paintless wooden house-fronts of the long village street" (293–94). This passage has been seen as Wharton's wish to rewrite her regionalist predecessors Mary Wilkins Freeman and Sarah Orne Jewett, but in linking moral depravity to poverty, Wharton seems just as intent on exposing the eugenic family studies of her day and their conclusions about the pathology of the poor. At the same time, Wharton's experience with her husband Teddy's mental deterioration showed just how much, in the jargon current in 1903, anxiety and overstimulation of the leisure class produced his lingering illness and mental fatigue. As Tom Lutz argues in *American Nervousness, 1903,* neurasthenia was linked to the "moral laxity or extreme moral sensitivity" ushered in with the new century and new American modernity (4). Lutz argues about Wharton that she ridiculed "the falsity of maintaining a neurasthenic mask" when it actually veiled anyone's egotism (237). By doing so, and thereby "locating moral responsibility in the manners and actions of individuals rather than in social structure . . . Wharton manages to seem both radical and reactionary at the same time" (237). In short, knowing too well from experience that high as well as low society had its share of insanity, incest, and moral bankruptcy, Wharton had to reconsider and ultimately reject eugenic assurances about the upper class and good breeding.

Having read Kellogg's influential treatise on natural selection suggesting the heredity of feeblemindedness and Robert Heath Lock's well-regarded *Recent Progress in the Study of Variation, Heredity and Evolution* (1906), in which he argues for the theories of variation and heredity that would underwrite his call for a "higher birth-rate . . . [for] desirables," Wharton would have also known the arguments of evolution disseminated by Darwin and his scientific progeny, who tried to account for what was considered a disquieting moral and mental diversity (Lewis and Lewis 146; Lock 288). The magazine culture which popularized the eugenic "decline" of the US population, and the racial inferiority of blacks and Jews, among other "lower orders," appeared in forums like *Century Magazine* (see Degler 48, 76), the same magazine which published Wharton's work since 1903, when it first commissioned her for a series of articles on Italian villas (R. W. B. Lewis 1975, 116). In *Summer,* she writes her first critique of the scientific racism and classism permeating the eugenics debate of her time. Contesting the biological theories of inferiority based on race and nationality, Wharton had also to confront the more general faith in evolutionary progress, especially as her own leisure class saw itself as the beneficiary of that progress. Yet being a member of that class never meant, for Wharton, an allegiance to it. In a sense, Darwinism forced her to change allegiances, from a belief in the cultural divisions between primitive and civilized cultures to a new value for the dismantling of highbrow and lowbrow distinctions. She no longer could afford—intellectually or financially—to rely on elite culture for her audience; she came to understand the necessity of appealing to a new, middlebrow, reading public.

The Eugenic Rhetoric

It is wrong to conclude, as some have, that because there may be no objective truth possible, there are not objective lies. There may be no objective canons of historiography, but there are degrees of accuracy; there are better and worse pieces of history. The challenge is precisely to maintain this tension between accuracy and mythic power.

—Linda Gordon, "What's New in Women's History?"

Wharton's criticism of American prudishness suggests how much she distrusted her audience's ability to judge sexual matters. In a letter dated 2 November 1934 to Minnie Cadwalader Jones (her sister-in-law), Wharton criticizes an "editress" of "Woman's Home Companion": "What a country! With Faulkner & Hemingway acclaimed as the greatest American novelists, & magazine editors still taking the view they did when I began to write! Brains & culture seem non-existent from one end of the social scale to the other, & half the morons yell for filth, & the other half continue to put pants on the piano-legs" (Beinecke Library). Her defiance of these conventional codes emerges during World War I, when her doubts about American taste were at their greatest.[1] The symptoms of a general blindness to the changing national and international scene, these American sexual values indicate one platform in the debate about moral decline, for Wharton saw her culture's obsession with sexuality as hypocritically linked to their fears of racial decline and degeneracy.

Indeed, World War I also occasioned a change in Wharton's attitude toward women's rights. As in the Twilight Sleep debate of 1914–15 (discussed in Chapter Three), abortion and other reproductive issues re-emerged as public issues during the war and became the stuff of fiction for Wharton, some forty-odd years after the supposedly conclusive passage of the Comstock Law of 1873, which outlawed the exchange of birth-control information through the mails in order to eradicate all public knowledge of abortion. From the teens through the thirties, eugenics or race hygiene becomes the focus of attention for those in reaction to American nationalist arguments. Even the most canonical of authors—Eugene O'Neill, in a one-act play, *Abortion* (1914), and Theodore Dreiser in *American Tragedy* (1925)—saw pregnancy termination not only as a plot device, but also as being at the heart of issues of identity and power.

In America, the Voluntary Motherhood advocates opposed birth control and were sometimes associated—especially by those who hoped motherhood would be an issue in the greater empowerment of women—

with the New Thought authors, who supported and sought to harness "mother power" as a radical force (Gordon 1982, 43).[2] While abortion rights advocacy represented some women's resistance to patriarchal control, others turned to New Thought for an antidote to patriarchal relations.[3] The abortion issue arose simultaneously with the New Thought phenomena: New Thought, at least in one manifestation, took the form of Mother Power, as Elizabeth Towne described it in her pamphlets and books.[4]

As part of the mind-cure movement, New Thought attempted to draw on psychic reserves, and was generally accompanied by liberal beliefs in individualism and powers of personality. Some women who were trying to deny powerlessness over their own bodies maintained New Thought to be part of women's magnetic power over men. Believing in the ability of New Thought to increase their control—less through traditional submission than through concentration—these women were drawn to these new social movements. Early Christian Scientists, influenced by Annie Payson Call's New Thought works, believed that calmness would lead to the end of "worry contractions" and that "the ability to drop contractions might be the secret of painless childbirth" (Parker 84). In the face of Comstockery, the moral and legal indignation over abortion and birth control, New Thought became an alternative to abstinence or eugenics.

While Jane Tompkins has documented how the ideology of such sentimental power pervades mid-nineteenth-century popular fiction, it is wrong to assume—as some critics have about Wharton's texts—that sentimental power predominantly organizes early twentieth-century domestic fiction. In fact, mind curists like Call found sentimentality to be women's greatest problem or error, arguing instead—somewhat paradoxically and sentimentally—for women's greater "magnetic" or psychological power (Parker 85). Wharton works through the same contradictions in *Summer* between personal life and popular psychological, medical, and legal movements promising greater power to women.

In *Summer,* Wharton first registers her participation in the cultural dialogue on reproductive rights, a dialogue which her 1930s fiction continues in relation to the rise of fascism. My reading of *Summer* takes its lead from Wharton's defiance of the legislation of private morality, for the novel's ending is not "sick," as Elizabeth Ammons has seen it (1980, 133), but a challenge both to the conception of women as mothers and to the way motherhood is constructed in eugenics discourse. That Ammons labels this book as "sick" indicates a trend in Wharton criticism that I would revise: to see *Summer* as dark realism, regional revisionism, partner of *Ethan Frome,* or even as a repudiation of a bourgeois, subversion theory of women's agency, is to miss its more profound cultural work.

Summer, as I will show, depicts Wharton's new response to the family
studies debate of her day and thus marks her movement into her career's
next phase of cultural engagement and revision.

Summer creates a case study of the controversies within twentieth-
century discourses of pregnancy and reproductive rights. Coupling these
issues to the debate about cultural degeneration and regeneration, Wharton makes pregnancy and abortion the subtext for the novel as bildungsroman; this debate necessarily takes readers into the realm of anthropology and sociology, where issues like "maternal" and "paternal"
instinct" were hotly argued (Degler 110). Charity's sexuality does seem to
lead inevitably to her motherhood, but not without Wharton's detour
through the possibility of abortion. Wharton demonstrates an acute
awareness of the popular obsessions with racial motherhood and racial
discourse, and about the fitness of some mothers over others. Like other
cultural critics, Wharton questions claims about the line drawn between
fit and unfit mothers, showing the fitness of Charity's mother Mary and
the unfitness of the "civilized" or "advanced" men and women of North
Dormer.

Critical interpretations of *Summer,* and particularly of its conclusion,
have been both contradictory and provocative. Two widely divergent
comments on the novel by Cynthia Griffin Wolff and Elizabeth Ammons
provide the misleading extremes. In her introduction to the Perennial
Library Edition, Wolff praises *Summer* as a bildungsroman "that deals
frankly with feminine sexuality as a powerful, life-shaping force" (v), and
she reads the novel's conclusion as a positive example of Charity's mature and "genuinely meaningful social [choice]" (xvii). For Wolff, this
meaningful social choice occurs when Charity, pregnant by a man who
has deserted her to marry someone else, tacitly assents to marrying her
own adoptive father, a man who has previously sought to seduce her.
Her pregnancy inhibits her further expressions of disgust at his incestuous claims, and she spends her wedding night alone, under Royall's
protection nonetheless.

On the contrary, Elizabeth Ammons recognizes the horror of the situation and sees the novel as "Wharton's bluntest criticism of the patriarchal sexual economy," and its main subject is "the incestuous nature of
patriarchal marriage" (133). While Ammons's reading is more strident
than Wolff's, acknowledging as it does Wharton's protest against the
social roles available to women, like Wolff's, it is too univocal. Ammons,
in stressing Charity's passivity, reads the conclusion as totally bleak.

In "Life's Empty Pack: Notes toward a Literary Daughteronomy,"
Sandra Gilbert more aptly reads this novel through a literary ancestress

and precursor, the George Eliot of *Silas Marner*. Focussing on daughter-hood and its "self-subverting power" (357), Gilbert emphasizes the inevi-table acquiescence of the daughter to patriarchal law. Lévi-Strauss's *Elementary Structures of Kinship* anchors Gilbert's reading of Wharton's investment in social order, in which women as chattel reinforce signs of kinship between men. As we will come to see, however, Wharton rejects the lessons of this patriarchal commodification of women as emphasized in a structuralist view of society, adopting instead an anthropological and functionalist view of incest, one substantially different from Lévi-Strauss's kinship model. Charity's inevitable domestication, Gilbert argues, depends on an ambivalent loss of the mother and an equally ambivalent "dependence on male legal and financial protection" (370). In Gilbert's view, *Summer* enacts but also complicates the Freudian father-daughter seduction and desire, as well as the daughter's entry into "mature (het-erosexual) femininity" as Freud defined it (375).

Yet patriarchy, as Wharton saw it, is not a monolithic force, impregna-ble to resistance and subversion. Reading Wharton's *Summer* as a record of the total repression of female desire forecloses any contradictions that undo this totalizing account. Wharton does not accede to what Tomp-kins calls the "lesson of submission" in the nineteenth-century sentimen-tal novel; instead, through her treatment of abortion, she offers an exam-ple of resistance—an antisentimental rhetoric of women's difference. Charity's ambivalence is clearly at the center of the book, as is Mr. Royall's. But her ambivalence, and Wharton's, does not center on the family romance as much as it questions the assumptions about "normal" American family life—especially as that standard was being constructed and legislated in the new battle for eugenic control. Royall's speech during Old Home Week is perhaps the novel's best articulation of this familial "norm": his directive to the audience is that they adopt North Dormer "for *good* . . . and not for bad . . . or just for indifference" (194). He continues: "Even if you come back against your will—and thinking it's all a bitter mistake of Fate or Providence—you must try to make the best of it, and to make the best of your old town . . ." (195). This familial logic prefigures Charity's return—for her baby's good—to Royall's fam-ily, yet that return is not without equal measures of resistance and ambivalence.

One major site of resistance to patriarchal ideology was, in Wharton's day as it is today, the abortion debate. Carroll Smith-Rosenberg has shown that in the face of the nineteenth-century movement to outlaw abortion, women advocated "disorderly conduct," particularly in print. The late nineteenth century saw professionals—from writers and physicians to reformers and feminists—increase their publishing as a way to interrogate patriarchal values:

> Marital advice books [were] addressed exclusively to bour-
> geois women readers. . . . [T]heir arguments constituted a
> new symbolic discourse that paralleled and opposed the male
> anti-abortion discourse. In their pages, images of marital
> rape, of unwanted pregnancies, or marriage as legalized pros-
> titution replaced male images of unnatural aborting mothers
> and willful urbane ladies. (243)

Wharton's novel can be read as part of this countermovement by women who wanted to resist the structures within which they were expected to live. Specifically, her interest in challenging "maternal instinct" theories is key to this countermovement during and after World War I. What marks this as a new turn in Wharton's career is that she renegotiates here what the culture might mean by "good" and "bad" mothering. Royall's cursing of Charity—once he sees her on Harney's arm at the July Fourth celebration—signals her appearance, bareheaded, as a sexual being rather than as a domestic one. She has violated his sense of sexual decorum by asserting her sexuality, just as he does the same for her by associating openly with Julia Hawes, a fallen woman. Charity's biological mother, too, had "fallen"; but the crucial difference between Charity and her mother is the difference in their degrees of passivity. While the Mountain people are "herded together in a sort of passive promiscuity in which their common misery was the strongest link" (259), Wharton takes pains to show Charity's deliberation in exercising her sexuality. Royall, how-ever, will exercise a romantic paternalism which attempts to keep Char-ity "decent." At the same time, he has already approached her in her room in order to seduce her, making her available to his desire but not desiring in her own right. Both Royall as father and as seducer seek to deny her autonomy. Male law, here embodied in Lawyer Royall, the principal attorney in the village, has its privileges.

   The Independence Day escapade in Nettleton is significant for another reason: Wharton reveals Royall's association with the secret societies common in nineteenth-century masculine culture as a method of institu-tionalizing the exclusion and suppression of women. "Like the young men of the party, [Royall] wore a secret society emblem in the but-tonhole of his black frock-coat. His head was covered by a new Panama hat . . ." (150–51). In *Secret Ritual and Manhood in Victorian America*, Mark Carnes argues that elaborate fraternal rituals in the nineteenth century allowed men to reenact "paternal roles replete with gender significance" (14); that is, to reinforce women's exclusion from men's secret world. In Wharton's earlier *Custom of the Country,* when Elmer Moffatt wants Abner Spragg to inform on an old business partner, Spragg fiddles with his Masonic emblem, a telling sign of Spragg's loyalty to conventional business values and his resistance to Moffatt's version of commercial ethics. Or, in *Hudson River Bracketed* (1929), Wharton shows these secret societies as facts of life in college towns and midwestern villages. In *Summer,* Wharton details how Royall's affiliation with these secret societies allows him to retain a camaraderie with young men; his drunken cavorting with Julia Hawes and company supports the illusion of his youth. Although Masonic lodges came to reject excessive drinking, early lodges promoted excess—of drinking or carousing—as part of a fraternal celebration of "the limitless possibilities of the secular world" (Carnes 23). While Royall's economic ambitions have been dampened by his diminishing returns as a country lawyer and insurance salesman in North Dormer, the secret society reinforces middle-class masculine comfort by providing a compensatory institution to the repressions of middle-class life and so buttresses his threatened self-image as provider, lover, lawyer.

The early nineteenth-century anti-Masonic crusade was underwritten by women militating against the secret rituals, including drinking, which "rendered men less pious" (Carnes 79). The secret society Wharton uses as a backdrop for *Summer* was still connected, however, with the old order of Masons, before the purge of alcohol and the addition of more religious, less secular rites and practices. The early nineteenth-century lodge constructed an alternative to domesticity, and Wharton draws on that earlier Masonic tradition. Selling insurance was one of the lodge's mainstays, so it is no literary conceit that one of Royall's sidelines is his peddling of these policies.

The lodge offered an escape, however, neither from capitalism nor from the demands of middle-class respectability, but from the ideal of domesticity represented by women like Mrs. Royall. Mrs. Royall, after all, forced Royall to leave Nettleton, which signified some vague failure or vague embarrassment, a move consistent with her need to remove him from the dissolute atmosphere of the lodge. As Royall remarks, "'I was a damn fool ever to leave Nettleton. It was Mrs. Royall that made me do it'" (28). Wharton's suggestion is that Mrs. Royall's humiliation stems from Royall's appetitive behavior—perhaps in drunkenness, sexual license, or both. Theirs is a face-saving move, designed to uphold domesticity and piety, and Charity's adoption is part of the same regulation of appearances.

Royall celebrates Independence Day in Nettleton with his lodge members, a celebration that includes Julia Hawes—a woman of the town, as the phrase used to go for describing young women outside the protection of patriarchal law. The secret society, as Carnes notes, was a place to work through the fundamental tension between mid-Victorian men and women, a tension founded in the domestic purging of social vices, especially intemperance, carnality, and degeneracy (90). This playing out of his anxieties about masculinity, while exorcising repressions in reveling with his drunken fraternity and women like Julia, bears a striking resemblance to Wharton's characterization of the men on the Mountain, the herd of "heathens" who run "amuck," as Royall and his secret society would do (71–73). If the Mountain is of a "lower order," so is Royall, as his affectation of higher civilization is belied by his indulgence in the fraternal rituals of escape—drinking, debauching, carousing. Charity may be determined to define her own sense of femininity, but Royall is also caught up in this socially inscribed drama of middle-class masculinity.

By stylizing this trial of civilization, Masonic rituals also helped middle-class men overcome their fears of a changing and unstable modern society. Part of that instability emerged from the influx of Eastern Europeans into the United States and in their failure or refusal to assimilate. Insofar as fraternal ties served sociologically to stave off cultural fears of outsiders, many of the early fraternal societies originated in nativist associations, including the United American Mechanics, Jr. (one of the first fraternal nativist organizations) and the Know-Nothings (see Carnes 2, 7–8). Wharton describes Charity as "swarthy" (8) and her Mountain heritage in terms of "gipsy-looking people" (63)—two code words that would have indicated her (fantasized) dysgenic origins. Wharton invokes these Eastern European associations also to suggest the presence of "lower races" against which certain lodges established themselves.

Charity herself is of these lower races, a liminal creature with all its allures and prohibitions. Charity is a child of a "half-human" mother—a "heathen" in Royall's words—and a drunken convict father, a father who requests Royall to rescue his child from the Mountain and the "bad mother" Mary, who relinquishes her daughter to Royall. Throughout the novel, Charity makes other connections to liminal figures: wondering whether she is related to Liff Hyatt, who has "the pale yellow eye of a harmless animal" (56); to Julia Hawes, in whom Charity sees "compensations" for shunning society and a "refusal to be snatched" from the figurative burning of wayward girls (106, 235); and finally, to her mother, with whom she identifies during her illegitimate pregnancy and in her desire to "save her child from such a life" (260). But Charity rejects Julia's example as she does the life of poverty Mary Hyatt had accepted for herself: "Was there no alternative but Julia's? Her soul recoiled from the vision of the white-faced woman [Dr. Merkle] among the plush sofas and gilt frames" (235). Yet Charity refuses identification with Royall, even once they recognize each other's desires as their own at the Fourth of July celebration.

Interestingly, Royall mainly identifies with Lucius Harney, an architect who visits North Dormer and who becomes Charity's lover. Talking with Harney produces in Royall a "sonorous satisfaction. It was a long time since he had had anyone of Lucius Harney's quality to talk to: Charity divined that the young man symbolized all his ruined and forgotten past" (68). The townspeople identify him as one of the "advanced" of Americans, more civilized because more urban and sophisticated. Accepting the primitive and its pleasures for the summer, Harney laughs at Charity's suggestion that the Mountain people are bad, although he is surprised by the "real architecture" made by these "sulky," "gipsy-looking" clans. For the moment, his "self-disgust" prevents him from pursuing Charity, but he gives in to his desire when Charity confesses Royall's attempted seduction (104), as if to suggest that the patriarch's acknowledgment of Charity as an object of someone else's sexual desire sanctions his own. Like Lily Bart, mistakenly identified after she leaves the Trenors' house, Charity Royall becomes a woman that a gentleman need not take any pains to respect.

The issue of identification is central to Charity's identity, since she tries to move beyond the oppositional stance she adopted earlier in the novel when she identified herself primarily by denying her common traits with others, like Liff Hyatt or Julia and Ally Hawes. After being discovered outside of Lucius Harney's house, she must defend herself against patriarchal misidentification. However, the strongest test comes when she discovers that her affair with Harney has made her pregnant. At that moment, she must choose from among the several mother figures of the novel a model for identification.

Reproductive Power and A New Narcissism

One of the narrative incidents distinguishing *Summer* from Wharton's earlier novels is the appearance of Dr. Merkle, a woman physician to whom Charity applies in order to confirm her pregnancy. Whether critics treat Merkle as "pseudomotherly" (Gilbert 370) or as "murderous" (Waid 113), they have not generally focused on this representation, though

I believe it is central to Wharton's novel. Consider the image of the woman physician of the day: according to Regina Morantz-Sanchez in *Sympathy and Science,* "the term 'female physician' referred primarily at that time to abortionists, the most notorious of whom was New York's Madame Restell" (188–89). "Nothing was so surprising to me during my first year of practice," remembered Eliza Mosher, "as the assurance with which women came to my office and asked for illegal operations. That's what they thought women doctors were for" (Morantz-Sanchez 220).

Wharton's portrait of Dr. Merkle, the female physician of *Summer,* draws on the popular knowledge of the abortionist. Wharton describes her as follows:

> Dr. Merkle was a plump woman with small bright eyes, an immense mass of black hair coming down low on her forehead, and unnaturally white and even teeth. She wore a rich black dress, with gold chains and charms hanging from her bosom. Her hands were large and smooth, and quick in all their movements; and she smelt of musk and carbolic acid.[5] (224)

Popular accounts of Madame Restell, whose trial in 1878 made the pages of *The National Gazette, NY Illustrated,* and *Puck,* recall Wharton's description of Merkle: "a handsome woman . . . with an ample figure, a dark complexion, luxuriant dark brown hair, and piercing black eyes . . ." (Browder 1). In addition, one *Herald* reporter described Restell as having black eyes and raven hair, two qualities Wharton repeats in her picture of Merkle (cited in Browder 20). Working from the 1840s through the 1870s, Restell gained fame for her procedures, especially her office and her professionalism, which persuaded clients that "she was no dowdy midwife, no quack, no criminal, but an intelligent professional, an informed woman of the world . . ." (Browder 15). That Merkle charges Charity five dollars for her first visit is not outrageous; indeed, as James Mohr reports, Restell's husband—under the pseudonym A. M. Mauriceau—advertised "Portuguese Female Pills" for five dollars a box (Mohr 63). The actual abortion, according to Browder, would cost twenty dollars for a poor woman, one hundred for a wealthy one (Browder 16).

Browder, Restell's most recent biographer (1988), argues that abortion was "more or less illegal" (12), but that in the political climate fostered by the Jacksonian Democrats, most citizens believed in "a God-given right to purge, puke, or poison themselves as they saw fit. In the face of such sentiment, New York's 1827 law against unauthorized physicians and its 1828 abortion law both remained unenforced" (14). A general tolerance for abortion—more or less contested by Female Moral Reform Societies and religious organizations—lasted until the 1870s and Anthony Comstock's crusade against all things "unnatural." Presumably everyone would have understood the sign outside of an office like Dr. Merkle's— "Private Consultations at all hours. Lady Attendants" (125, 140)—as indicating a private acceptance of a known social reality.

> This woman with the false hair, the false teeth, the false murderous smile—what was she offering her but immunity from some unthinkable crime? Charity, till then, had been conscious only of a vague self-disgust and a frightening physical distress; now, of a sudden, there came to her the grave surprise of motherhood. She had come to this dreadful place because she knew of no other way of making sure that she was not mistaken about her state; and the woman had taken her for a miserable creature like Julia. . . . (225)

Merkle offers no sentimental or domestic arrangement of a medical question, but a straightforward business proposition to Charity. In Wharton's original version of the novel, however, her depiction of Merkle is harsher: not only is "unthinkable crime" originally written as "secret murder," but also the "grave surprise of motherhood" was first rendered as "reverence" and then "awe." The passage reads as follows: "Was it possible that this creature imagined she had come there to ask her to [Wharton crossed out the word "murder"] destroy her child? The thought was so monstrous that she sprung up, white & trembling, one of her great rushes surging through her" (Ms. 138, Beinecke Library). The final passage is much more ambivalent about Merkle and Charity's fate: the "grave surprise" of motherhood is more doubtful than Wharton's original "reverence" or "awe" would suggest. In *Edith Wharton's Letters from the Underworld*, Candace Waid reads the original phrasing as proof of Wharton's identification with the father against "murderous mothers" (113, 117). But this reading does not explain Wharton's distrust of public legislation of private morality, upon which both her aesthetic and ethics are based.

Dr. Merkle's maternal or even pseudomotherly behavior brings to light the equivocal position of the mother in early twentieth-century society. Charity has no access to her biological mother; her adoptive mother is dead; this pseudomother is "false": where once the mother, in nineteenth-century culture, was assumed to socialize her daughter, here the mother's power is doubtful. Merkle's vague foreignness—her pronunciation of "noospaper" provides just a hint of her (perhaps German) difference—is suggested in her stereotypical focus on the financial transaction of the abortion. The presence of the "bushy-headed mulatto girl" as the doctor's helper completes the picture of foreignness and racial lower orders associated with sexual transgression. Dr. Merkle, however, is both motherly and alien, a woman who will take Charity in during her pregnancy, while Mary Hyatt gave her up. In exploiting the muddle between the "good mother" and "bad"—like the roles of the fathers elsewhere—Wharton subverts the conventional sense of maternal culpability, especially how it can be limited or legislated according to eugenic doctrines.

Charity sees Merkle's "falseness" but recognizes in turn that the doctor provides a needed service to women, one that Charity rejects in favor of maternity. It was not unusual for women to go to a female physician for advice about labor, but it was unusual for someone like Charity to be ignorant of the possibility of termination, according to the demographics of abortion statistics (see Francome). Instead, in Wharton's scheme of things, Charity makes an anomalous place within the structure of North Dormer society: she keeps the baby to remind her of Harney, to affirm her vitality, and to remind Lawyer Royall that he has no share in the paternity. Charity takes control of the sexual act in deciding to keep her child, just as she has taken control first by rejecting Royall's forced attentions, then by entering willfully and joyfully into sexual relations with Harney, and later, on her marriage night with Royall, by having no intercourse at all.

Pregnant, Charity decides to seek out her mother on the Mountain, only to find her lying dead on a filthy mattress: "But she did not look like a dead woman; she seemed to have fallen across her squalid bed in a drunken sleep, and to have been left lying where she fell, in her ragged disordered clothes . . . one leg [was] drawn up under a torn skirt that left the other bare to the knee: a swollen glistening leg with a ragged stocking rolled down about the ankle" (248). When Charity is presented as her daughter, one of the Mountain people comments, "What? Her too?" (249). Not only have the Mountain people had so many children that the presence of one more pregnant woman is a matter of complete indifference, but here, too, the essential similarity between mother and daughter, between mother and mother-to-be, is taken for granted.

Lawyer Royall, the most educated man in dreary North Dormer, is presented as the exemplar of civilized ways. Yet, through Royall, Wharton undercuts the value of his civilization. The name he has given his adopted daughter constantly and insidiously reminds her of her origin on the Mountain and the nature of her indebtedness to him: "She knew that she had been christened Charity . . . to commemorate Mr. Royall's disinterestedness in 'bringing her down,' and to keep alive in her a becoming sense of dependence" (24). From her early childhood, Charity is also aware of the duality of the connection and grasps Lawyer Royall's dependence on her. When he fails to send her off to boarding school after his wife's death, Charity realizes he has been undone by "the thought of losing her" (25). From that point on, she knows that "lawyer Royall ruled in North Dormer; and Charity ruled in lawyer Royall's house . . . she knew her power, knew what it was made of, and hated it" (23). Depressed and stultified himself, Royall seeks to control Charity's sexuality, as Wharton shows how disinterestedness can mask a repressed desire for control.

Yet another reason for Charity's return to the Mountain is that she has never repudiated her mother, the source of her "low" origin, another "dark inheritance" that Lawyer Royall and his dead wife have tried to suppress in Charity. As Royall reminds Lucius and Charity, "'They all know what she is, and what she came from. They all know her mother was a woman of the town from Nettleton, that followed one of those Mountain fellows up to his place and lived there with him like a heathen" (207–8). Charity, however, has never come to identify with her adoptive father or with his class affiliation in North Dormer. Thus, she is left in an unbounded space without maternal identification, threatened with sexual violation by the oedipal father (see Jessica Benjamin 97). That she does not repudiate her mother forces Charity either to repress her desires or to act them out, perhaps guiltily, but certainly out of conscious choice. Charity fends off the father's seduction and asserts her independence from both maternal and paternal power over her, even though that independence is complicated by her father's economic and legal status and her mother's invisibility. Nevertheless, Charity inherits her mother's sexual legacy. Witness Harney's talk about his attraction to the Mountain and Charity's reaction: "on top of that hill, there [is a] handful of people who don't give a damn for anybody" (65). Harney's desire not to "give a damn" expresses the reality that he gives too much of a damn about social order and that he eventually will marry Annabel Balch rather than Charity out of conventional respect for the status quo. Through her experiences with Harney, she confronts her origins and rejects his erotic domination: "An unknown Harney had revealed himself, a Harney who dominated her and yet over whom she felt herself possessed of a new mysterious power" (149); that power, Sandra Gilbert convincingly argues, comes from her seeing Harney and Royall as "rivalrous" doubles (368).

Charity's search for her mother and her own origin on the Mountain reveals traces of her transgressive desire. A hybrid of both cultures, the pregnant Charity represents that threat of the intermingling of the high and the low—of civilization (law, society, custom) and the mountain (body, nature, appetite)—the grotesque body of the mother incorporated in her own pregnant body. From the time of her adoption, Charity has been alienated from this "low" origin. That she returns to it reveals her desire for amalgamation, just as Royall's desire for her marks his return to the repressed—symbolic incest—and expresses what Stallybrass and White generally call "the symbolic contents of bourgeois desire" (191). Walter Michaels writes that *Summer* blurs the distinctions between North Dormer and the Mountain and between the anthropological distinctions of nature and culture: "For if the Mountain, as the site of 'passive promiscuity' . . . , is a place where one might end up sleeping with a member of one's family, North Dormer turns possibility into fact" (519). Michaels's reading is on target in that the symbolic incest suggested in the "civilization" of North Dormer confuses the distinction established by an anxious culture between itself and the lawless "other." By turning symbolic incest into marriage, Wharton shows the tenuousness of these relations, but not to bolster convention as Michaels suggests. Rather, Wharton undermines popularly received anthropological distinctions between the civilized and the primitive. It is, after all, civilization which produces the Mountain as an outlaw culture, and not the other way around. North Dormer stigmatizes the poverty found in the Mountain, creating rigid social institutions and marginalizing the rural poor. According to eugenics thinking, poverty is the mark of the dysgenic, a pathological and therefore ineradicable inherited trait. However, as Wharton shows, Charity's liminality is the mark of her character and her name, a difference she foregrounds in order to sustain her embattled narcissism.[6] Charity's hatred of Royall's desire—from which her power comes—is made explicit when he comes to her room drunk, saying he is a lonely man and intimating his intentions. "This ain't your wife's room any longer," she reminds him (29). Charity responds not with fear, but in disgust at a sexual confrontation beyond her power. Royall asks for trust as a paternal figure, then reveals his sexual expectations. By giving this relation an incestuous nuance, Wharton implies that desire cannot be contained by patriarchal categories. Royall cannot act both as her father and her lover; that he wants both roles suggests the problematic excess of the patriarchal desire for power.

Royall claims to be all things to Charity: father, lawyer, husband. Yet in one gesture—her affair with Harney—she reveals the clear contradiction in patriarchal and psychological economies. Royall cannot play all the middle-class masculine roles at the same time, even if he needs to do so in order to shore up his failing ego. Wharton understood that middle-class patriarchal power depends on the male's ability to shift roles, as she showed the respectable lawyer finding the consolations of the fraternal lodge. If he cannot seduce Charity himself, Royall wants to force Harney to marry her, thereby literally enforcing the law-of-the-father over her: "'I'll have him here in an hour if you do [want him]. I ain't been in the law thirty years for nothing . . .'" (118). Either way, whether Charity marries Harney or Royall, she remains under the law, although she consciously rejects Harney and Lawyer Royall's command. Wharton suggests that the woman who believes sexuality offers any sort of escape from patriarchal society is deluded. Without an attendant legal equality, sexual freedom lands women right back under phallocratic law. Charity rejects the seduction and the law by which her father would exchange her to Harney; ultimately, she rejects their institutionalization of desire. Yet, by manipulating Royall's desire for her, Charity shows that he, too, cannot live comfortably within a patriarchal order which bars the incestuous desire by which he might be controlled.

As with boarding school, so with marriage: Royall cannot bear to give Charity up. To see Charity as doomed to "perpetual daughterhood" (Ammons 1980, 141) is to miss her new relation, which is actually more ambiguous. Having revealed his desire, Royall cannot exercise the law over her. Neither can he claim her completely as his wife, pregnant as she is by another. In marrying Royall, Charity demands that society must acknowledge and accommodate the hybrid and the anomalous. Choosing to remain within North Dormer rather than live on the Mountain publicizes Charity's resistance to the outlaw status to which she would be consigned by the social powers that be. While Charity's mother seems grotesque, figured as "other" to bourgeois desire, Charity herself demands a share of the symbolic space within the domestic and dominant scheme of social relations. Her resistance forces Royall to admit that *his* desire cannot be contained within patriarchal relations either. Unlike Simon Rosedale in *The House of Mirth,* who still desires Lily but will only marry her if she regains her community status by blackmailing Bertha, Royall wants Charity despite her loss of exchange value. In accepting Charity, Royall must also accept, in the person of the baby and the rival, the displacement of the very patriarchal descent he is supposed to uphold. These relations are mystified in the name of a disingenuous benevolence that is patently transparent. Charity in turn becomes less fixed by the roles she inherits—of daughter, scorned lover, wife—and seems intent to keep herself poised for the ongoing battle she will wage with Royall.

Charity's Narcissism of Little Differences

Unconventional as the marriage is, so too is Wharton's demythologizing of motherhood. Wharton's representation of Charity's sexuality contests the dominant image of "the mother [as] a profoundly desexualized figure" (Jessica Benjamin 88). But why is it important to see the mother as sexualized? Charity's acceptance of Royall's marriage proposal is less a submission to an idealized other than it is a recognition of her own newly won identity, an ambivalent integration of both maternal and paternal powers. Lawyer Royall prefers to live in a world where patriarchy is compromised, and where he must keep the living proof of it around him, rather than accept a world where patriarchal rules do not obtain. Charity does, too. Rather than reduce or controvert the ambivalence of Charity's acceptance, I would foreground it as part of the struggle to assert herself: until her pregnancy, Charity reacted adversarially to both Royall's and Harney's domination; afterwards, she acts as an agent in determining the nature of her relation to Royall. In this light, the novel does not exemplify Wharton's "fatality" (Gilbert 378), since agency, not fatality, is at the center of Wharton's concern about eroticized motherhood. What is more, Wharton historicizes this struggle within the frames of the eugenics debate and an abortion decision in order to suggest how idealizing motherhood thwarts her heroine's sexual desire.

Here, as well as earlier in *The Custom of the Country* and later in *Twilight Sleep*, Wharton debunks the hereditary view of the "good mother," the woman who finds her greatest satisfaction in the maternal "instinct" and the propagation of a fit race. Bad mothering is not, for Wharton, a legacy of a "psychopathological curse" (Badinter 261). She may suggest that the Mountain represents just such a curse, but Charity's case need not be the same. Denouncing the myth of hereditary unsuitability, Wharton disputes the eugenicist argument, an attack she will repeat in her 1927 and 1928 novels, *Twilight Sleep* and *The Children*. She worried about the medicalizing of the "bad mother," as well as the moralizing of hereditary and eugenicist discourse. As she came to see in the twenties, eugenics arguments were often directed against women like herself—women who refused to have children in favor of an intellectual life.

Yet as a deliberate response to the cultural idealization of motherhood, this novel focuses as much on the question of what constitutes a good father as it does on the cultural valuation of a good mother. In *Summer,* Wharton's challenge is double-edged: while debunking the myth of the bad mother, she sees the "pathogenic" or bad father as central to family life, to the "good parenting" that is at stake in the eugenics debate (Badinter 288). Royall is an absent figure for identification, as is Charity's mother, so Charity forges an alternative identity for herself. Charity wants freedom, while her adoptive father wants her submission. When Royall offers her seduction rather than protection, thereby making him not so much absent as symbolically incestuous, Charity substitutes Harney—who seems omnipotent to her in his crossing of class boundaries—as her object of identification. The ability to see herself in rhetorical alignment, instead of agonistic opposition, allows Charity the sense of contingency she needs in asserting her desire.

If we see Charity's relation with Harney and her initial rejection of Royall's desire in this light, then her erotic experience with Harney is only part victimage and, more tellingly, partly an enactment of her desire for recognition (Jessica Benjamin 126). Thus, she must reject the notion of sexuality as economic exchange: she forgoes her "value" and her "power" and gives herself freely to Harney—a "different and less straightforward affair" (*Summer* 63)—frustrating the homosocial economy that Royall's desire and rule typify. No "victim of the perilous venture," Charity chooses mutual desire throughout; even in the confines of North Dormer, her desire is less a risk to herself than it is disruptive of things as they are. Unlike her relation with Royall—who violates her room if not her body ("He put his foot across the threshold, she stretched out her arm and stopped him" [29])—Charity's relation with the outsider Harney allows her separation from North Dormer and from the possibility of incest, a possibility with all of her relations both in North Dormer and on the Mountain. In rejecting the oedipal configuration, Charity sounds Wharton's death knell for the family as a functioning unit.

Lest I sound too celebratory in this reading of Charity's desire, I do want to qualify her sense of power with a Freudian proviso: she does succumb to the narcissism of little differences, seeing herself as distinct from the other young women of North Dormer. When we see the loss of uniqueness women face in debates about the potentiality of motherhood and their reproductive rights, this narcissism of distinguishing little differences is understandable. Whether or not Charity's public sexuality saves her, she must continually readjust her sense of self in order to accommodate her visions of these other women's fates. Where at first she prides herself for being "contemptuously aloof" from the activities of the other girls (61), she comes to recognize how everyone else takes her for one of them. She has a fear of being the "other woman," of having the same romantic delusions other girls had of being rescued from North Dormer: "If [Harney] wanted her he must seek her: he must not be surprised into taking her as girls like Julia Hawes were taken . . ." (106). She does not go to see Harney in his room. She knows only too well that he would welcome her: "It was simply that she had suddenly understood what would happen if she went in. It was the thing that *did* happen between young men and girls, and that North Dormer ignored in public and snickered over on the sly. . . . It was what had happened to Ally Hawes's sister Julia, and had ended in her going to Nettleton, and in people's never mentioning her name" (105). With Harney, Charity does not want to seem like other girls, expecting presents in return for her sexual openness. This novel sets up a pattern that reappears in other Wharton novels: when a woman receives a gift of jewelry, as Charity does from Harney(as Susy Branch in *Glimpses of the Moon* and Kate Clephane in *The Mother's Recompense* do), there is hell to pay.

While Charity wants to see her sexual relation as countercultural, Harney and Royall make it so clearly economic that it smacks of degradation, prostitution, and shame, the same shame Charity sees in Julia Hawes's status as a whore. Once Charity realizes that "she had given [Harney] all she had . . . she [understands] . . . the case of girls like herself to whom this kind of thing happened" (198). And when Dr. Merkle takes Charity for an abortion case like Julia's, Charity's narcissistic daydream ends. Yet her denial of the sexual exchange operative in American culture does not compromise or negate her sexuality. Wharton foregrounds this contradiction in Charity's case—between women's sexual agency and their victimage—to suggest that the rhetoric of reproduction is much more complicated than the eugenicists believe, for the eugenicists fail to account for women's sexuality. Charity's position remains a liminal one: married to the man who is and is not her father, pregnant with a baby whose only link to "its unknown father" is the blue broach Harney had given to her.

Julia's sister, Ally, who is Charity's friend and a "good girl" (another disruption of the hereditary thesis regarding women's crimes), speaks the most haunting words of the novel when she talks about her sister's abortion: "She came as near as anything to dying . . ." (125). Charity, too, faces her mother's dead body and potentially her own death when she rejects abortion and chooses childbirth. Reproductive choice is not beyond Charity's control, and in her choosing to have Harney's baby and marry Royall, the dynamics of all of her choices become clear. Those choices might be ambivalent ones, but they nevertheless have real consequences in uniting the heredity in the mother's body, the putatively "advanced" cultural inheritance of the father, and the social adaptability of her adoptive father. In this way, *Summer* suggests Wharton's growing interest in a cultural criticism that questions America's myths of exceptionalism and progressivism, based as they are on the troubling assumption of eugenic and dysgenic hierarchies of civilized and uncivilized communities.

Old Maids and Good Mothers

As Hamilton Cravens argues in *The Triumph of Evolution* (47), the eugenics movement brought people together from the right, left, and center in the years before World War I, creating as strange a set of bedfellows as the more recent case when Catharine MacKinnon and Andrea Dworkin found themselves aligned with members of the right against pornography. Similarly, Wharton's sexual politics did not find her allies in fellow artists like Charlotte Perkins Gilman or Gertrude Atherton, Kathleen Norris or Mary Baker Eddy. While these other writers advanced a conservative agenda, designed to celebrate racial motherhood, Wharton continued to muddy the issue of genetic purity. Another Wharton novel deals with the issue of counter-eugenics, *The Old Maid* (1924), and is something of a wish-dream, one that deals with one woman's struggle to keep her illegitimate child without publicizing her pregnancy. Charlotte Lovell cares for Tina, establishing a home for orphans where no one will suspect she is Tina's mother. The family explains Charlotte's strange calling by saying that she was shocked by the "degradation of the 'poor whites' and their children" in Georgia (65). Wharton's reference here to the proverbial "white trash" of the dysgenic documents suggests the cultural commonplace eugenics occupied, especially in narrative accounts about the Jukes, the Kallikaks, the families who have not bred well. In the novel, the English and Dutch Ralstons represent the old stock of Europeans, a family into which Delia and Charlotte Lovell want to marry. Taking up the generational thinking common in eugenics tracts, Wharton mocks its genteel pretensions: "Two marriages with Dutch Vandergraves had consolidated these qualities of thrift and handsome living, and the carefully built-up Ralston character was now so congenital that Delia Ralston sometimes asked herself whether, were she to turn her own little boy loose in a wilderness, he would not create a small New York there . . ." (61). The belief that traits were "congenital"—attributed to heredity and not to environment— was a mainstay of eugenics thought. Thus, for Wharton, inheritance becomes the crux of her argument against eugenic prejudices. When Joe

Ralston asks his fiancée Charlotte to give up her orphanage lest his own unborn children might "catch things," Charlotte balks; Delia, however, mouths the same precautions against the "contagion" of "poor people [who] were so ignorant and careless, and their children, of course, so perpetually exposed to everything catching" (68–69). The weaker stocks seem the source of social disease. Charlotte fears that her child will be sent to an institution or asylum (such as Vineland, New Jersey, where H. H. Goddard developed his theory of the Kallikak family). Delia cannot imagine her cousin Charlotte's child "growing up on charity in a Negro hovel, or herded in one of the plague-houses they called Asylums" (75).

The resonant word is "asylum" for Wharton, who had plenty of exchanges with doctors about asylums and institutions through Teddy's and her own neurasthenic breakdowns. If heredity were a significant cause (as the eugenicists argued), then it would not matter where Tina Lovell—"made of different stuff" (77)—was raised. Her innate tendencies would obviate any deleterious effects of the environment, whether this involved a hovel or an asylum. But Wharton's novels complicate the eugenics argument by showing incest as possible in civilized breeds, nobility possible in marginal ones. Here Wharton's characteristic ambivalence about motherhood does not arise from good or bad mothering, but from the social legislation of breeding. As in *Twilight Sleep*, the subject of Chapter Three, Wharton assails the easy elitism of her day. It is one of her major imaginative and political leaps.

In writing *Summer,* Wharton anticipates anthropological arguments, especially those of Malinowski (whom she would befriend in the thirties), against father-rights and the genetic argument about bad mothers as the source of eugenic decline. In doing so, she does not advocate mother-rights, but a more complex notion of culture than the sentimental one she had seen before World War I.[7] *Summer* may not be a blueprint for the new family, but it raises the questions about families and authority to which Wharton returns for the next decade. In the novels of the twenties, Wharton shows how contradictory identities really are: how the individual is always in the process of reconstructing one's identity, pushed and pulled by different cultural directives. Nonetheless, Wharton challenges the notion of the instinctual—the genetic, somatic, and biological theories of human behavior that would obviously limit the range of human motives to "scientific" ones. By showing how precarious the notion of identity is, how fixed social roles allow women only an illusion of security, Wharton contends against the biologism dominating popular eugenics. The limit of that struggle, as the next chapter shows, is the question of race.[8]

2

Why Gentlewomen Prefer Blondes: *The Mother's Recompense*

Edith Wharton's racial politics embarrass her critics. Notably, her anti-Semitism has been observed in critical commentary on *The House of Mirth, Twilight Sleep,* and the Beatrice Palmato fragment.[1] In the course of *Twilight Sleep,* Wharton's conventional racial references include one to Pauline Manford's spiritual leader, the Mahatma, as "the nigger chap" and to the Jewish film mogul Klawhammer as the "Dirty Jew . . . the kind we used to horsewhip" (46, 315). Her prejudice against African Americans and "coloured" foreigners is perhaps less known, but equally disquieting. While this chapter is not out to rehearse those politics, I will show how Wharton's racial views conflict with her sexual politics, creating contradictions in her fictions she did not often recognize, much less know how to resolve. I am not out to excuse her reprehensible stand on race, for she clearly made choices about which groups she believed could assimilate. Instead, I situate her work in the popular fiction of the twenties and thus dispute the standard critical view of her work during the period in which Wharton seemed to devote herself only to private dramas and intimate experience.

To that end, this discussion brings together several strains of Wharton's concerns in the mid-twenties: the emergence of mass culture and its effects on artists, as well as her audience; the rise of the Harlem Renaissance and other artistic communities competing for cultural dominance in America; and her even greater sense that technological progress ushered in a modernity which conflicted with the cultural values she held most dear, of stability, integrity, and intellectual and moral depth. In explaining Wharton's nostalgia for permanence and her lament over the standardization of mass culture, I introduce Antonio Gramsci's analysis of Taylor-ism and Fordism in order to show how Wharton found the rise of corporate capitalism to be the beginning of the end of her old New York, to which she said good-bye somewhat regretfully. Gramsci's theory of hegemony eerily registers Wharton's main attack on the "new tolerance" in America. According to both Wharton and Gramsci, this "new tolerance" is really an old fascism in disguise.

This chapter addresses Wharton's sympathies with and her ambivalence about the "new America" she diagnoses in *The Mother's Recompense*. In order to explore the dimensions of this new social order, I will discuss the sympathy Wharton had with Anita Loos and the antipathy she developed for Carl Van Vechten, two popular authors of the twenties. The second part of this chapter deals with the ambivalence about ethical values Wharton tries to resolve in her 1925 novel, the contradictions she saw at work in her culture but which she may not have realized were also dividing her fictions.[2]

The Mother's Recompense focuses on Kate Clephane, a woman who left her husband and three-year-old daughter, Anne, to escape the suffocation of marriage to a man who was "always the slave of anything he'd once said" (41). After eighteen years and the deaths of both her husband and mother-in-law, Kate receives a request from her daughter to return from the Riviera to New York. Wharton's novel asks us to scrutinize the old New York that Kate left in contrast to the new New York, where the unvarying "American Face" reflects this "mannerless age" (71, 52). Wharton sets this new America—with no morals, manners, or respectability of its own—against the Riviera, where all sorts of petty criminals and refugees from American scandals have settled and created their own society. When she returns to Anne and finds that her daughter is engaged to her old lover Chris Fenno, Kate debates whether to tell Anne of her affair with Chris or let her marry him, which raises the issue of symbolic incest. Kate chooses to return to Europe rather than to cause Anne "sterile pain"; she rejoins her social set on the Riviera, where her group never questioned her absence and where individuals had "no more substance or permanence than figures twitching by on a film" (262).

This and the many other references to film and to popular culture in *The Mother's Recompense* betray Wharton's preoccupation with mass culture and its amusements in the twenties. More important, such details reveal Wharton's cultural preference not for some imaginary age of innocence, but for an age of substance and permanence. Placing her work in the context of one of her favorite novels of the twenties, Anita Loos's 1925

Gentlemen Prefer Blondes, and one of her most hated, Carl Van Vechten's
1926 *Nigger Heaven,* I foreground Wharton's competing demands for a
"new America," demands issuing in part from her nostalgia for the stability of the "old America" and her fears concerning these new preoccupations. Wharton's 1925 novel is part of a larger cultural constellation of
popular twenties fiction, with Loos's and Van Vechten's and another best-
seller of those publishing years, Bruce Barton's *The Man Nobody Knows*
(1925). Advertising culture (and Wharton gave fuller voice to her distrust in
the Vance Weston novels in the late twenties) raised the dangers that one
might not buy—not to mention *write*—fashionable commodities, and she
was clearly skeptical of such politics of taste.

For Wharton, public interference in the private matters of sexuality
and reproduction was the great offense of post–World War I politics and
the rise of fascism. Wharton's own political attack is aimed most specifically at women of privilege. As Wharton writes in *Twilight Sleep,* "[Soci-
ety] ladies always seemed to be the same, and always advocated with
equal zeal Birth Control and unlimited maternity, free love or the return
to the traditions of the American home; and . . . they . . . [never] seemed
aware that there was anything contradictory in these doctrines. All they
knew was that they were determined to force certain persons to do things
that those persons preferred not to do" (5–6). Her writing during and
after World War I addressed the dangers she saw in these sexual politics
and such routinization of daily life as the new vogues of Taylorism (the
cult of efficiency that became a social ideal) and Fordism (the corporate
appropriation of private life) demonstrated for her. As Martha Banta
defines it, Taylorism was "a historical 'given' of the early twentieth century, which fostered the dream of a 'contained' (often excessively controlled) society, and the narratives (also excessively controlled) that
sprang up out of the sense of urgency either to defend or to deny flat-out
assertions that the Answer to All had been found at last" (Banta 1993, x).

Taylorism and Fordism—like many of the other *isms* of modern life—
elided many of the issues dismaying Wharton because these economic
and social movements did not seem to face the production of culture or
the challenge to social control. Yet, at this point, I want to suggest why
Wharton would recognize class and sex as restrictive categories, but not
race. What inducement was there for her to see through the construction
of social position to some alternative social vision, one based on mutuality rather than dominance? One perceives in Wharton's fiction a special pleading for women's freedom—from whatever class—that she
could never extend to blacks and Jews, to racial "others." Wharton does
invite her readers to identify with her often marginalized heroines, but in

unconventional ways. However, her narrative strategies, as we shall see, offer other identifications, other ways to identify than those her culture usually furnished in flappers, autonomous heroes, or—in Barton—Jesus Christ as consummate businessman. Wharton's narrative sets up a process of identification, then, which presupposes a sympathy with the class and gender perspective she embodied in Kate Clephane. Unable or unwilling to imagine the racial other, Wharton's sympathies end there.

Propaganda versus Art: Wharton's Battle

Confronting the popular culture of Van Vechten and Anita Loos, on the one hand, and the propagandizing of Upton Sinclair for radical new social theories about blacks, Jews, and assimilation, on the other, Wharton found herself in the midst of a generational conflict. Unwilling to become either the popular writer or the ideologue, Wharton took another road in negotiating a variety of these social visions: the abundance theories of the Christian Scientists versus the bolsheviks' labor solutions. In her novel, she plays these alternatives out against the backdrop of a family torn apart by the shifts in allegiance to popular versus traditional ways of relating. Her method shifts with *The Mother's Recompense* insofar as she adopts a cultural dialogic, immersing herself in the rhetoric of the day in order to critique it. She finds that this dialogic means her negotiating with the psychology, psychoanalysis, and politics of sexuality that are played out in capitalism and radicalism.

Both Anita Loos's *Gentlemen Prefer Blondes* and Wharton's novel of the same year see women's lives as being prescribed by the contradictions of their contemporaneous political and economic scene. Taylorism and corporate management provide the impetus for both Loos's Lorelei and Wharton's Pauline Manford and Kate Clephane, no less than they do for Van Vechten's heroines. Indeed, the contradictions between personal (especially sexual) freedom and corporate abundance theory mark the popular writings of the mid-twenties: as Jackson Lears argues in *No Place of Grace,* the mind-cure movement was of a piece with the whole "abundance therapy," thereby linking the psychic concerns of the domestic front with the industrial growth advocated by "corporate liberal ideologues—social engineers who spoke of economic rather than psychic abundance but who shared the interest of mind-curists in liberating repressed impulses" (54). Wharton sees no value in either psychic or economic abundance theories, which for her only led to a greater repression and intolerance. She posits her own theory of "sterile pain" in answer to these liberal ideologues and social engineers advocating a false liberation and an unchecked narcissism.

Taylorism, meanwhile, advocated scientific management of labor and tried, as Martha Banta argues, "to accommodate the drift of the age toward reform measures as a way to fend off revolution" (1989, 210). Antisentimental in orientation, Taylorism proposed a way of (seemingly) reconciling the ideals of individualism in a collectivized, albeit atomized world of mechanical labor. Rather than worry about these social contradictions, the rhetoric of Taylorism joined radical individualism with communal ideals of labor, without regard to the personal and gender conflicts embedded in these views (Banta 1989, 216, 219). Both reformers and bolsheviks are identified as the enemy because they object to the dominance of capitalism as the only goal of American democracy. Somehow, happiness had to be found in the isolated work of and for American capitalism, even though this "happiness" depended on the repression of communal life and, as Gramsci points out in *Prison Notebooks,* suppression of erotic life (Banta 1989, 226). Later in the twenties, Antonio Gramsci's meditations in "Americanism and Fordism" point to some of the same conclusions: the First World War diffused psychoanalytic practice so that psychoanalysis "increased [the] moral coercion exercised by the apparatus of State and society on single individuals" (Gramsci 280).

Gramsci's claims about Fordism in American culture hit the same target as Wharton had through her fiction; for Gramsci, the post-war period

> involved a particular repression of sexual instincts. . . . The crisis was made even more violent, and still is, by the fact that it affected all strata of the population and came into conflict with the necessities of the new methods of work which were meanwhile beginning to impose themselves. (Taylorism and rationalisation in general.) These new methods demand a rigorous discipline of the sexual instincts (at the level of the nervous system) and with it a strengthening of the "family" in the wide sense (rather than a particular form of the familial system) and of the regulation and stability of sexual relations. (299–300)

Gramsci notes that Ford and other industrialists were keenly interested in the sexual lives of workers, in and outside of the family. The sexual instinct was regulated and rationalized in order to create the most efficient worker, the greatest good for the industrial-capitalist complex. Both Loos and Wharton reject this mechanization of labor and desire and, along with it, the fascist control of sexuality. Again, Gramsci: "'Womanising' demands too much leisure. . . . It seems clear that the new industrialism wants monogamy: it wants the man as worker not to squander his nervous energies in the disorderly and stimulating pursuit of occasional sexual satisfaction. . . . The exaltation of passion cannot be reconciled with the timed movements of productive motions connected with the most perfected automatism" (304–5). In her repeated musings on Taylorism, from *The Mother's Recompense* through *Twilight Sleep*, Wharton questions this subjugation of sexuality to automatized work. In this case, Chris's "womanizing" not only keeps him from his literary work, his writing, but it also chains him to the overheated stimulations of mass culture; Wharton represents him as so devoted to his sexual satisfaction that he can ignore the symbolic incest of his relation with Anne. He becomes the sexual automaton that is the logical extension of Gramsci's critique of sexuality under Fordism. While Chris is perfectly guilt-free, Kate is motivated by guilt: first her guilt is over the affair with Chris, and then it is ruined by the conjecture that the new American tolerance might actually forgive her for it. Wharton's heroines resist any sexuality that serves either the state or the status quo, although Kate ends up fighting alone against her culture's repressions and its evasions.

Thus, productive and reproductive labor (for Gramsci and Wharton, respectively), not intellect or sexual instinct, became the guiding principle of pre-Depression life. The only ethics of culture were business ones; no wonder that Barton's life of Christ as consummate businessman in *The Man Nobody Knows* was such a popular success in a culture bent on commodification and newly uncertain ethical standards. As Barton writes, "To create any sort of reception for a new idea today involves a vast expense and well-organized machinery of propaganda. Jesus had no funds and no machinery. . . . Every one of His conversations, every contact between His mind and others, is worthy of the attentive study of any sales manager" (Barton 49, 58). According to Banta, "Living in a pinch . . . between individualist theories and collectivist facts, the new man suffers the constant threat of fragmentation" (228).

The New Woman suffers, too. Hers is a double privation since both her gender and her class contribute to her alienation from her labor. Consider, for example, Wharton's reference to Frederick Taylor, the inventor of these new work models: Kate's maid Aline works in "spare Taylorized gestures" (6). Aline is the model of efficiency and devotion, although it does not prevent her from raising an eyebrow at her employer's social conduct: the Taylorized gesture, as we will see in another maid, is a guise behind which marginalized classes and races conceal their awareness of the anxiety at the heart of the leisure class. Or consider *Twilight Sleep:* "What was the use of all the months and years of patient Taylorized effort against the natural human fate: anxiety, sorrow, old age—if their menace was to reappear whenever events slipped from her control?" (114). Such detail is important to Wharton precisely because of the way in which business and technology have infiltrated the domestic realm. Wharton did not ignore social movements as large as these, nor could she afford to. In order to appraise the "new America" in *The Mother's Recompense,* she had to internalize its new directives toward social engineering or, as Banta explains, "the grand design" of industrial management which would contain human needs by managing and constructing them (1993, 17). In particular, Wharton writes of the social threat of fragmentation within the New—even Taylorized—Woman exemplified by Kate Clephane. What Wharton does not write is the drama of the working-class maid Aline or the black maid Phemia, whose "spare Taylorized gestures" barely conceal an awareness of the sexual anxieties of their employers.

Granted, what Wharton feared in her vision of the 1920s flapper society was an uncontrolled sexuality, a sexuality she feared the most from races (and occasionally the working classes) she understood the least. She believed the stereotype of blacks as slaves to their passions and reacted violently to the thought of Harlem life. In an unpublished letter to her friend Gaillard Lapsley dated 1 April 1927, Wharton expresses her hatred of black culture:

> Have you read "Nigger Heaven"? It is so nauseating (& such rubbish too) that I despair of the Republic—
> I thought the whole thing was made up, but the other day Mr. & Mme. Bourdet (of "La Prisonniere") came to lunch, & they told me they had been to New York for the "premiére" of the play there & had been taken by the "Jeunes" into nigger society in Harlem "et que cétait comme dans le livre." And now I must stop & be sick—(Beinecke Library)

What is "sickening" here for Wharton is that black Harlem epitomizes the uncontrolled sexuality she associates also with white flapper society, but the middle-class black intellectual set Van Vechten depicts threatens her popularity as well. There are few other references to her hatred of blacks in either the published or unpublished letters; what is telling about this response is that it comes on the heels of Van Vechten's celebration of a growing African-American culture in the Harlem Renaissance. Publicly, Wharton wrote Van Vechten off as propagandist; privately, her consciousness of race relations underwrites the racial subtext of *The Mother's Recompense.*

About one thing Wharton had no ambivalence: the propaganda novel. In a letter dated 19 August 1927 to Upton Sinclair, she denounces *Oil!*, his 1927 novel about the Teapot Dome oil debacle that was also a call for socialism, as descending into a "political pamphlet. I make this criticism without regard to the views which you teach, and which are detestable to me. Had you written in favor of those in which I believe, my judgment would have been exactly the same. I have never known a novel that was good enough to be good in spite of its being adapted to the author's political views" (Lewis and Lewis 500–1). Similarly, Wharton saw Van Vechten's work as sheer proselytizing for the ascendancy of Harlem culture, even though a debate about the values of propagandistic novels is one of the problematic themes of *Nigger Heaven*.[3] Van Vechten's hero Byron Kasson struggles with "the Negro problem," and his girlfriend Mary Love cautions him about overreaction: "These propaganda subjects are very difficult, Byron, very difficult, that is, to make human. It is hard to keep them from becoming melodramatic, cheap even. Unless such a story is written with an exquisite skill, it will read like a meretricious appeal to the emotions arising out of race prejudice" (204). How far is this from Wharton's own aesthetic? On the surface at least, Wharton's objections are similar to Van Vechten's, insofar as Van Vechten struggles with propaganda and aesthetics in *Nigger Heaven*. Similarly, Wharton's literary goal was to "make human" the social contradictions she observed in American social relations. Despising melodrama as cheap, Wharton praised a finer sensibility, a broader awareness of emotional motive.

Instead, Van Vechten focuses on the "exotic low life" (107) of cabaret Harlem, which he saw divided between black intellectuals and people who were "slaves to their passions," people who frequented the Black Venus, the Harlem after-midnight hang-out. Black women were especially afflicted, given the limits he imputes: "There's only one success for a woman, Adora announced, at least for a coloured woman, and that's a good husband, and a good husband for a coloured woman means a rich husband" (29). Consider this statement in the light of Anita Loos's Blonde Venus Lorelei, the blonde whom gentlemen prefer. Her search for a good husband—a good provider, a sugar daddy—is predicated on the notion that the only good spouse is a rich one. While Wharton can see vindication in Loos, she sees only contempt in Van Vechten's propaganda, although Loos's novel is no less propagandizing than Van Vechten's—or Wharton's for that matter.

Whether Wharton expresses an unconscious fear of competition for a popular audience she often mistrusted is not the issue; rather, Wharton's allegiance to a restricted cultural politics defines her social vision here. Van Vechten is alert to the issue, taking Wharton to task in *Nigger Heaven* for her views: "I don't see any sense in writing about this [the new Negro intellectual], Byron protested, rather hotly, Mary thought. It's too much like Edith Wharton's set" (107). Byron, the would-be author in *Nigger Heaven* who has been recently graduated from Penn, objects to Wharton's intellectualism and elitism, the two qualities she had come to represent for Van Vechten. For Wharton, Van Vechten made the artistic sin of stepping out of his "own set"—upper-middle class whites—and into Harlem, thereby writing a novel that is unabashed about its status as propaganda and about his ironic critique, as Langston Hughes saw it, a notion that Wharton could only begin to grasp. She saw so little to take seriously in the Harlem life of arts and ideas that she just could not make the imaginative leap. The black intellectual society in Van Vechten's novel debates the future of the Negro writer (42–43), an idea Wharton barely comprehends. In that debate, Van Vechten's characters worry over the fact that "the white editors are beginning to regard Negroes as interesting novelties, like white elephants or black roses." Filled with references to both white and black authors and texts—Jean Toomer, Sherwood Anderson, Gertrude Stein, Wallace Stevens (57, 100–01, 111–12)—Van Vechten tries to integrate black culture into white; at the same time, he establishes the integrity of Harlem life.

Even scarier than this claim to someone of Wharton's stripe is that the assimilation of the Jews provides a model for middle-class blacks. One need only remember Wharton's representation of the "glossy Jew" Rosedale in *The House of Mirth* to conjure her fear of assimilation and the erasure of racial boundaries. One of Van Vechten's characters says: "Look at the Jews. A lot of Nordics despise them, but they can't ignore them. They're much too important financially" (51). Byron himself imagines that a mass revolution might be possible, "a mass that might even assume an aggressive attitude" (189). And if the revolution is not forthcoming, intermarriage and miscegenation—both contested by black intellectuals—remain possible: "I read somewhere, said Byron, about a fellow who holds a theory that this . . . this . . . flair the white man has for our women will eventually solve the race problem. We'll all be absorbed in the white race!" (183). Van Vechten challenges high- and low-cultural hierarchies, along with the politics of cross-class and cross-racial assimilation; on the contrary, Wharton's fiercely defended individualism no longer constitutes a stay against the masses.

Wharton's ethics are antagonistic to views like Van Vechten's. Only once in *The Mother's Recompense,* for instance, does Wharton mention race, in reference to the "negress" who is the maid at Chris Fenno's house. Kate remains oblivious to her presence at the Fennos' Baltimore home, but it is Phemia, the maid, who informs Anne about Kate's confrontation with Chris at his house. Anne explains to Kate, "'Mother,' she broke out, 'the day I went to Baltimore to see him the maid who opened the door didn't want to let me in because there'd been a woman there two days before who'd made a scene. A scene—that's what she said! Isn't it horrible?'" (157). When Anne presses her mother, Kate slips and asks whether "the negress" really said that Anne looked like the woman who had made the scene. With this slip—for Anne had never said the Fenno maid was black—she knows that her mother intervened in her engagement, compelling Chris to break it off. She dismisses her mother with the claim that she must "manage [her] own life in [her] own way" (161). Kate does not see Phemia as a threat to her secret or her privacy; she does not recognize Phemia and does not imagine how she could be the key to Anne's knowledge that it was Kate who got Chris to break off the engagement.

As Kenneth Warren remarks about Henry James's references to race and ethnicity, Wharton's, too, were often "throwaway" comments intended more as anchoring dialogue in the colloquialisms of the day (20). But they also reveal more about the possibilities both James and Wharton saw for social equality; for James, this meant imagining intimate connections in public spaces with racial others, an intimacy Warren sees as troubling to James (22): "James's remarks emerge from a context in which the social distribution of consciousness and feeling was racially and politically inflected" (25). Wharton resisted seeing other races as having their own cultures, as her letter to Lapsley shows, or as being able to contribute to her culture, except in the most circumscribed or unusual way. Wharton's narrative hinges on Phemia's revelation to Anne that her mother had caused a scene with Chris in his parents' house. Wharton puts Phemia to use as a narrative device, without, I submit, fully understanding the implications of the black maid as the central consciousness of these fateful scenes and as the agent of Kate's estrangement from her daughter. Phemia recognizes the likeness between mother and daughter and reveals it to Anne, whereby Anne trips up her mother's contact with "the negress" (158). Insofar as Wharton herself is by this time a "new American," this moment makes emblematic how the "new America" is not as tolerant as its liberal ideology promotes. Wharton uses the black maid as an agent of fictional consciousness at the same time as she denounces the idea of a Harlem culture as generating a new social and aesthetic set of premises. While Wharton self-consciously indicts "American faces" as blank, uniform, and lacking individuality, she unconsciously attributes black American faces with an uncanny recognition and powers of discrimination.

Wharton's denial of the politics of her fiction notwithstanding, her narrative choices—like the one above—do have political meaning in their refraction of the cultural dialogue around her. Her fiction displays the fractures of the twenties, in both private and public worlds. Wharton's refusal to recognize Harlem culture reveals just how much she wants to maintain a cultural authority guaranteed by her race and class and, simultaneously, to oppose paternal authority and domination. In dismissing the "tone" of this novel as "grudging, perhaps even querulous," Cynthia Griffin Wolff claims that the tone "verges on both of these without achieving the sure edge of satirical devastation. . . . Published in the same year as *The Great Gatsby, The Mother's Recompense* was no match for the work of the younger writers when it came to capturing the mood of that strange era [the jazz age]" (1977, 372). My point is, however, that Wharton readily compared herself to other controversial writers—like Loos and Van Vechten—whose social criticism took turns every bit as complex as Fitzgerald's. And like Fitzgerald, Loos, and Van Vechten, if not Upton Sinclair or Bruce Barton, Wharton encodes her political views in the intimacies—and lack thereof—among her characters. Kate's failure is that she cannot imagine any intimacy or shared knowledge with the black maid with whom she shares a crucial revelatory moment. The fact is that Loos and Van Vechten both went further in their progressive notions of race relations—even Lorelei recognizes the dehumanizing force of the word "nigger" (28–29)—than Wharton ever did, or could.

Wharton did not often recognize the contradictions in her fictions, much less know how to resolve them; nevertheless, her ambivalence points to the psychic terrain of the 1920s and larger social issues that remained repressed. If anything, her hard line against dissidents and radicals during World War I was mostly forgotten in the twenties' cultural amnesia. All around her, the middle class especially was split generationally, the younger generation bitter and disillusioned by the authority and authoritarianism of the older. As one historian of the twenties argues: "Young people have an uncanny sense of what infuriates their parents: in a decade of strong nativist feeling and race prejudice they gravitated toward the most forbidden emblems of independence, Negro dancing and Negro jazz" (Sklar 20). Perhaps Wharton had this same conservative sense that the force of her moral authority was being countermanded. Occasionally disillusioned herself after the war, she takes up her anxiety about the "new America"—largely represented by Harlem culture, jazz, and flappers—in a novel playing out these generational conflicts. Neither flapper nor ossified member of the middle class herself, Wharton can support neither Harlem Renaissance nor the old nativism. She is as ambivalent as her heroine Kate Clephane is about the New Woman's role. Even though she rejected the previous century's Know-Nothingism, Wharton does not know what to embrace in her own time.

By 1925, Wharton could no longer afford to turn her back to or evade these challenges. Later, in the thirties, Wharton would write: "[Gross, her maid] and I can think of nothing but the Lindbergh baby, and I cannot reconcile myself to the idea of living in a world populated by such fiends. I turn back to my Reminiscences, and try to forget what the world is like now in remembering what a safe little place it used to be when we were young!" (to Minnie Jones, 21 March 1932, Beinecke Library). Perhaps indulging in grand nostalgia, perhaps in more of her complex irony, Wharton preferred to imagine a world free from moral monsters and criminals, a world ready for her particular aesthetic and ethical reform. Wharton the *gentlewoman* prefers blondes like Lorelei because the author sees in her adventures an effort at economic security unanchored by marriage and outdated morality, a freer Undine Spragg.

The Power of Contradiction

As much as Wharton admired Fitzgerald's *The Great Gatsby,* especially the "perfect Jew" he rendered in Wolfsheim (see Lewis and Lewis 481–82), she admired Anita Loos's *Gentlemen Prefer Blondes* even more. Although her famous letter to Fitzgerald links her with his interest in illustrating the shallowness of the twenties, Wharton's relation to Van Vechten and Loos is more significant, given her sense of competition with them for a popular audience. She describes Loos's novel as a masterpiece in a letter to John Hugh-Smith (26 January 1926, Beinecke Library), and she elaborates on her praise for this popular novel in her letter's postscript: "I don't know if the Blonde's trick of speech is southern—but I somehow know it's *all right*—& that Undine at last is vindicated!" (see Lewis and Lewis 491).[4] Wharton here refers to her heroine of *The Custom of the Country* (1911), but I would argue that she also takes Lorelei Lee as a model heroine for Pauline Manford in *Twilight Sleep.* Loos's novel is the story of an uninhibited young woman's social education; Lorelei runs rampant over American culture, including corporate America, where she is quite comfortable with the new sexual freedom of the twenties. Wharton needed this vindication about Undine because she felt Undine relentlessly and unduly criticized.[5] In *The Mother's Recompense*, Wharton shows the delicate balancing act involved in women "managing" their own lives. As in *The Age of Innocence*, Wharton seems, both literally and figuratively, to look back to the past and to see how the exigencies of the present must be met.

The once extremely popular *Gentlemen Prefer Blondes* is important for Wharton because it validates the writer's strategies of counter-identification: the identificatory process is located in a heroine every bit as ambivalent or conflicted as any Wharton might have created. Loos, like Wharton, sketches out how white women negotiate male power. A case in point is Loos's portrait of Freud, loosely veiled in Lorelei's diary as "Dr. Froyd." Lorelei's escort Mr. Eisman takes her to a "famous doctor in Vienna" to keep her from "trying to reform the whole world" (Lorelei's cover for her sexual exploits):

> So Dr. Froyd and I had quite a long talk in the english landguage. So it seems that everybody seems to have a thing called inhibitions, which is when you want to do a thing and you do not do it. So then you dream about it instead. So Dr. Froyd asked me, what I seemed to dream about. So I told him that I never really dream about anything. I mean I use my brains so much in the day time that at night they do not seem to do anything else but rest. So Dr. Froyd was very very surprized at a girl who did not dream about anything. So then he asked me all about my life. I mean he is very very sympathetic, and he seems to know how to draw a girl out quite a lot. I mean I told him things that I really would not even put in my diary. So then he seemed very very intreeged at a girl who always seemed to do everything she wanted to do. . . . For instance did I ever want to do a thing that was really vialent, for instance, did I ever want to shoot someone for instance. So then I said I had, but the bullet only went in Mr. Jennings lung and came right out again. (155–56)

Loos celebrates Lorelei's uninhibited sexual freedom as it subverts the repression of psychoanalytic coercion. Her lack of inhibition (really, her ability to act without repression) becomes a comic paradigm for the way Wharton's heroines struggle with social demands. Lorelei—like Undine before her and Pauline Manford after her—seriously questions Freud's theory of repression. *The Mother's Recompense* is, in this respect also, an extended meditation on Wharton's battle with the popularization of psychoanalysis. Lorelei suggests what Loos (and Wharton) could not say outright: that "Dr. Froyd" did not know what women want, that his psychology of women left out the economics of women's oppression, relying as it did on seemingly universalist claims about complexes and instincts. But Wharton saw these psychological complexes and instincts as less individual ones and more determined by the new American efforts to standardize taste, culture, and personality.

Loos's novel also vindicated Wharton on two other social fronts—Christian Science (along with other mind cures) and bolshevism, both of which interested Wharton as much as they did Loos. Lorelei parodies the former as her religion of permissiveness. When dealing with Mr. Spoffard's mother (Mr. Spoffard was one of Lorelei's most ardent suitors), she espouses her own brand of Christian Science:

> So then I ordered luncheon and I thought some champagne would make her feel quite good for luncheon so I asked her if she liked champagne. . . . But I told her that I was a Christian science, and all of we Christian science seem to believe that there can not really be any harm in anything, so how can there be any harm in a small size bottle of champagne? . . . So then we had luncheon and she began to feel very very good. So I thought that we had better have another bottle of champagne because I told her that I was such an ardent Christian science that I did not even believe there could be any harm in two bottles of champagne. (165)

Like Pauline Manford of *Twilight Sleep,* Lorelei can reconcile mind cure with bodily pleasure. Lorelei's emphasis on "education"—the euphemisms throughout for her exploits in Europe—is but a guise for her own imperialism of the self. While Mr. Eisman, her industrialist benefactor, hunts down a button factory to buy in order to extend his corporate empire, Lorelei matches him move for corporate move on the seduction front. Thus, Loos suggests that women need to rely on the same sort of abundance theory advanced in business. Bruce Barton's *The Man Nobody Knows* and its thesis of Christ as corporate executive was the bestseller of 1925–26; no less surprising, then, is that Lorelei's business sense about seduction makes her as popular as Barton's pseudo-secular hero. Here Loos, like Wharton, was in the business of justifying women's necessary shift from the home into corporately-informed sexual management. To "manage," as Susy Lansing does in *The Glimpses of the Moon* (1922) and as Wharton's other heroines of the twenties do, is the necessary enterprise of the modern woman.

Lears contends that the 1880s through the 1920s—what he terms the antimodernist period—marked the end of sentimental power and the beginning of a cultural nostalgia for the authenticity of nineteenth-century life. He documents the response to the crisis over modernism that resulted in arts and crafts movements, neurasthenia, and new cults of medievalism that arose to cure people of the dis-ease or the "crisis of cultural authority" at the time. Lears intimates that many modernist women neither raged against the end of sentimental power nor grew nostalgic for separate spheres. What Wharton and Loos saw, for instance, was a way for women to break free from the domestic restraints of nineteenth-century domestic cults. In turning toward the abundance theories of culture—theories that suggested the rich possibilities of tapping into new forms of social power—Loos's Lorelei and Wharton's twenties' women could relinquish domestic norms for potentially liberating ones. Lorelei was a mystery to more than Loos's "Dr. Froyd": she would be the mysterious new New Woman of corporate America.

To the degree that women's liberation was imagined in the twenties as a kind of corporate psychic-sexual power, the New Woman was expected to countervail the anxieties bolshevism intensified, especially as revolution was imagined to be engineered by Jewish financiers. Not surprisingly, the Bolshevik Revolution figures in Loos's novel, Atherton's 1923 *Black Oxen* (discussed in the next chapter), and Wharton's letters of the twenties. Stuart Ewen's *Captains of Consciousness: Advertising and the Social Roots of the Consumer Culture* explains why the fear of bolshevism struck such a chord in the twenties. As Ewen contends, "We must not take lightly the assertion heard among businessmen of the twenties that in mass production and mass consumption lay the answer to the growing threat of what was shorthandedly termed 'bolshevism.' In the corporate ideology of the 1920s, the goods of the marketplace were sold to the public with the 'liberating' and 'democratic' lingo which had up till then been heard among those whose attack was on the corporate premise of the market economy itself" (201). At the same time Gertrude Atherton was writing about rejuvenating the middle-aged body in *Black Oxen*, consumer capitalism also gave rise to advertising as a way to revitalize post-war culture and stave off bolshevik agitation. Similarly, like Loos and Atherton, Wharton invoked bolshevism as a specter threatening woman's new freedoms in general, her sense of the "inner life" in particular.

While Wharton responded to the fear of bolshevism, she did not think advertising was the solution to the problem bolshevism represented. The "quieter universe" she hoped for did not reemerge in post-war culture, nor did the demand for quieter books. Hence, to fend off both bolshevism and the rise of mass culture—two varied but related threats—Wharton wrote novels designed to counter what Ewen calls the "commercialization of creativity" (66). Moreover, Wharton felt the need to address the growing incursion of advertising in the arts. If advertising was "the answer to bolshevism," and itself a "fundamental process of Americanization," then Wharton would challenge this "new America" with more traditional, because aesthetic and ethical, values (Ewen 88, 93).

Wharton's ethical values had to counter—or at least take into account—the fear of bolshevism that often went hand-in-hand with anti-Semitism, especially as Henry Ford characterized US and international Jews in the *Dearborn Independent* and in the publication of the Protocols of Zion in the early twenties, which he finally retracted as a forgery in 1927.[6] Arguing for Jewish subversion of American life, Henry Ford was bent on proving that bolshevism was a Jewish plot. Along with the anti-Semitic propaganda Ford published from 1920 to 1924, he included attacks on women's clubs, which as Elinor Lerner cogently argues, were posed as leading questions: one of these, "entitled, 'Are Women's Clubs "Used" by Bolshevists?' presented interconnections between the memberships of various feminist and peace groups. This 'interlocking directorate' was held to represent an international Bolshevik conspiracy. The Spider Web Chart, as this diagram of women's multiple affiliations was called, became a major tool in conservative attacks on women's groups" (322–23). In short, women were implicated—innocently or not—in public, political conspiracy theories.

Bolshevism also figures as a threat to Lorelei's friend Mr. Eisman, a crucial instance of Loos's defense of Jewish business since she refutes the Jewish/bolshevik connection established in the popular press. Eisman only gives Lorelei a "little thing" instead of the biggest square cut diamond in New York, and she is moved to ponder capitalism:

> I mean he kept talking about how bad business was and the button profession was full of bolshevicks who made nothing but trouble. Because Mr. Eisman feels that the country is really on the verge of the bolshevicks and I become quite worried. I mean if the bolshevicks do get in, there is only one gentleman who could handle them and that is Mr. D. W. Griffith. . . . And when I saw how Mr. Griffith handled all of those mobs in Intolerance I realized that he could do any-

thing, and I really think that the government of America ought to tell Mr. Griffith to get all ready if the bolshevicks start to do it. (19–20)

Dwelling on the fear of bolshevik power in the twenties, Lorelei echoes as well the cultural prejudice about the end of American business and individualism. J. C. Furnas quotes a March 1919 *Harper's Bazaar* in his *Great Times: An Informal Social History of the United States, 1914–1929*, in which the *Bazaar* warned: "There is a plague abroad in the land . . . bolshevism . . . [and] the cure is a thorough inoculation with Americanism" (259). Although Loos's Mr. Eisman fears the effect of unionism on the capitalist market, Lorelei would assuage his fears by bringing Griffith to bear on the situation, a Griffith who in *Intolerance* "celebrated the people en masse as hero" (Sloan 75).[7] Lorelei resolves the problem by suggesting a liberal solution—tolerance and populism—to a reactionary political intolerance of bolshevism. By invoking the mass appeal of such popular entertainment as film, Loos's Lorelei would manage the threat of bolshevization through the mediation of popular culture, a strategy that may ultimately have proved to work.

Loos and Wharton seize on bolshevism as the threat of collectivization, a political threat to bourgeois individualism, just as Freudianism in the twenties was also an affront to that individualism. In addition, bolshevism was also seen to jeopardize the only way women could conceivably "rise" in American culture. Although Wharton may not have celebrated the new narcissism of twenties culture, she did recognize the value of women's increasing individualization. Wharton admires Lorelei, who can voice sexual expression in the context of economic success, what Wharton would like but cannot have in Kate Clephane, her heroine of *The Mother's Recompense,* who is too clearly locked in to the old values of serial sexual monogamy. In making Kate pay for her rejection of marriage and conventional motherhood, Wharton responds paradoxically to Kate's decision to allow Anne and Chris's marriage. While applauding Kate's decision not to cause "sterile pain," Wharton shows how Kate's sacrifice for the sake of her daughter also limits Anne's emotional depth. Kate survives as an individual, but Anne's narcissism demonstrates "that one may be young and handsome and healthy and eager, and yet unable, out of such rich elements, to evolve a personality" (71).

If Loos's *Gentlemen Prefer Blondes* celebrates that triumph of the female individual over an increasingly difficult marriage market in a grim international economic scene marked by the rise of fascism, Wharton's 1925 novel imagines just how precarious that market could be for women.

This novel begins with Kate's reminiscences about gambling: she is on the Riviera, thinking over the "lost joys" of her winnings in the old days. Gambling testifies to the spirit of New Womanhood. Lily Bart and Undine Spragg, before Kate, are consummate gamblers, as is Loos's Lorelei herself. Chris Fenno had also gambled in the name of stimulating his artistic genius: "To be capable of that thought-play, of those flights, and yet to need gambling, casinos, rowdy crowds, and all the pursuits devised to kill time for the uninventive and lethargic!" (15). This gambling does not pay off, for the moment which gave success to Undine, like Lorelei, has passed. As Tom Lutz argues in *American Nervousness, 1903,* "Ways of spending one's nerve force—the paradigmatic examples are masturbation, gambling, and other forms of illicit sexual or financial activity—constituted a waste, a drain on nerve force without any corresponding reinvestment" (3–4). While Kate had gambled on finding freedom in leaving marriage and motherhood, she discovers upon her return that she has lost her family, but not her self.

While earlier novels like *The House of Mirth* and *The Custom of the Country* concern women's entry into society, Wharton's later fictions are typified by a character's retreat into mass culture, represented by the gambling casinos of Nice, Hollywood film, and self-help and the personality-improvement schemes so popular in the twenties. For Wharton, these cultural pastimes were at a remove from the ethical responsibility she believed fiction ought to promote. As she writes in a 6 May 1924 letter to Edward Sheldon, "I believe the movie has killed imagination, and that the allusive, the elliptical and the metaphorical are going to be, to this young generation, as much of a 'dead language' as English is rapidly becoming to them" (Lilly Library). As Paula Fass argues in *The Damned and the Beautiful,* what prevails in this youth culture, instead, is a widespread cultural conservatism masquerading as sexual liberation (see Fass 290–92). For Wharton, Kate's own immersion in that culture "was to escape from reality and durability [. . .] one plunged into cards, gossip, flirtation, and all the artificial excitements which society so lavishly provides for people who want to forget" (5). Seizing on the new "American Face" as blank and uninspiring, Kate denounces the whole cult of personality associated with mass culture, particularly in flapperhood and in narcissism. The only value she initially cultivates is an alienated nostalgia for the old society. Yet there is an important difference between Lily or Undine and Kate since Kate's is an escape from, rather than to, the artificial excitements of leisure-class society. She wants to pay with guilt, and the feeling that the new society may pardon her past indiscretions scares her as much as the symbolic incest—or her confession of it—does: "She would have felt herself befouled to the depths by Lilla's tolerance" (192). Kate's guilt at least confirms her sense of identity over and against the blankness and terror of the undifferentiated mass of people who now populate her old New York social scene, a world where a smooth indifference reigns and renunciation has no meaning. She asserts her difference from the "facial conformity" of any number of women in the social world of the "new generation" (121). Kate's greatest fear is to end up like any of them, and John Clephane's sister Enid was the representative of the facelessness of the American personality: "If she had conformed to the plan of life prepared for her, instead of turning from it and denying it, might she not reasonably have hoped to reappear on the scene in the form of Enid Drover?" (201).

As I have argued here, Wharton saw her culture immersed in a rampant individualism and overdetermined personal authority the effects of which Loos might parody but which Wharton could successfully dramatize. Nothing could deflect the horror of the symbolic violation Kate imagines. Kate recoils from Anne's engagement to Chris Fenno; denying the jealousy she feels, Kate imagines her horror at incest: "Was that why she had felt from the first as if some incestuous horror hung between them? . . . The very grave, she thought, would be hardly black enough to blot out that scene" (221–22). When she tries to confide in Fred Landers, he disavows the shame she feels, overcoming "his strongest feelings, his most deep-rooted repugnance" (271). But Fred, too, prefers to avoid the truth (254): "She remembered his first visit after her return; remembered how she had plied him with uncomfortable questions, and detected in his kindly eyes the terror of the man who, all his life had tried to buy off fate by optimistic evasions" (255). Kate's own evasion no longer works, and she must decide to confess or to return to Europe. Just when she is able to face the new America, Kate finds that America prefers to ignore its moral dilemmas on all fronts. Anne and her friends will idealize the mother, but Anne will not take Kate on the mother's own terms.

The Waning Power of the Mother

The struggle over the mother's cultural authority in the face of the new America is the focus of *The Mother's Recompense*, a nearly transparent reflection of Wharton's own struggle with her controlling mother. It is so much the focus, as it was of twenties life, that Wharton blocks out all other contemporary crises of authority, most particularly those of race and cultural difference. The problem does not lie in a singular dysgenic or "bad mother"—a notion Wharton dismissed in *Summer*. The cultural issue at hand for Wharton was, instead, the denial of motherhood altogether, whether by idealizing the mother out of existence or by negating her influence. Kate's daughter wholeheartedly adopts a therapeutic self, undergirded by an illusion of choice in selecting Chris Fenno as a mate, when really she is reinventing her mother's mistake: "Anne had inherited her capacity for such all-obliterating bliss" (207). In Wharton's vision, twenties culture promoted an autonomy too easily co-opted into a Freudian setpiece, itself popularized by an emerging capitalism. The sentimentalized good mother validates individualist notions of breaking free, separation, atomized boundaries, and domination—all values which ultimately serve what Gramsci calls Fordism. More important, the sentimentalized "good mother" is a racialized figure, a white woman who can assert the so-called natural primacy of a mother-daughter relationship.

Although Eve Sedgwick's influential *Between Men* (1985) has inspired a number of interpretations about the exchange of women in society, the exchange of men between women—in Wharton, between mother and daughter—has been generally left untheorized. Kate finds the exchange of Chris between mother and daughter horrifying; everyone else ignores or denies it. Characters talk about buying off pain or pleasure, even as Wharton sees them buying off repressions, too: "Her duty—how [Chris] used to laugh at the phrase! He told her she had run away from her real duties only for the pleasure of inventing new ones, and that to her they were none the less duties because she imagined them to be defiances. It was one of the paradoxes that most amused him: the picture of her flying from her conscience and always meeting it again in her path, barely disguised by the audacities she had dressed it up in" (97). This significant passage highlights Kate's dilemma: no matter how the trick of evasion works for Chris or even for her daughter Anne, Kate intuits that evading the contradictions is only a form of imperfect repression. She encounters again and again her maternal duties in being forced to take care of Chris, then Anne, then both of them. In the Taylorized world she sees before her, Wharton finds no place for mothers, whose influence has been surpassed by the new vision of personal liberty and its emphasis on sexual freedom.

While Lorelei flies in the face of respectability, Wharton demonstrates just how much her characters cling to it as a stave against modernity, against the flappers' sense of the "new tolerance," as Kate Clephane calls the tolerance of racial and cultural pluralism of the kind Wharton found so "nauseating" in Van Vechten's novel. Flapper culture, for Wharton, permits women's sexual freedom without diminishing the threat of the "natural enemies" of women, including such official guardians of culture as "lawyers, judges, trustees, [and] guardians" (8). Banished when she left her daughter in her husband's care, Kate has been prevented from seeing Anne for twenty years until both her ex-husband and ex-mother-in-law have died. While the judicial system saves Lorelei from prison when she shoots her employer and persuades the jury of her intended innocence, Kate imagines that being an independent woman—one who has left her daughter and husband behind because of her domestic unhappiness— imperils her culture. Because she is a sexual entity, she is also seen as a criminal by her society, which views mothers as self-sacrificing: "She had 'lost' Anne: 'lost' was the euphemism she invented . . . because a mother couldn't confess, even to her most secret self, that she had willingly deserted her child" (13). Kate had left the "oppression of her married life" (13), only to discover that her new freedom was an "asphyxiation of a different kind, that was all" (14). Now Kate pays the cost to the "outraged goddess of Respectability" (23), not so much out of moral crime but a sense of penance.

Compared to Loos's Lorelei, Wharton's Kate Clephane is cautiously conservative: "As she looked back, she saw herself always with taut muscles and the grimace of ease; always pretending that she felt herself free, and secretly knowing that the prison of her marriage had been liberty compared with what she had exchanged it for" (58). The prison-house of marriage, in other words, is no different from that of the stifling social atmosphere of the new modernity. The Great War saw at least a temporary necessity for women's work outside the home, but the end of it meant the return of independent women into domestic oblivion. Moreover, the war erased social differences and the hypocritical respectability Wharton denounced in earlier novels as well as in *The Mother's Recompense:* "Then the war came; the war which . . . was chiefly a healing and amalgamating influence" (24). What Wharton laments—indirectly for the most part, yet sometimes explicitly—is that women's novels (and their heroines) found too little cultural work to do. Lorelei's triumph is that she has no unconscious and invents the "job" she does; she does whatever she wants to do in the name of "education" or seduction. Wharton's understanding of women changes from 1913 to 1925 because the work of women—and of women novelists—changes. In the 1913 *Custom of the Country,* she writes a satirical critique of the forces which distort Undine; in 1925, however, she elaborates on the political and social forces which plague women—from Taylorism to Freudianism, Fordism, and eugenics. Wharton suggests that life without work leaves women in a void, resulting in their retreat to mass movements, to drugs, and to conservatism. The twenties liberation movements, which promised sexual liberation for the flapper, mark the return of the imperfectly repressed: the growing Fordism of the culture and the increasing fascism of American morality. She saw the dangers of Fordism and fascism or, to recall her words from *Twilight Sleep,* the dangers in "[forcing] certain persons to do things that those persons preferred not to do" (6).

The Return of the Imperfectly Repressed

Wharton's critique of Taylorism, Fordism, and US ambivalence and intolerance takes the symbolic form of a focus on incest, the central problem of this novel. The "new America" treats incest as a cultural fact; symbolic incest is no longer taboo since, in Wharton's view at least, the new tolerance admits anything. Wharton's novel curiously extends the Freudian model made explicit in *Totem and Taboo* (1913), where Freud first articulates the custom of the mother-in-law taboo, claiming that civilization depends on the banishment of the mother-in-law since she acts as a temptation to familial disruption. In effect, this happens in *The Mother's Recompense,* but not to the end Freud theorized. Kate's renunciation of her life in America, in her second exile, reproduces the denial of intimacy Wharton laments. Celebrating the autonomous self—the self-made man or woman—the culture of the twenties destroys the relational self upon which true intimacy (as Wharton saw it) depends. While Wharton's Undine may have been "vindicated" by Loos's Lorelei, Wharton herself does not celebrate a culture which turns selves into Taylorized subjects (whose sexuality is channeled into production) or flappers, whose motto "anything goes" includes symbolic incest.

In this novel, Wharton exploits the Freudian model of incest, particularly the notion of the taboo, arguing instead that a social model of incest pertains in America. Anne's marriage to Chris Fenno cements a new social relation. The mother-in-law must be excluded, not because, as Freud argues in *Totem and Taboo,* hostility is bred between son- and mother-in-law, but because she threatens the rise of the nuclear, atomized family. Freud argues that "the figure of the mother-in-law usually causes such an interference, for she has many features which remind him of her daughter and yet lacks all the charms of youth, beauty and spiritual freshness which endear his wife to him" (15). This is the new social formation of the twenties: the atomized couple versus the extended family which used to populate New York. Throughout her fiction of this period, Wharton means to show how motherhood is a sentimentalized construct, not a universal instinct; she does so by showing the effects of

Kate's abandonment of her daughter, the use of "Twilight Sleep" (a drug used during childbirth), and parental rejection in *The Children*. Rather than present these effects as psychological or psychoanalyze her characters, she traces the social consequences of abandoning parental responsibility. Ammons rightly focuses on "Mothers and Flappers" and "The Mothers" as the focal questions Wharton adopted, but Wharton's answers are not necessarily conservative. The symbolic incest theme, for example, allows her to play out her resistance to Freudian psychoanalysis through her emphasis on the structural effects of trading the communal family for a much more attenuated version of it.

While Wharton is ambivalent about how to resolve the new problem of the family, she clearly rejects Freud's reliance on unconscious drives in order to advance her own social theory of familial relations. Consider the inversion Wharton constructs on the following Freudian scenario:

> A mother's sympathetic identification with her daughter can easily go so far that she herself falls in love with the man her daughter loves; and in glaring instances this may lead to severe forms of neurotic illness as a result of her violent mental struggles against this emotional situation. . . . And very often the unkind, sadistic components of her love are directed on to her son-in-law in order that the forbidden, affectionate ones may be the more severely suppressed. (15)

However, in *The Mother's Recompense*, it is really Chris's desire that is skewed; having had an affair with the mother, he now desires to extend the mother's desirability by marrying the daughter. Chris's view of the mother and daughter as fungible shows the play of masculine desire that Wharton critiques. Chris can act out this patriarchal fantasy at the expense of his mother-in-law, whose banishment is less a psychoanalytic than a social necessity. What Freud calls a "streak of irritability and malevolence" in the son-in-law's range of feelings reveals his "temptation" to incest. How else to explain Chris's gravitation to Kate's daughter Anne, except as a fulfillment of the Freudian scenario: "the not uncommon event of a man openly falling in love with the woman who is later to be his mother-in-law before transferring his love to her daughter" (1950, 16). Kate's plan of outlasting Chris by Anne's side—and thereby making marriage impossible between Anne and Chris—backfires when Kate grasps Chris's own power in the situation: "He had only to hold out till the wedding; after that she would be a mere mother-in-law, and mothers-in-law are not a serious problem in modern life" (208). Chris dismisses the affair by an act of forgetting: "Chris Fenno was a young man—she was old enough to be, if not his mother, at least his mother-in-law" (219). The Freudian directive against mothers-in-law—the source of so many jokes about them—holds true for this novel.

Were Wharton to stop at this, it might be accurate to call the novel a response to Freudian analysis and leave it at that. Yet she complicates this perspective by showing its transformation in her cultural context. Another exchange—or transference—provides a useful example: symbolically enough, the exchange of the family jewels between the Clephane women. As in most ritual exchanges, the giver displays power. "John Clephane was fond of jewels, and particularly proud of his wife's, first because he had chosen them, and secondly because he had given them to her. She sometimes thought he really admired her only when she had them all on" (61). One of Kate's central memories was of old Mrs. Clephane, her mother-in-law, handing over the jewels upon her marriage to John. And, upon her return to New York, Anne restores these jewels to her mother (63). This ritual transaction reinstates Kate's "place" as Anne's mother: to give, receive, and to repay, are for Marcel Mauss, the three stages of the ritual. How can Kate repay when she is destitute? With her self: first, as ornament for her husband's jewels; second, as a negation of her sexual self to serve in the background of her daughter's ascendancy to autonomy.

It is no accident that Anne's primary fetish, the jewels, is one Lorelei shares in *Gentlemen Prefer Blondes*. With Wharton's women, however, the exchange of jewels signifies a show of power, rather than a sexual transaction, as Loos suggests it does with Lorelei. The daughter's gift to the mother, instead of the reverse, reveals how much relations have changed from Wharton's girlhood to those of contemporary capitalism. In contrast to the kinship relations that marked the nineteenth century, as *The Age of Innocence* portrays them, this "new America" engenders the new narcissism and market relations from which Anne's power derives.

Authority has become the province of the young and, in fact, Wharton explains that the ritual nature of exchange underwrites culture's failure, a topic she had taken up earlier in *The Glimpses of the Moon* (1922). In that novel, Susy and Nick Lansing are repaid for their aid in Ellie Vanderlyn's affair with jewels: a pearl pin and a sapphire bangle, an exchange which disrupts their marital harmony, when Susy realizes the social costs of the gifts. As a meditation on gift exchange, this novel suggests how closely aligned Wharton's understanding was with anthropology's analysis of gift-giving. Anne's "gift" of respect to her mother, like the return of the jewels, is actually just the opposite: "Anne's very insistence on treating her [mother] as the mistress of the house only emphasized her sense of not being so by right: it was the verbal courtesy of the Spaniard who puts all his possessions at the disposal of a casual visitor" (70). We see here a daughter displacing a mother and celebrating the completeness of her victory by disavowing it. The ritual of the gift props up the symbolic violence of displacement of one member of the culture (here, one generation) against another.

The displacement of the mother for the cult of the daughter—and her greater sexual freedom—is a sign of Wharton's times and "the era of taking things for granted . . . and in that respect Anne was of her day" (206). Contemporary views of American culture suggested that an "exaggerated mother-love" dominated the twenties scene, along with a sentimentalizing of sex and motherhood (Kuttner 437–38). Writing in 1922, Alfred Kuttner, translator of Freud and a drama critic, remarks tongue-in-cheek:

> The problem of how to handle sex in America has been solved long ago. The way to do it is to sentimentalize it. If Freud, instead of saying that the incestuous longing of the child for the parent of opposite sex is a natural impulse, though normally sublimated during the period of adolescence, had put the same idea into the phraseology of so many of our popular songs which reiterate the theme about mother being her boy's first and last and truest love, he would have encountered no opposition. . . . He would have gone over with a bang, though he probably would have been quite as amiably misunderstood as he is now viciously misunderstood. (436)

Kuttner goes on to suggest the dangers of the "cultic proportions" of mother worship "in our fiction, in our motion-pictures, in the inferior position of the American husband, and in such purely matriarchal religions as Christian Science where a form of healing is practised which is not very far removed from a mother's consolation to her boy when he has bruised his knees" (438). All of this mother love goes hand-in-hand with a violent rejection of even the mention of Freud's "incest-complex."

In the post-war era, motherhood becomes the ground for reinterpreting American culture. While motherhood used to be middle- and upper-class women's occupation, Kate Clephane—after a twenty-year absence—tries to return to the time when being a mother counted, when being divorced still carried weight (83), despite what she knows to be true about social institutions. Wharton recurs to the point that neither motherhood nor family can give women the anchor they need. Kate's abjection comes in the form of her cultural dislocation from the nineteenth-century values which kept woman's position stable but weighed them down. As Marianne Hirsch writes, "This novel makes utterly and starkly clear . . . that mother and daughter cannot coexist as adult *sexual* women" (119). Because the culture cannot tolerate the eroticized mother, Kate must choose between the desexualized and erotic roles, thereby relinquishing the erotic role to her daughter. As the Freudian model has it, the mother can then only identify with the daughter's sexuality. But Kate does not want to choose; neither did Undine Spragg before her or Pauline Manford after her. Her insistence that Chris confess to their affair demands that the culture recognize the sexual mother as an alternative to the sentimentalized mother.

In Wharton's 1923 novel *A Son at the Front,* John Campton, an artist schooled in nineteenth-century virtues, rededicates himself to art after his son George dies at the front. His art is not political per se, but it is nevertheless invested with a sense of social purpose. The book ends with Campton's intent to design a memorial statue for his dead son. For Chris Fenno in *The Mother's Recompense,* too, the war was crucial: it "transformed him; made a man of him" (116). He has ostensibly abandoned the life he led as "a boy . . . [as] a sort of intellectual rolling stone, never sure of what he wanted to be or to do, and always hurting and offending people in his perpetual efforts to find himself" (116). While the war may have made American men into more serious artists, it provided no aesthetic security or commitment for women, as it has for Campton and for Fenno, now a poet. Even when Wharton doubts the aesthetic commitment that the war engendered, as she does in her Vance Weston novels in the late twenties and early thirties, she offers a crucial difference: masculinity offered a pointed critique of post-war alienation, but women were still adrift. Indeed, celebrating motherhood no longer provided an answer to the question of what women could do, and Lilla's flapperhood and Anne's narcissism made Wharton equally uncomfortable. Wharton critics have argued that she laments the passing of the "old social code" (120), but while that may be true in the historical retrospect played out in *The Age of Innocence,* it is no longer the case in the contemporary analyses that followed in *A Son at the Front* and *The Mother's Recompense.*

While she does not write nostalgically about the "blessed anonymity of motherhood" (64), Wharton sees how motherhood used to provide women with some sort of sentimental influence over others, or to provide them with some office to perform. Consider Bronislaw Malinowski's views on motherhood as spelled out in his 1930 "Parenthood—The Basis of Social Structure": "Motherhood is always individual. It is never allowed to remain a mere biological fact. Social and cultural influences always indorse and emphasize the original individuality of the biological fact. . . . [M]otherhood in each culture [is] a relationship specific to that culture" (1962, 62).[8] Neither flapperism nor sexual liberation nor socialism were Wharton's solutions for the culturally specific problem of American motherhood as a trope for the problem of individualism. She wanted human relations based on something other than psychoanalysis, eugenic or population policies, Birth Control Leagues, or other legislations of sexuality. Her novels speak to a desire to see intimacy as less a tyranny and more a privilege, albeit a privilege limited by racial categories.

Thus, *The Mother's Recompense* also predicts what amounts to a crisis in individualism. As much as Kate finds Chris's oedipalization horrifying, she is speechless at Anne's narcissism.[9] The Oedipus complex gives way to something more chaotic, atomized, overwhelming: flapperism, what Wharton posits as a narcissistic evasion of public life and responsibility. It isn't flapperism alone that causes Kate's fears, since these extend to the breezy intolerance Anne Clephane embodies. Anne's parents split, leaving the daughter with no option but to identify with the father's power. Throughout the novel, Chris is aligned with and mimics Anne's dead father, who represents for Kate the patriarchal authority she flees and which Anne embraces: "Now, as then, a man's hat and stick lay on the hall table; on that other day [when Kate left John Clephane for Hylton Davies] they had been John Clephane's, now they were Chris Fenno's. That was the only difference" (222). Rather than maintaining the tension between Kate's nurturance and John's authority, Anne pledges allegiance to the father's dominance and social power. Having lost that nurturance in Kate's abandonment of her, she reproduces her father's authority in herself and in her supreme dedication to Chris.

The novel argues, then, that the ascendancy of paternal authority emerges in post-war culture in the banishment of the sexualized or erotic mother. Twenties culture is the culture of paternal authority, internalized and appropriated by both genders, the result being the compensatory (however illusory) power of the flapper. Anne could be like her flapper friend Lilla Gates, marrying into the powerful Horace Maclew line, but she chooses instead to adopt her father's authority. The flapper, providing a crude facsimile of individual liberty, imitates a male's vision of women's sexual freedom. A woman's vision, Wharton suggests, would be that of the erotic mother. Wharton's novel moves beyond the Freudian scenario of son- and mother-in-law incest in order to contextualize post-war social psychology as the rise of paternal authority through the exclusion of maternal power. *The Mother's Recompense* begins with the daughter's authority over her mother, making way for the new narcissism Wharton's novel attempts to derail. As Wharton sees it, the culture promotes autonomy and hedonism—the ability to do anything one wants with whomever one wants—as its only value. Completely foreign is the value of a private morality with public meaning. At the same time that the new individualism was preached, it really sold a profound conformity, so much so that upon her return Kate sees the young generation as "merged into a collective American Face" (51). This "new tolerance" cannot sustain the pressures of the individual's need for recognition, since it is predicated on acting out desire and aggression in equal doses, as Loos's Lorelei does in celebrating the omnipotence of her desire. Private life has been Taylorized, mass-produced, collectivized; individuality has become an effect of advertising and wealth.

Hence, the novel's focus is the violence between generations, leading to the abjection of the older and the weightlessness of the younger generation. Kate reflects: "As a matter of curiosity, and a possible light on the new America, [she] would have liked to know why her husband's niece . . . had been singled out, in this new easy-going society, to be at once reproved and countenanced. Lilla in herself was too uninteresting to stimulate curiosity; but as a symptom she might prove enlightening" (73–74). Kate tries to grasp the "new America" (as Tocqueville had) by looking at the image of its women—in this case, the flappers—a move much like Thorstein Veblen's in his 1899 *Theory of the Leisure Class*. But Kate slips, sometimes like Wharton herself, into "the attitude of caution and conservatism" (74). Although Wharton can applaud Loos's satire, her own reaction is more skeptical, perhaps even more disbelieving, than her earlier works had been. *The Mother's Recompense* is written by an author more cautious than ever before.

Caught between sentimental inauthenticity and modernist irony, Wharton sees no way out for women, since modernism, like Taylorism and Fordism, had done little to change women's purposes. Women need, in Loos's oft-repeated parodic phrase, education and occupation. Kate Clephane mocks Chris Fenno's speeches, which sound to her like those "learned by heart out of some sentimental novel" (88). Yet Wharton makes the distinction clear in her gender politics: for men, there can be old and new selves. "It all came to the question of what he wanted; it always had. When had there ever been a question of what *she* wanted? He took what he chose from life, gathered and let drop and went on: it was the artist's way, he told her" (91). Wharton's distrust is evident here: "A real mother is just a habit of thought to her children" (155). While

Kate rejects precisely this habitualized way of thinking of herself, she also reviles the role of "the other woman" in Anne's life and in Chris's past (159). Ammons (1980) and, more recently, Katherine Joslin both interpret Wharton's struggle as "the clash in manners and morals between pre-war and post-war American culture" (Joslin 1991, 118).

Yet Wharton's novel is much more confused about these cultures, given that it is not just a question of class and elite society but also of gender and race. The generational split in *The Mother's Recompense* reveals less about the values of old New York versus the new America, a split which polarizes pre- and post-war America; rather, it suggests a much more contested view of culture, less tribal in mentality and more standardized according to the demands of the twenties' contradictory directives to individuate by consuming mass culture, a Taylorization of the individual that suggests how a culture of managed desires regulates one's motives.

While Kate sees the larger picture with respect to the repressed relations designed to advance a self-protective and self-promoting autonomy, the heroine of *Twilight Sleep,* Pauline Manford, tries to ignore those contradictions; unlike *The Mother's Recompense,* the later novel is a comic portrait of Pauline Manford's failure to resolve those contradictions, even to make a virtue of not resolving them by developing a kind of negative capability for living with them. Kate Clephane, however, cannot ignore them. That which the representatives of the "new America" want to evade returns in other forms as caution, conservatism, even reactionary political thinking. Anne insists that mother and daughter can be "perfect pals" (109); at the same time, Anne exerts her authority by reminding Kate that she abandoned her daughter out of her desire for autonomy, a desire that mothers are supposed to surrender for their children. "Mothers oughtn't to leave their daughters," Anne says (186). While the culture reminds mothers that their love is "dangerous," any alternative to mothering seems absent or unavailable. Mothers, as Wharton represents them, are either willfully absent, comic contradictions, or exiled once they become mothers-in-law.

In a sign of her symbolic power, Anne reestablishes their connection at the Drovers' Long Island estate. Kate has gone there to tell Anne about her affair with Chris, but Anne silences her before she can confess by invoking the new economy of pleasure and pain: "After all, we've all got to buy our own experience, haven't we? And perhaps the point of view about . . . about early mistakes . . . is more indulgent now than in your time" (186). Anne feels herself able to purchase her way through life, a consuming passion that Kate never had. Instead, Kate had acted on her desire, not on her ability to buy "indulgence." Anne's power over her mother "fitted in with the new times. The old days of introspections and explanations were over" (206). In short, Anne manages to banish the ambivalence her mother feels by taking for granted what her mother could never do. Like Loos's Lorelei, Anne can deny the crisis of authority after World War I and assert instead her own reckless passions. If for Lorelei this meant shooting a man, for Anne it means capturing Chris. Fred Landers, Anne's guardian, describes her as "a young woman of considerable violence of feeling" (199). While the culture is steeped in ambivalence—what Lears defines as "the [cultural] dialectic between latent impulse and manifest behavior"—the flappers of the new America assert a new self-possession and authority, a violent individualism, over the ambivalence of the Mothers. The signs of excessive indulgence clearly visible in Anne, the "cult of the child," like the prolonged adolescence of the flapper, before too long lead to the cult of the celebrity Wharton denounces in *Hudson River Bracketed* and *The Gods Arrive*.

At the end of the novel, Kate returns to Europe and to "the narcotic tricks of evasion" she had denounced while living in the new America: "She still had to go on cramming things into her days, things good, bad or indifferent, it hardly mattered which as long as they were crammed tight enough to leave no chinks for backward glances" (266). For Wharton, backward glances are not evasions, but acts of courage. Kate thinks, "'One has to have something to help one out—' It was the old argument of the drug-takers" (268). As Cynthia Griffin Wolff argues, Wharton's satire begins with post-war America's "refus[ing] itself to pain" (1977, 374). The connections among evasion, responsibility, pleasure, and meaningful work are never as clear again in Wharton's work.

Thus, Wharton's novels reject the reactionary trend in the old social code and the tribe mentality. With the end of World War I, she sheds that old mentality for the ambivalence of post-war society. Some evasions prove clarifying, like Kate's flight from the oppression of marriage, but the larger cultural evasion of gender politics frightens Wharton. In that evasion, she sees the possibility of a return to the culture which made Lily Bart ornamental and Newland Archer ineffectual. Wharton is ready for a brave new politics, a gender politics supporting women's desire to alleviate the social contradictions by which they are forced to live. While decrying propaganda, Wharton inadvertently writes novels in 1925 and 1927 that, like Loos's *Gentlemen Prefer Blondes,* are themselves propaganda for a new conception of mothering and family—and despite these advances she kept on decrying the Harlem Renaissance. Wharton could not understand how the new discourses on race and African-American culture challenged the racialized mothers of *The Mother's Recompense* and *Twilight Sleep,* who are the hopes on which Wharton hangs her new political vision.[10]

The Mother's Recompense tries to fuse these irreconcilable cultural directives: Freudianism and bolshevism (arguing for collectivization of culture), behavioralism, new tolerance, and Wharton's own social and racial prejudices. The novel might be one of the few in which the daughter is spared, fortunately or not, the mother's paralyzing ambivalence. In her next novel, *Twilight Sleep,* Nona Manford is shot because of her mother's crises; like Nona, Lily Bart had earlier become the agent of her mother's revenge. Unlike other mothers, Kate is helpless in the face of her daughter's determination: "[Kate's] unrest drove her forth again into the darkening street, drove her homeward with uncertain steps, in the mood of forlorn expectancy of those who, having failed to exert their will, wait helplessly on the unforeseen" (216). But Wharton worries that the daughter's determination is a kind of blindness; the mother's indeterminacy, at least, provides her with a larger cultural vision disavowed by the younger generation.

While denial is the rule of the new culture, Kate Clephane feels nostalgic for the women's communities—and even their harsh rule-bound dictates—over the laissez-faire individualism of the present. The culture is mobilized against bolshevism and Freudianism and the modes of collectivization both suggest. Both are ideologically denounced since, as Anne Clephane's behavior shows, they militate against the sort of individualism embraced by the new America wherein, as Elizabeth Fox-Genovese has it, women then do the "dirty work" of capitalism (31). This conflict produces the quandary at the center of her twenties novels.

Wharton could be progressive about one issue—in her rejection of genetic engineering and the sentimentalizing of motherhood—while at the same time be reactionary about another. Although she could understand motherhood as a cultural issue in need of revision, she remained blind to the political program of racial stratification she implicitly endorses and explicitly keeps out of her fiction. And yet her very focus on ethics is itself a politics worth pursuing, despite her prejudice. *The Mother's Recompense* rejects a sentimental maternalism; in 1927, *Twilight Sleep* will reject the politicized legislation of this ideology. Not incest but drug-taking becomes Wharton's metaphor for life in the twenties. *Twilight Sleep* (1927) would take its title from the drug given to women in labor, to help them forget the pain of childbirth, a move Wharton could only view with irony.

3

Eugenics and a New Politics:
Twilight Sleep and *The Children*

The Lorelei that Wharton found so vindicating in Anita Loos's *Gentle-men Prefer Blondes* was a typical figure in novels of the twenties. Two years before Loos's novel and four years before Wharton's own novel about the fads of youth, *Twilight Sleep* (1927), Gertrude Atherton published *Black Oxen* (1923). This novel about the famous "reactivization treatment," which used X-ray stimulation of the ovaries to rejuvenate older women (a practice that leaves women sterilized), goes through the same catalogue of cultural options available to middle-aged women that Wharton will pursue in 1927: flapperhood, psychoanalysis, "the fetish of the body" (42), and finally medical remedies—like twilight sleep or the X-rays of the Steinach Treatment. Atherton's heroine, Mary Zattiany, endures these X-ray treatments in order to regain her youthful energy and sex-magnetism and to advance her political cause of saving children in post-war Austria; in doing so, she forgoes a romance with the American drama critic, Lee Clavering, in order to marry a European man who is more mature than Clavering and capable of advancing their mutual political cause.

Atherton's earlier novel deals with two of the same important cultural topics that Wharton features in *Twilight Sleep*: eugenics and its relation to women's social and reproductive power. Furthermore, the two writers seem to agree on at least one thing, the necessity of overturning what Atherton called "The Reign of Youth!" in favor of a mature woman's political power (124). Although Atherton rejects the "feministics" of the Lucy Stoners (156), a women's group devoted to "the inalienable individuality of woman" (156), she finds that the beauty treatment developed in Europe allowed her heroine to turn her renewed mental energy to Aus-

PAVILLON COLOMBE
ST BRICE-SOUS-FORÊT (S&O)
GARE: SARCELLES
TÉLÉPHONE: ST BRICE-SOUS-FORÊT 2

Letter from Edith Wharton to Gaillard Lapsley about eugenics craze (13 August 1925). Yale Collection of American Literature, Beinecke Rare Book and Manuscript Library, Yale University.

will incline me toward the Compostela tour, reluctant as I am to miss a chance of Salso mitigated by you.

All this is conditional, however, for great are the mysteries of heart & arteries, & Kresser may say he doesn't want me to go on any long "randangs" yet. — I believe my own impartiality is complete, because I find life so absorbingly interesting that I wouldn't willingly disobey, & then get come up with! —

So this is just to explain, & to say that I'll write again the day after tomorrow. If Kresser says it's Compostela, I'll send you all particulars about Salso, with a letter for D. Zoia —

Walter & I thought that the enclosed wd

trian and European politics: "Power, after sex has ceased from troubling, is the dominant passion in human nature" (336). The power of a fifty-eight-year old woman who looks twenty-eight (due to the Treatment) fascinates Atherton. While many of Atherton's younger characters insist that woman's power lies in eugenic reproduction, and while her middle-aged characters contend that the race might benefit from "eugenics, birth control, sterilization of the unfit, and the expulsion of undesirable races" (180), Atherton finds political power more fascinating than reproductive power, and she bemoans the "epoch of the submerged woman," where woman's only power could be social rather than national or even international. When Mary Zattiany leaves her youthful lover of thirty-four for her old lover, in what is to be a political marriage, Atherton ends the novel abruptly: this "master passion," power, outvies the illusions of love (336). While eugenics is the power of the young, Atherton suggests, politics is the power of the mature.

In reviewing this novel for *The Nation*, Carl Van Vechten would use the occasion to take another swipe at Wharton, as he did in *Nigger Heaven*: he praises Atherton's glamor and vitality, two qualities he finds missing in her staid literary rival, Wharton (see Leider 305). Wharton's literary rivalry notwithstanding, *Black Oxen, Twilight Sleep*, and *Nigger Heaven* are important signs of the twenties' obsession with the fetishizing of youth that the flapper signifies. While Atherton condones reactivization, and undergoes the procedure herself as a way to compete with flapperhood, Wharton is much more skeptical about such rejuvenating effects. Perhaps Wharton would not have found Atherton so troubling had they not been pitted against each other so often in the popular press. In any case, Wharton took a different tack on twenties narcissism, refusing to validate it as Atherton had implictly done in *Black Oxen*. Although she might have been considered more conservative than Atherton, Wharton provides in her 1927 novel a far more radical and far-reaching cultural critique than she had previously attempted. Perhaps buoyed by Loos's success, Wharton writes a sweeping social comedy about contemporary efforts at rejuvenation.

In challenging the gender ideology of her class and of her society, Wharton manipulates the conventions of the realist novel to reconcile popular fiction with cultural criticism. My aim here is not to discount the viciousness of Wharton's anti-Semitism, or her hatred of black culture. However, while critics enjoy claiming that Edith Wharton liked both her gardens and her society well-pruned, I argue that her late fictions unflaggingly address the politics of intimate experience in the context of social debates. To that end, her characters often echo social policy, transformed as it is by Wharton's own bias against the legislation of private morality. Writing literature and writing culture, for Wharton, drew on a public unconscious, one associated for her with fascism. In Nancy Armstrong's terms, "individual works and kinds of writing gather force, not as they exemplify [an] individual imagination, genre, or tradition of ideas, but as they enter into an unwitting conspiracy that extends throughout the figurative operations of cultural production to shape the lives of real people" (357). I will show how the cultural codes Wharton challenges are the same "figurative operations" employed in eugenic tracts, medical discourse (of the twilight sleep movement), and debates about women's rights. Both *Twilight Sleep* and its author need to be defended against the charge of political quietism and of collaboration with reactionary politics. To the extent that Wharton tries to redefine the nature of political writing, rejecting a reflectionist political literature and political allegory of the sort Atherton had written time and again, Wharton's novel suggests that the contradictions in women's lives do not allow them an unambivalent political position. Wharton continues to think against herself and more consciously reveals her own political stance.

The Question of Eugenics—or, The Inquisition

Our upper middle class is similarly annihilating the lower middle class by evoking its envy and teaching it habits of dress, living and amusement which can only be maintained by dispensing with children.
—R. B. Cattell, *The Fight for Our National Intelligence*

In the twenties, Edith Wharton's letters no longer concern her war work, but instead cast a critical eye upon reproductive politics. For example, she encloses three documents to Gaillard Lapsley in her letter of 13 August 1925 (Beinecke Library). These documents concern "The Library League" and its "Creed of CHRISTIAN Citizenship"; in them, the League distinguishes itself from the Klan Kraft, another version of the Ku Klux Klan, though its goal of racial purity was similar to its predecessor's. With a heavy pencil line, Wharton marks the following paragraph from the advertisement of the League for the Cambridge don's notice:

> The European spirit of Marxian Materialism is slowly but surely undermining constitutional government—an inheritance received from our Anglo-Saxon ancestry whose tradi-

tions were based not partly but wholly on the fundamental
faith of the Christian religion.

The proposed goal of the creed, drafted by George Whitefield Mead, is to
unite theology and biology: "eugenic in practice, theologic in principle"
is their motto. "The outstanding objective thereof is CHRISTIAN educational work along theological lines. But, in so far as we know, there is no
existing organization the outstanding objective of which is CHRISTIAN
educational work along biological lines." The group hopes to follow in
the lines of "the Christian Endeavor movement founded by Dr. Francis E.
Clark or the Boy Scout movement founded by Colin H. Livingston."
Along with this advertisement, Wharton sends her friend a copy of another letter from Riverda H. Jordan, Professor of Education at Cornell
University, to Mr. E. Cosgrove of the League, which professes Jordan's
devotion to this cause.[1]

Wharton's letter contains her strong response to the advertisement:
"Walter [Berry] and I thought that the enclosed wd interest you. It is an
amazing commentary on the chaos lá-bas, & makes me long for Holy
Church & the long arm of the Inquisition" (see Letter 1, Beinecke Library).
Wharton ironically equates the Christian Creed—and Jordan's response—
with the whole endeavor to root out Marxists, assimilated Jews, and here-
tics. In general, she is against such Inquisitions; in particular, she is vehemently against those prejudices represented by Fordian culture.

Nonetheless, interest in eugenics was at its height in the twenties.
According to Richard Hofstadter, the eugenics fervor took on "fad"
proportions in 1915 and the years following (138). This reformist enthusiasm had consequences for social policy:

> Rural living would counteract the dysgenic effect of urban
> society. The abolition of child labor would cause the poor to
> restrict their breeding. Compulsory education would have the
> same effect by making the child an expense to its parents; but
> it should not be supplemented by subsidies to children of the
> poor in the form of free lunches, free textbooks, or other aids
> that would lower the cost of child care. (142)

The eugenic fad meant there would literally be no free lunch for children,
no governmental free ride for the poor. More important, the eugenics
movement sought to make children an economic punishment for the
poor, while maintaining child-rearing as a privilege for the rich.

The call for eugenics generally sought on the nationalist front for a collective legislation of American breeding. In particular, books like *The Fight for Our National Intelligence* (1937) documented the "sex delinquencies" that "defective" women committed promiscuously when school failed to teach them propriety (110).[2] Positive eugenics, a corollary to the larger eugenics imperative usually associated with population control, was the movement to increase the birth rate among the socially fit, the wealthy, and the intelligent, a move often based on controversial I.Q. scores. Among the eugenically fit, then, birth control was meant to encourage birth, not restrict it. Contraception scared positive eugenicists because it fostered a decrease in birth rate among "desirable" mothers. The positive eugenicists wanted to substitute birth selection in lieu of birth control. The fear was that women of all sorts, eugenic and dysgenic, would opt for fewer children, when the hope was that superior women would choose a family of four or larger.

Raymond B. Cattell's research findings in favor of positive eugenics can be summarized as follows: two social groups destroy civilization, "Civilization Wreckers, Unlimited" and the "National Suicide Club." The former is composed of women like "Mrs. Smith," who is "the pitiful victim of a slavery worse than any of ancient times" (i.e., motherhood): she represents the unemployed and "subcultural" (111). Cattell (a clinical psychologist) argues: "Blindly, unconsciously, [the Wreckers] gnaw away at [civilization's] foundations, impoverishing themselves and other people, converting their misery into an acid corroding the foundations of society" (111). On the contrary, the "National Suicide Club" claims as its members the well-to-do, upper middle-class men and women with "social pretensions." "Mrs. Haslam," who represents the National Suicide Club, has her first child at thirty-one: the child has an I.Q. of 120, but his mother claims not to be able to "afford" a second child, having chosen a social life over motherhood. Cattell describes the Haslam family with contempt:

> [They] live in an atmosphere of assertive overcompensation, trained to social climbing. Their bridge game, product of intensive training, is the terror of the neighbourhood, whilst their dominance on the committee of the suburban tennis club is unquestioned. In clothes and cars they go from strength to strength. In fact, they and their like are so successful that in two or three generations they will be as extinct as the Dodos. (112)

The salvation of the race, then, depends on mothers of the right class keeping in check their selfish desires for social climbing and the privatization of personal desire. The Scylla and Charybdis of modern culture are, on the one hand, the reproduction of the unfit and, on the other, the extinction of the upper middle class.

Cattell's research was done in England, but he is quick to point out that the same results obtain in America (14). More important to Cattell than the object of analysis is the premise that eugenics recreates the distinctions between high and low culture. Thus, his cultural argument is passed off as one about nature. For Cattell, popular culture entertains the eugenically unfit, since the lower classes require mindless distraction:

> Unfortunately it is far from true that "little things please little minds." The most stupendous spectacles need to be staged to entertain a Roman rabble, whereas an Isaac Newton can sit in an orchard and be infinitely intrigued by a falling apple. If with much labour and sorrow and educational expenditure you convince a youth of I.Q. 80 that he likes Shakespeare you may rest assured that your cruelty will receive no permanent justification, for in a while he will be enjoying himself at a gangster film, unconsciously following the wise injunction, "to thyself be true." (53)

Citing Shakespeare here just to make sure that we know to which group he belongs, Cattell goes on to argue that cultural values and superiority are "intuitively self-evident," however egalitarian he sounds in his claim that "each mental capacity is entitled to its own amusements" (53). "It would take one into deep waters to discuss adequately why for a tired man's recreation Aldous Huxley is preferable to all-in-wrestling, or why, for inspiration Beethoven is superior to bull fighting. . . . But that does not invalidate the judgment that some amusements are intrinsically 'higher' than others, more favorable to the tone of a civilised society and endowed with more permanent satisfactions" (53–54). I do not want to take on Cattell's arguments about the superiority of high culture over low or popular culture; instead, let us consider the ideological assumptions behind them. Cattell worries about the "unconscious" seduction of the low, the transgressive desire which is part of the cultural unconscious and even refers to Freud's *Civilization and Its Discontents* to support his claim that society is in danger of taboo violation. Eugenics is his answer to this taboo.

For Cattell and others, the decline of culture leads to the subsequent decline of birth-rates from the educated, assumed to be superior parents as well as to have superior tastes. "A Faraday, a Pasteur and the lesser but still unusually good mental capacities of big business organisers of the Ford type, actually increase the real wealth of the community and probably only use up on themselves a fraction of the wealth they create" (64). Leonard Darwin seconds this argument in *The Need for Eugenic Reform* (1926):

> What is needed is a dual campaign. . . . The poor and needy bring upon both themselves and others a vast amount of unnecessary suffering and inconvenience by the production of large families which they cannot properly support, whilst the best stocks are being exterminated by the selfish use of contraceptive methods, generally in ignorance of the harm thus being done to the nation. (Darwin 407; see also Kevles 88–89)

The world needs to reproduce Fords (both the man and his machine) as examples of the "best stocks" in order to assure the propagation of American mental capacity. The eugenicist argument generally assumed that superior wealth meant superior genetic health; environment or social prejudice had ostensibly little to do with individual progress.

Almost all of Cattell's arguments come back to gender, which is quite typical in the rhetoric of the eugenicists. "Deterioration of the Civilised Woman," "Prostitution and the Cigarette," and "The Girl Who Goes Right"—all titles of addresses he delivered at The First National Conference on Race Betterment in 1914—summarize his argument. "Both in our schools and in welfare work we select the most intelligent girls of each generation to be celibate teachers and social assistants and leave the less intelligent to provide the race of children which is to become the next generation. . . . We are the victims of a confusion of moral thought and the slaves of blind habits which compel us to maintain traditional social and educational standards even though it has to be done at the terrible cost of consuming our biological capital" (101–2). Biological capital is at stake, not the social or intellectual kind. Cattell fears we have overinvested in democracy at the expense of biological preservation, an expenditure that results from the feminization of culture: "Let us examine the fact that the so-called 'masculine' characteristics obtain little expression in a community that is becoming a collection of nurses and which offers to self-assertion only the old outlets of war and crime" (105). War and crime are the retrograde expressions of masculinity; eugenics, for Cattell, is the positive expression of masculine control over the "collection of nurses" comprising civilization. As Stephanie Shields explains in "Functionalism, Darwinism, and the Psychology of Women: A Study in Social Myth," the "real threat" to female domestic education and women's rights was the "'feminization' of the American male" (746). "The War against Dullness" (one of Cattell's chapter titles, vaguely reminiscent of Alexander Pope) is a battle of the sexes, of masculinized culture versus a feminized one.

Wharton herself was to involve herself even more intimately in this discussion when she writes explicitly about eugenics and eugenic training in *The Children* (1928), a novel to which I will return at the end of the following discussion of *Twilight Sleep*. There, the new Princess Buondelmonte suggests that she needs to take her step-children away from Judith Wheater's clan because Martin Boyne, the children's guardian, does not raise the children with an eye to the guiding principle of eugenics. The Princess, Wharton tells us, has taken her degree cum laude "in Eugenics and Infant Psychology, at Lohengrin College, Texas" (277). She reminds Boyne that the children need to be psychoanalyzed and "their studies and games selected with a view to their particular moral, alimentary, dental and glandular heredity" (278). When the nurse states that her own family consisted of fourteen children, the Princess argues: "In the United States such matters will soon be regulated by legislation . . ." (291). Such strange allusions in the novel as these suggest Wharton's preoccupation with reproductive engineering, a fascism she saw threatening the intellectual climate in American and Europe as another "Inquisition."

Positive Eugenics

We can understand the twilight sleep furor in the context of women's reproductive choices and the eugenics debate which ensued in 1914 and 1915. Twilight sleep, the compound of morphine and scopolamine administered by physicians and nurses at elaborate birthing establishments, proved one answer to the question of proper birth control. Twilight sleep was thought to provide, as Judith Walzer Leavitt explains, "a 'better race for future generations' since upper class women would be more likely to have babies if they could have them painlessly" (1980, 156). What is crucial for my purposes is that the central issue of twilight sleep was one of women's power since it was a method by which women could gain some say over the birthing process: "Feminist women," Leavitt argues, "wanted the parturient, not the doctor or attendant, to choose the kind of delivery she would have" (1980, 148). For Leavitt, the twilight sleep movement proved a way for women to exercise their power over childbirth rather than relinquishing it to doctors and midwives. At the very least, the twilight sleep movement made the debate over obstetric conditions a public issue rather than a private and individual one. The contradictions here are obvious: how could women gain control by going to sleep? So goes Adrienne Rich's argument in *Of Woman Born* (published sixty-four years after the initial debate): her chapter "Alienated Labor" suggests the opposite of Leavitt's conclusion: "As long as birth—metaphorically or literally—remains an experience of passively handing over our minds and our bodies to male authority and technology, other kinds of social change can only minimally change our relationship to ourselves, to power, and to the world outside our bodies" (185).

Marguerite Tracy and Constance Leupp initiated the controversy over twilight sleep in *McClure's Magazine*. In the June 1914 issue, they quote Professor Krönig of the Frauenklinik at Freiburg: "The modern woman, on whose nervous system nowadays quite other demands are made than was formerly the case, responds to the stimulus of severe pain more rapidly with nervous exhaustion and paralysis of the will to carry the labor to a conclusion. The sensitiveness of those who carry on hard mental work is much greater than that of those who earn their living by manual labor. . . . As a consequence of this nervous exhaustion, we see that precisely in the case of mothers of the better class the use of the forceps has increased to an alarming extent, and this where there is no structural need of forceps" (43). A "robust woman" might have no trouble giving birth, but a sensitive woman—especially of an upper-class background—generally did. One of the chief consequences of the argument for twilight sleep is the "modern woman's" freedom from dependence on lower-class midwives. The higher cost and "science" of twilight sleep were ways to smooth over the class issue. The twilight sleep movement proved to be a positive eugenics, making childbirth "a costly science" (October 1914), albeit a painless one. "But, just as the village barber no longer performs operations," Mary Boyd and Marguerite Tracy claim, "the untrained midwife of the neighborhood will pass out of existence under the effective competition of free painless wards" (69).

Moreover, the twilight sleep method became available only to women of a certain class despite the original argument that all women ought to have access to comfortable childbirth. In the *International Socialist Review,* Sam Schmalhausen suggests in 1914 that "the sucklings of the proletariat have committed the irrevocable folly of having chosen poor parents . . . [and therefore] the beneficent childbirth must remain the superadded luxury of the wealthy mother" (234). "Gaining power" for upper-class women was class power: the rhetorical strategy of "denaturalizing" pain was designed precisely to reassure upper-class women of their superiority over working women. They lose power over their bodies in sleeping through childbirth, but they disassociate themselves from lower class "robust" women and, thus, can argue the "naturalness" of painless childbirth in a curious recuperation of the primitive. In *Pain, Pleasure, and American Childbirth,* Margarete Sandelowski also points to the slipperiness and complexity of eugenics and twilight sleep: by manipulating the idea of "natural childbirth," the twilight sleep method was considered "natural"; the "unassisted," unnatural. The argument became a rhetorical one, articulated in terms of the nature versus culture debate (19).

One such rhetorical argument occurs in Henry Smith Williams's *Twilight Sleep* (1914). Williams's and Schmalhausen's descriptions of the link between twilight sleep and race hygiene are similar; Williams's, however, is without irony, since he finds the hypodermic method a salvation of the race: "The women of primitive and barbaric tribes appear to suffer comparatively little in labor; . . . it is civilized women of the most highly developed nervous or intellectual type who suffer most. . . . This seems at once to suggest that the excessive pains of childbirth are not a strictly 'natural' concomitant of motherhood, but rather that they are an extraneous and in a sense an abnormal product of civilization" (39). He is particularly concerned that the middle class will adopt birth control rather than selective breeding. Pain, for him, is unnatural, since primitive mothers do not feel it. He warns against the "archaic spirit" of middle-class women's "illogicality," since they believe that the "natural" physiological functions of childbirthing ought not to be tampered with (89). Williams argues:

> The truth is that in assuming an upright posture and in developing an enormous brain, the human race has so modified the conditions incident to child-bearing as to put upon the mother a burden that may well enough be termed abnormal in comparison with the function of motherhood as it applies to other races of animate beings. . . . Moreover, the cultured woman of to-day has a nervous system that makes her far more susceptible to pain and to resultant shock than was her more lethargical ancestor of remote generation. . . . Such a woman not unnaturally shrinks from the dangers and pains incident to child-bearing. (90–91)

The "natural" becomes the battleground for racial and class power and eugenic "hygiene."

As Wharton thus saw them, eugenics and twilight sleep were related cultural movements because of these rhetorical strategies. By attacking twilight sleep, Wharton questions as well the eugenics movement she likened in 1925 to the "long arm of the Inquisition." In 1927, her most political novel—*Twilight Sleep*—appears and exposes the contradictions at the heart of the twilight sleep debate while pointing to the larger social significance in the eugenics fervor. At the same time that twilight sleep forced women to lose control over their bodies, it allowed them some element of choice. Wharton's target is the contradictory nature of these choices offered to women. Was twilight sleep a feminist answer to the fears of childbirth, and thus a way to women's power, or was it a conservative gesture for advancing the cause of positive eugenics? or both?

Wharton's Brave New World

> The copy of my new novel, "Twilight Sleep", wh. I sent to John, was seized as contraband, & on his applying for it at customs, was told this applied to books "When they were thought to be pornographic"!!!!
>
> Fame at Last—
>
> —Wharton to Gaillard Lapsley, 11 June 1927

In a letter to Mrs. Winthrop (Daisy) Chanler dated 25 March 1932, Wharton praises her friend Aldous Huxley's *Brave New World* as a "masterpiece of tragic indictment of our ghastly age of Fordian culture. . . . He wrote to me that I had 'put the case' already in 'Twilight Sleep'. . . ." Wharton declares that she was much "set up" by Huxley's "recognition of the fact!" (Lewis and Lewis, 547). A best-seller in its day, *Twilight Sleep* has not been much of a hit with Wharton's critics. R. W. B. Lewis writes in the biography that this "seriously and variously marred" novel (523), "referring to the comatose condition in which most women of gentle birth, according to the author, pass their adult life," is her "most overplotted" work (474). He condemns its ending as melodramatic, as does Cynthia Griffin Wolff, who passes an even harsher judgment on it:

> *Twilight Sleep* is chaotically plotted; some of this anarchy is undoubtedly intended as a reflection of the disjointed quality of life in postwar America. Nevertheless, Wharton does not manage to prevent the novel from falling into dreadful melodrama at the end when Pauline's first husband invades Dexter

Manford's home one night, brandishing a pistol and prepar-
ing to redeem the family's honor. Even worse than the plot,
however, is the sloppy management of the social criticism.
(1977, 376)

On the contrary, Millicent Bell in *Edith Wharton & Henry James: A
Story of Their Friendship* sees the novel as successful. She suggests that
Wharton's novels of the twenties "are unsentimental, even austere stories
of personal passion, deftly placed in a medium of ironic social observa-
tion" (298), including presumably this one. Most recently, Mary Suzanne
Schriber has described this novel as a satire and a critique of women's
limited sphere (169).

Why this indifference at best, dismissal at worst and, above all, the
critical depreciation? I account for the range of critical judgments—even
the praise of it as "good, acid reading"—by highlighting the cultural contradictions of the novel rather than reducing them to a "higher harmony"
of form (Royde-Smith 442). Following Edmund Wilson's 8 June 1927
review in *The New Republic*, which welcomed this novel demonstrating
Wharton's renewal in a new age (78), I would stress that *Twilight Sleep*
renders the alienation inherent in the eugenic position as making women
victims of the very ideals they are trying to advance. The melodramatic
ending notwithstanding, *Twilight Sleep* is filled with her most searching
contemplations of the cultural contradictions Pauline Manford embodies.

One reason *Twilight Sleep* has been dismissed as chaotic and anarchic
is that it does so much "cultural work," to borrow Jane Tompkins's
phrase in *Sensational Designs,* and some of it is difficult to recover. One
of Wharton's most comprehensive novels, it assumes its readers are familiar with the popular fads of the twenties. The work is not so much
farce, as Q. D. Leavis claims in "Henry James's Heiress," but an uncertainty, a confusion, about women's choices within a contradictory political and domestic scene. Despite its high comic spirits, it remains a dark
companion piece to *The Mother's Recompense.*

Dominating the novel's social scene is Pauline Manford, who is absorbed with finding genius and spiritual cults, fighting off wrinkles and
large hips, and managing her family. One of Pauline's typical thoughts is
represented as follows: "She felt a twinge of regret at having so involved
herself with the Mahatma. Yet what did Episcopal Bishops know of 'holy
ecstasy'? And could any number of Church services have reduced her
hips?" (73). Her second spouse, Dexter Manford, is a successful lawyer,
having arranged for Pauline's divorce from her ineffectual first husband,
Arthur Wyant. Dexter is bored with Pauline and infatuated with his

daughter-in-law, Lita, married to Jim Wyant, Pauline's son by Arthur. Arthur—the first husband, referred to as dear old "Exhibit A"—is crippled by gout, a sign of his age. Nona is the child of Pauline's second marriage. The melodramatic ending occurs when Arthur Wyant, armed with a pistol, discovers Dexter Manford in his daughter-in-law's, Lita's, bedroom; Arthur, however, ends up shooting Nona, who has rushed in because she anticipated her father's adulterous desires. Family order is preserved, symbolic incest repressed, and everyone evades the scene and retreats. The novel ends.

In the first few pages Wharton's ironic tone sets the stage for her satire of modern life to follow. Pauline Manford's schedule is the focus; Freudian psychology is the locus of attack. Pauline schedules her cure— psychoanalysis—in the fifteen minutes between breakfast and interviewing the cook. Moreover, Wharton likens this search for psychic health to visits to "faith-healers, art-dealers, social service workers, and manicures," juxtaposing as she does the appointment with her therapist, then her cook (4). All add up to Wharton's rejection of the instant gratification of solving problems in fractions of an hour.

Wharton's novel plays with these evasions of pain and the new therapeutic culture of the antimodernist period.[3] Wharton's characters all desire to escape pain, what she herself will call the tendency to "[buy] off suffering with money" (307). Wharton documents the use of drugs to buy off such suffering in many of her works: Lily Bart takes chloral for sleep, perhaps suicide; Ramy uses drugs in "Bunner Sisters" to forget his dehumanization; drugs serve as a recreation in *The Mother's Recompense* and in *Twilight Sleep;* and finally, the most institutionalized drug, twilight sleep, is administered to mothers who can afford it. Pauline's embrace of twilight sleep epitomizes the cultural view of childbirth Judy Trenor expresses in *The House of Mirth.* Judy Trenor remarks about her maid's going off to the bedside of her sister: "It was simply inhuman of Pragg to go off now. . . . She says her sister is going to have a baby—as if that were anything to having a house-party!" (42). For Pauline Manford (as for Judy Trenor), childbirth need not be "anything" but a twilight sleep:

> Nona had rather feared that [Lita's] perpetual craving for new "thrills" might lead to some insidious form of time-killing— some of the drinking or drugging that went on among the young women of their set: but Lita had sunk into a state of smiling animal patience, as if the mysterious work going on in her tender young body had a sacred significance for her, and it was enough to lie still and let it happen. All she asked was that

nothing should "hurt" her: she had the blind dread of physical
pain common also to most of the young women of her set. But
all that was so easily managed nowadays: Mrs. Manford (who
took charge of the business, Lita being an orphan) of course
knew the most perfect "Twilight Sleep" establishment in the
country, installed Lita in its most luxurious suite, and filled
her rooms with spring flowers, hot-house fruits, new novels
and all the latest picture-papers—and Lita drifted into motherhood as lightly and unperceivingly as if the wax doll which
suddenly appeared in the cradle at her bedside had been
brought there in one of the big bunches of hot-house roses
that she found every morning on her pillow. (14)

We need to remember here that twilight sleep promised "untraumatic
birth" (Leavitt 1980, 128). As one mother put it after having had twilight
sleep: "The head nurse . . . gave me an injection of scopolomin-mor-
phin. . . . I woke up the next morning about half-past seven[,] . . . the
door opened, and the head nurse brought in my baby. . . . I was so happy"
(quoted in Leavitt 1980, 147). Wharton parodies these advertisements in
McClure's for Twilight Sleep establishments (advertisements which included, among others, one in Boston's Back Bay). For Wharton, forgetting the delivery reduces it to just another commodity in the vast realm of
commodities which Pauline and her daughter-in-law Lita sought. Childbirth under twilight sleep allowed women to distance themselves from
their bodies; biology need not always equal a painful destiny.

For Pauline, childbirth is a mode of production "and babies something
to be turned out in series like Fords" (15). To mechanize childbirth,
Wharton argues, is to make women unaware, out of control, once again.
Her protest is against inscribing women in medical discourse, or insert-
ing women and reproduction into the discourse of capitalism. Or worse,
that with twilight sleep, women, hating pain, would become more com-
plicit with their own dehumanization, and thus become more efficient
and more willing to be machines (as Henry Smith Williams had argued
would happen). Moreover, twilight sleep helped turn medicine and ob-
stetrics into capitalist production, given the expense of the procedure and
the move of women in labor out of the home and into the hospital.
Twilight sleep "capitalized" childbirth: to reproduce is to engage in a
kind of business, collapsing the domestic world into a business practice
and relations of production.

According to Wharton's notebook for this novel, "Lita is—jazz"
(Beinecke Library). Lita's favorite activity is dancing; as a dancer, she is

potentially in line for a big Hollywood contract. In contrast, Pauline Manford is Taylorized (after Frederick Taylor's *Principles of Scientific Management*) and runs her life according to a schedule designed to capitalize on her indomitable energy. She wonders: "What was the use of all the months and years of patient Taylorized effort against the natural human fate: against anxiety, sorrow, old age—if their menace was to reappear whenever events slipped from her control?" (114). Pauline Manford squashes Lita's desire for a Hollywood career because it would take Lita out of her control and into the public realm.

If Pauline and Lita seem to be at odds, it is only a seeming opposition, one that pits the New Woman against the twenties flapper. Carroll Smith-Rosenberg glosses these stereotypes in *Disorderly Conduct:* "From being the dangerous, sexual competitor of the New Man, the New Woman had become a repressed, at times ludicrous, figure. As such she no longer threatened the New Man. Rather, he had made her the enemy of the 'liberated' woman of the 1920s—the flapper" (282). Dexter Manford prefers Lita (the flapper) to his aggressive and controlling wife (the New Woman), thereby instigating the conflict at the center of the novel. But Lita and Pauline, both frustrated, are manipulated by this opposition which occurs in the male vision of Dexter's dream life. As Smith-Rosenberg has it:

> The New Man could portray the New Woman as the enemy of liberated women because he had redefined the issue of female autonomy in sexual terms. He divorced women's rights from their political and economic context. The daughter's quest for heterosexual pleasures, not the mother's demand for political power, now personified female freedom. Linking orgasms to chic fashion and planned motherhood, male sex reformers, psychologists, and physicians promised a future of emotional support and sexual delights to women who accepted heterosexual marriage—and male economic hegemony. Only the "unnatural" woman continued to struggle with men for economic independence and political power. (282–83)

Dexter sets up this opposition—between the New Woman who is his wife and his domestic angel mother—and benefits from the disruption. He can have Pauline as manager (having neutralized the radical goals of the New Woman) and Lita as erotic partner, incestuous complexities aside. Dexter's complaints about his wife take the form of a sentimental recollection of his mother, however distorting:

He had a vision of his mother, out on the Minnesota farm,
before they moved into Delos—saw her sowing, digging po-
tatoes, feeding chickens; saw her kneading, baking, cooking,
washing, mending, catching and harnessing the half-broken
colt to drive twelve miles in the snow for the doctor. . . . And
there the old lady sat at Delos, in her nice little brick house, in
her hale and hearty old age, built to outlive them all.—Wasn't
that perhaps the kind of life Manford himself had been meant
for? . . . Using his brains, muscles, the whole of him, body and
soul, to do real things, bring about real results in the world,
instead of all this artificial activity, this spinning around faster
and faster in the void, and having to be continually rested and
doctored to make up for exertions that led to nothing, nothing, nothing. . . . (79–80, first and last ellipses Wharton's)

Recognizing later that the dream of a western farm is "rubbish," he is
paralyzed by frustrating feelings of unreality and weightlessness. Finally, he
wants a woman who will anchor him to the real, as his mother did; and if
not a woman like his mother, then "a woman lifting a calm face from her
book: a woman who looked so absurdly young to be [his children's]
mother" (81). Dexter feels an intense nostalgia for the woman in the home,
for a domestic influence, which Pauline's worldliness negates.

   In short, Lita and Pauline are in the double-bind of the domestic
hegemony. Pauline cannot afford to let Lita go to Hollywood, since
Pauline is in charge of the domestic sphere and requires a daughter to
command. And in keeping Lita in line and at home, Pauline provides
Dexter with the sexual partner he desires. Such are patriarchal capitalist
relations: in failing to recognize the dual systems of patriarchy and capitalism, Pauline mistakenly assumes her freedom from pain amounts to
freedom in capitalism. But this snare contradicts what Wharton otherwise knows to be true: that women under capitalist patriarchy form an
oppressed class on their own, regardless of the class they enter upon
marriage. Twilight sleep, Alvah Loft ("The Busy Man's Christ") and his
"Spiritual Vacuum-cleaning," psychoanalysis, and eurythmic exercise are
all the various manifestations of a consumer culture designed to palliate
women caught in this binary opposition—New Woman versus flapper—
arranged to preserve patriarchal order (179).

   Both victim and beneficiary of these social arrangements, Pauline believes in the efficacy of the corporate mind and committee work; as in the
pursuit of culture in "Xingu," she wants to discover a spiritual "quick
fix" and joins a committee in which to do so—the League For Discover-

ing Genius—which will also discover a "universal simplification" (226). Edith Wharton's social scene is "a world which believed in panaceas" (55), even though Wharton does not. Her novel repeatedly attacks popular ways of reducing cultural conflict and contradiction—Freud, drugs, Oriental thought, Alvah Loft, alcohol, twilight sleep, golf—testifying to the writer's attempts to demystify cultural fads and motives, eugenics among them. The culture preaches and practices evasion and, indeed, the novel repeats the initial evasion: after Nona is shot, everyone leaves the country for an extended vacation, as Carol Wershoven suggests (131).

Pauline Manford's most telling moment comes at the Mother's Day Association meeting, where she comes close to making a spectacle of herself. Celebrating the capaciousness of a mother's heart (96), Pauline launches into the speech she was planning to give at the Birth Control banquet: "Personality—first and last, and at all costs. . . . That's what every human being has a right to. No more effaced wives, no more drudging mothers, no more human slaves crushed by the eternal round of house-keeping and child-bearing" (113). With a look of horror, Nona alerts her mother to the error, and Pauline quickly catches herself and reverses direction: "That's what our antagonists say—the women who are afraid to be mothers, ashamed to be mothers, the women who put their enjoyment and their convenience and what they call their happiness before the mysterious heaven-sent joy, the glorious privilege, of bringing children into the world—" (113). Later, she feels uneasy, but "reconciles these contradictions" simply, by meditation: "Did not the Mahatma teach that, to the initiated, all discords were resolved into a higher harmony?" (115).

In *Edith Wharton's Argument With America*, Ammons interprets this scene and the novel as follows: "This omnicompetent woman adroitly turns the faux pas to advantage (when it dawns on her what day of the week it is and therefore where she is) by attacking everything she has just finished arguing. The incident sums her up. She is able to endorse position as well as opposition on every issue because she really has no convictions; her life consists of fads" (164). According to Ammons, who finds the twenties novels "stale" (158), Wharton celebrates motherhood in these novels, but does not do it well: "sickened by the flapper," Wharton was "obsessed by the subject of good and bad mothering" (184). For Ammons, Wharton's attack on Pauline Manford is "sound" (165), but I dispute the grounds for this judgment.

Why are we moved in general to read mothers in terms of good and bad oppositions? In Wharton's scheme, contradiction cannot be reduced so easily by binary opposites. In other words, the contradictions of twenties culture—involving here, specifically, Pauline's search for the end to pain—is an attempt to forget her abjection in a culture of masculinist and racist hegemony (a cultural privilege which Wharton all too often supported). The source of her discomfort is not physical so much as ideological. To Ammons's reading I would add the claim that Wharton was bothered by this failure to resolve contradiction. As Wharton writes in her notes for the novel: "Bright elderly women with white hair, eurythmic figures & finely wrinkled faces, who advocate either birth control or unlimited maternity. They always seem to Nona to be the same women & Pauline is never troubled by the contradiction between the 2 theories" (uncatalogued mss., Beinecke Library). Troubled as she may be by the contradictions she sees all around her, the novelist will not resolve them either by blaming or absolving Pauline. Instead, *Twilight Sleep* avoids traditional plot closure—ending neither with marriage, nor insanity, nor even Nona's death—but with a silence which marks the family's inability to be healed. Blake Nevius reads the novel as continuous with Wharton's theme from 1927 to 1928, when she wrote *The Children:* "Once again, the generation which reached middle age following the war is arraigned, the indictment is on the score of irresponsibility, and their guilt is objectified in the blighting of their children's lives" (211). Blaming the mother, however, misses Wharton's subtlety entirely.

Rather than condemning Pauline Manford for her politics, Wharton is much more ambivalent about the culture which produces such contradictions. She questions the notion of natural relations; in fact, her emphasis in *Summer* and *Twilight Sleep* on veiled incestuous relations between father figures and daughters-in-law brings to the fore the cultural construction of sexuality. If New Thought, twilight sleep, and even Henry Ford's anti-Semitism sought to bring the twenties closer to "nature," over and against culture, Wharton's novel questions the value of these oppositions.

By reading *Twilight Sleep* as a fiction about Pauline's failure as a mother, we reinforce the essentialist notion of femininity, of motherhood as erasing otherness. If we look at Pauline from the point of view of the child (and I would include her two husbands—Arthur Wyant and Dexter Manford—as reinforcing these points of view), then she does seem a failure. Melanie Klein's psychoanalytic criticism suggests that no matter what the mother looks like—Pauline Manford or Joan Crawford or Mother Hubbard—every child feels murderous impulses toward her (see Suleiman 355). Because the narrative point of view is that of a child looking to Pauline for support—especially here, with Nona being the most sympathetic of Wharton's children—Pauline is bound to fail.

What happens if we read the novel from Pauline's point of view, taking into consideration all of the contradictions and choices surrounding her which I have already laid out? Beth Kowaleski-Wallace reads *The Custom of the Country* as one that challenges our expectations of Undine Spragg's mothering, arguing that the act of reading Wharton's 1913 novel "metaphorically positions the reader as child in relationship to Undine's failed maternity" (45). Hence, our reactions against Undine are based on our own inabilities to identify with her as mother, from our child's-eye view. As one contemporaneous reviewer put it, "Pauline is more in the forefront of the narrative than any one else, with Nona perhaps a few steps behind. And the story is generally told as seen through their eyes (especially Nona's, Pauline being highly myopic) . . ." (Hutchinson 432). Like Undine's, Pauline's searches for fulfillment can be read as discontent with the choices she can possibly make, choices which result in inevitable contradiction.

Indeed, the novel lets us glimpse Pauline only as mother and family manager, only as the child's mirror—or as our own search for the "good mother." Susan Suleiman writes about the mother's predicament: "Just as motherhood is ultimately the child's drama, so is artistic creation. In both cases the mother is the essential but silent Other, the mirror in whom the child searches for his own reflection, the body he seeks to appropriate, the thing he loses or destroys again and again, and seeks to recreate" (357). Wharton's mothers, either Pauline or Lita, both seek some sort of self-expression, even in its mass-produced form of acting, mind cure, psychoanalysis, and dancing. Granted, for Wharton these are problematic expressions of a healthy adjustment to society, but what if these expressions cater to and are produced for constricting the mother's body and limiting her creative acts to recreation of the species? Is this a culture in which Motherhood has its own special form of production and commercialization? To produce babies like Fords is the first step toward the production of a ready-made culture for women.[4]

Leaving behind the mores of old New York, Wharton's late fictions challenge the ideology of domesticity and sexual nature. While Lewis, Nevius, Wershoven, and Wolff suggest that Pauline is to blame for the failure of the family and see woman as mirror for her children in *Twilight Sleep,* I contend that Pauline's contradictoriness is neither the mirror nor the cause of her children's contradictions. Her fragmentations refuse a vantage point from which the children could see themselves. Pauline's "flightiness"—as it is denigratingly called—is of her own creation. She refuses the traditional role of mother for a less glorified—but nonetheless her own—role.

It is not surprising that Nona, the holdout for traditional values, is the martyr of the novel. Nona represents the family glue; she is the "mother" who cannot be other. Hence, Nona's lack of personality—her blankness—suggests what Wharton thought about the extremes represented by mother and daughter. One leads to living in contradiction, the other to martyrdom. Yet even Nona comes, after she is shot, to embrace her mother's contradictions when, at the end, she wants to join a convent where no one believes in anything. This is neither nostalgia nor progressivism, but a look at patriarchal and capitalist relations in the face.

Wharton's novel refuses us the possibility of identifying with any of the characters and also refuses to offer us a mirror image of ourselves or our mothers in the family. In refusing this mirror, Wharton disrupts the dominant image of the maternal in her time as the self-sacrificial angel. Full of contradictions from Ford to twilight sleep, mind cures, and maternity, the novel does not give us the easy comfort of "higher harmony" or a formal solution, no easy binaries between good and evil to be transcended at the end. What has disturbed critics is not so much the melodrama but Wharton's ambivalence about the culture which produces easy remedies and whose binaries—nature and culture, the New Woman and flapper—she has dismantled. Perhaps this is enough to suggest Wharton's politics on eugenics and on women's desire to control their bodies. She saw twilight sleep institutions and the other activities which Pauline supported as essentially elitist, because those organizations drove wedges among women along class lines. If Wharton deprecates her antagonist Pauline, it is not out of a nostalgia or sentimentalizing of the sort Dexter feels. Rather, Pauline is degraded for her insistence that cultural standards are class dependent and meant to apply "to different categories of people" (224). Earlier in the novel, Pauline questioned the contradiction of appearing on the Mother's Day and Birth Control boards at the same time. She decided that in "encouraging natality and teaching how to restrict it, . . . it was sufficient . . . to say that the two categories of people appealed to were entirely different, and could not be 'reached' in the same way. In ethics, as in advertising, the main thing was to get at your public" (115).

The same holds true for novel-writing. Wharton gets at her public not by condemning Pauline but by forcing her readers to analyze themselves. From our vantage point, it is easy enough to condemn Pauline and Lita for their frivolities and failure to choose. Nevertheless, before condemning them, we need to remember that the early feminists' search for freedom was often contradictory. G. J. Barker-Benfield, in *The Horrors of the*

Half-Known Life, notes that women in the twenties manifested a desire "for greater obstetrical care" which also meant turning "away from the 'natural,' domestic scene of childbirth" as a "function of . . . emancipation" (67). What we see as "natural childbirth" was the opposite in the twenties, thereby demonstrating once again the arbitrariness of the "natural."

Twilight Sleep is chaotic, but no less brilliant for being so. The chaos Wharton represents in the novel is not one of plot but of the culture—and of women's place within it. Pauline ponders this chaos in the novel: "Wasn't everybody talking about 'the return to Nature,' and ridiculing the American prudery in which the minds and bodies of her generation had been swaddled?" (110). Wharton's novel shows how impossible it is to locate "Nature," since—as we have seen with Dexter—Nature is the locus of nostalgia and an agent in Dexter's condemnation of Pauline's culture. Choice, as Wharton has it in novels like *Twilight Sleep,* is always contradictory and never easy.

Maternal Indifference

> What cannibals marriage makes of people . . .
> —Edith Wharton, *The Children*

Writing to Royal Cortissoz on 11 October 1928, Wharton describes playing with her brother's friends, "men 15 or 20 years older than I was, who were the most delightful of comrades & play-fellows. Looking back now, I see there were Boynes among them, but I was all unconscious then . . ." (Lewis and Lewis, 518). Wharton's 1928 novel *The Children* brings to consciousness the attention of these older men, intellectual comrades who had peopled her childhood and, one assumes, her adulthood, too. Coupled with *Twilight Sleep,* this work makes a compelling argument for the new politics of the family Wharton contemplates in the twenties. Martin Boyne—the forty-six-year old bachelor-hero of the novel—is the central consciousness, but the novel is told from a child's perspective.[5] Wharton was always told she "didn't know anything about children" and referred to this novel and its infant, Chipstone, in a letter to Elisina Tyler, ten years later, as "the baby I had dreamed of, and never met" (16 April 1937, Lilly Library).

In *The Children,* Wharton abandons whatever uncertainty she had about eugenic control. The novel charts the disasters of the millionaire couple—Cliffe and Joyce Wheater—as parents, focusing not so much on the genetic success of parents, but on their social failures. Certainly, there is no innate "maternal instinct" in either of the two Mrs. Wheaters: Mrs. Wheater #1 is Joyce Mervin, mother of Judith, the twins Terry and Blanca, and the baby Chipstone; Boyne describes her as "aimlessly abundant," as one whose self-described "great unhappiness" is her weight (9, 16). Mrs. Wheater #2 is the film star Zinnia Lacrosse, who gave birth to Zinnie—now one of the three "step"-children accompanying the other Wheater children across Europe (22). The other two stepchildren, Bun and Beechy (Beatrice and Astorre), had an Italian lion-tamer and tightrope dancer for their mother, and Prince Buondelmonte, Joyce Mervin Wheater's second husband, for their father. Bun and Beechy are "foreigners," whose erratic, emotional behavior is chalked up to their Italian parentage. The biological parents abandon them to Joyce and, thus, to Judith—the eldest daughter and the caretaker of them all. In featuring this disarray, Wharton's novel suggests just how wrong the eugenics movement could be. Thrown together by their second-honeymooning parents, the children wind up raising each other. The father of the clan, Cliffe, is only interested in Chipstone—the eugenic gem—as his heir; Terry, the invalid, survives, as Chipstone dies from meningitis.

Although a financial success for Wharton (the book was chosen as a Book-of-the-Month Club selection for that year and earned her $95,000 [Lewis and Lewis 509]), *The Children* has not been considered one of Wharton's literary successes, perhaps because the novel is unremittingly bleak and so decided about its politics. Boyne's first objection to the Wheater clan is that they are "very unmodern" (19) for having so many children, a claim that tenuously links him to the eugenic concerns of the day while his other views of parenting remain orthodox, since they focus exclusively on good mothering. Good mothering was ostensibly the source of race superiority; divorce, a source of dysgenic poison.

Wharton's counterexample of the good mother, the Princess Buondelmonte, arrives with her training in eugenics and infant psychology to offer a view toward the moral guidance and religious education of her stepchildren Bun and Beechy, a perspective Wharton describes as a "forensic" or didactic thesis (277). "Her glib command of the subject" of eugenics leads her to question Boyne on the children's history—whether they, in fact, had "ever been properly psychoanalyzed" (278). Her grasp comes from her training in Texas at Lohengrin College (where her grandfather had been the College's first president), an experience that seems all too remote to Boyne, as it does to Wharton. The princess's view of the children's mock-battle leads her to believe that "the old militarist instinct" must be eliminated in the future eugenic training she has planned for them (282); she wants to replace play as they know it with the "newest feats in scientific gymnastics" and games called "Ambition" (289, 294–95). Bun's response undermines the princess's training: "Are you really and truly my father's new wife? Then you must tell him he's got to send me a gun at once, to shoot everybody who calls me and Beechy a wop" (283). Immediately afterwards, Judith reminds the princess of the parents' abandonment of the children: "And now that they're big enough to cut up their own food and be good company, I suppose you and he think it would be fun to come and carry them off, the way you'd pick out a pair of Pekes at a dog-show . . ." (286). (If there were any doubt that Wharton's sympathy lies with the children, her reference to her favorite dog breed, the Pekinese, should clinch it.)

What Jessica Benjamin writes about contemporary feminism holds for Wharton's novel here: "The puritanical tendencies within the feminist movement are often linked to a tendency to elevate the desexualized mother whose hallmark is not desire but nurturance" (91). Exactly this tendency—which polarizes male rationality and female nurturance and essentializes nurturance and parenting—leads to the oppositional politics Wharton rejects (see Jessica Benjamin 206). Consider how Wharton describes Boyne's early relation to Judith: ". . . He was already busy at the masculine task of endowing the woman of the moment with every quality which made life interesting to himself" (35). His relation is one of intellectual domination as he explains the aesthetics of the Italian basilica to her, but it also thinly veils his desire for erotic companionship. Only by continual reminders that she is a child can Boyne remember his rendezvous with Rose Sellars, a woman his age but with less sexual attraction because less available to erotic or intellectual domination. When Judith is away from the children, Boyne recognizes her as an adolescent, "a child of fifteen or sixteen," "almost plain," and reducible to "a bundle of negatives" (35–36). "But outside in the sunlight, with the children leaping about her, and guiding her with joyful cries toward the outspread tea-things, she was instantly woman again—gay, competent, composed, and wholly mistress of the situation . . ." (36). This "little-girl-mother" intrigues him precisely to the extent that she is an ambiguous sign to him in the way Rose Sellars is not (38). Rose may be "clever" and "original," but she is not erotic (39). The novel highlights, then, Boyne's struggle with "cataloguing"—or characterizing—Judith into the acceptable feminine roles of the day: the adolescent girl or the asexual mother.

Privatized and polarized notions of motherhood—not dysgenics or "racial suicide"—prove for Wharton to be at the crux of the problem. As much as Wheater rhapsodizes about the "heredity" of the children (50),

Wharton shows how unhealthy their social environment is. As Joyce herself declares, Judy is one of those modern children (like Nona for Pauline Manford) who mothers her own mother (54). When Judy confronts Martin with her knowledge of her mother's sexual interest in Terry's tutor, Gerald Ormerod, the bachelor is shocked. "I suppose," she told him, "You think I oughtn't to say things like that about mother—but what am I to do, when they're true . . .?" (61). Prematurely exposed to sexuality—as Martin sees it—Judith recognizes the precarious situation of the children when it depends upon her mother's "maternal instinct." Everywhere the naive Boyne is forced to see the sexualized mother and the failure of his culture's category of nurturing mother. For his part, Martin "would have given the world to believe either that she was five years older than she said, or else that she did not know the meaning of the words she used" (62).[6]

The subtext of this novel is neither heredity nor mass culture but how parental irresponsibility distorts children's lives. Judith announces that children know better how to care for each other, and she cites Doll Westway as her best friend and model (130). Doll Westway used to steal money from her mother in order to pay bills, and Judith out of necessity learns to do the same. Boyne is again outraged, although this is because Judith's moral sense seems to be created from "depths of pain and disillusionment" he cannot fathom, not from the conventional sense of childhood innocence he expects (144). Boyne knows that, similarly, Cliffe Wheater has no conception of making a home for his children. Insofar as Cliffe and Joyce Wheater refuse to see their resemblance "with a down-and-outer like Charlie Westway" (149), Doll Westway's suicide offers no cautionary tale to them. And, in fact, Syb Lullmer, Doll's socialite mother and Wheater appendage, so thoroughly misses the import of her daughter's death that she can only regret that Doll had resisted her "maternal counsels" (159). Judith, too, talks about her best friend's death as "the shortest way out" of the "abyss of precocious knowledge" gotten from hotel life and promiscuous parents (248). Although Joyce likes to think of herself as a sacrificing mother who puts her children first, the children's flight from Venice culminates in Wharton's mocking of the parents' deluded claims to represent "the real labouring classes" rather than "high-brows" (164–65).

Yet Boyne is equally disgusted by Rose Sellars's proposition that they adopt Terry and Blanca and separate the Wheater children, a separation Boyne has worked to prevent. Her intent is to make the twins "useful members of society" (251), an echo of eugenics arguments of the teens and twenties. In the meantime, the children send Boyne a wedding

present—a baby cradle—since they expect Boyne's marriage and parenthood with Rose to be imminent. Martin unconsciously keeps his boots in
the cradle, a sign to Judith at least that he cannot imagine the sexual and
social commitment of having his own children. When Boyne proposes
marriage to the fifteen-year-old Judith, she misunderstands it as an offer
to adopt her and all of the Wheater clan. Crushed, Martin resolves to
leave for Brazil where he can forget his unrequited love.

Ultimately, Boyne clings both to his passion and to his sense of propriety, heading to South America after his failure to keep the Wheater clan
intact. Torn between work and fatherhood, eventually he chooses the
former since it allows him to be "his own master" (239). Moreover, his
rationalization suits him, since it is consistent with his preference for a
life in which there is "no one that he need be on his guard against or at his
best before; no one to be tormented or enchanted by, no one to listen to
and answer. 'Decidedly, I'm a savage,' he thought . . ." (239). But
Wharton makes clear that his notion of savagery is simply alienation
from cultural prescriptions for parenting. Boyne's uncompromising dream
of passion is at odds, however, with a culture of accommodation and
compromise, the accommodation which the Wheaters compulsively exhibit in their personal relations. Mrs. Wheater is a prime example of this
horror of relinquishing an ideal of self: her decision "to let herself turn
frankly into an *old woman*" comes in reaction to Syb Lullmer's "hopeless
attempt to keep young" by dyeing and drugging herself (326). Wharton
sees this social life as an endless round of compromise and reaction, a
complete surrender to accommodating a culture continually in flux.

"Tierra del Fuego" marks the spot of Boyne's vision of escape, of
savagery, of bachelorhood (240). As Judith Sensibar suggests, Martin
goes to Brazil as a "highly successful civil engineer—the cultural hero of
Manifest Destiny" (582). In this light, this immersion in Brazil is an
imperialist appropriation of the primitive. Boyne refuses to compromise
his—or Judith's—values and heads to the South American territory to
repudiate his complicity in the Wheater clan's dispersal. Thus, as she had
before in *The Reef* and would again later in *The Buccaneers*, Wharton
sets European dissolution against South American "primitiveness," with
primitiveness becoming a museum piece—the Incunabula—which Joyce
Wheater and the Lawyer Dobree view at the Paris museum (324). An
immersion in South America—like the immersion in "Xingu"—washes
away memories of the kind of taboos Boyne wants to forget.[7] Yet Wharton inverts the general terms of the primitive: modern life, for her, is
sexualized and promiscuous; South America and Xingu are realms where
one escapes the eroticized world of the 1920s. Indeed, the novel's last line

belies Boyne's vision of Brazil as escape: he is "a lonely man," neither a savage nor a carefree bachelor.

Another way to read the end of this novel is to focus on its symbolic implications. At moments of his most intense passion, after he proposes to Judith and after he breaks for good with Rose Sellars, Boyne misplaces his umbrella. This lapse of memory can be associated with the symbolic significance of dreams; in Freud's "Symbolism in Dreams," forgetting the umbrella suggests a genital re-membering. He experiences the choice between fatherhood and a distinctly unerotic companionship with Rose as a symbolic castration. Thus he prefers his loneliness to the fear of complying with the conventional compromises of his culture. Wharton sees these compromises as emerging from the regulating of sexuality (through eugenics, through standardization, through technology and ideology), in contradiction to the unlegislated sexual desire that is so often associated in modernism with the primitive. For Wharton, the truly primitive and barbaric occurs *in* modern society; South America, by contrast, signifies a refuge from the promiscuity—the symbolic mutilations—of the twenties.

Primitivism and Cultural Repression

Perhaps at no other time in history than in the twenties and thirties was reproduction tied so intimately to war: women were supposed to be "race warriors," protecting the purity of the eugenic stock. However, the thirties saw a crucial shift in eugenics thinking, since the effects of Hitlerism made social scientists denounce racial thinking (see Degler 202–5), but the nineteenth-century Wagnerian "Twilight of the Gods" was already over for Wharton. Social movements like twilight sleep and eugenics proved, for Wharton and friends like Huxley and Malinowski, to accelerate the feared decline.

Wharton denounces American culture for "moral forcible feeding, for compelling everybody to be cleaner, stronger, healthier and happier than they would have been by the unaided light of Nature," as Dexter Manford pronounces in *Twilight Sleep* (190). Pauline Manford's reflections on philanthropy, genius, and American individualism are even more to the point: "Every contact with the humanitarian movements distinguishing her native country from the selfish *laissez faire* and cynical indifference of Europe filled her with a new optimism, and shed a reassuring light on all her private cares. America really seemed to have an immediate answer for everything, from the treatment of the mentally deficient to the elucidation of the profoundest religious mysteries. In such an atmosphere of universal simplification, how could one's personal problems not be solved?" (225–26). At this point, however, I would take this ironic celebration of America's "simplification" in a different light. Seeing Wharton's passing reference to the "treatment of the mentally deficient" as another indictment of the eugenics policy Wharton feared, I would highlight her own simplification of the race problems of her culture. Whereas Wharton sees the contradictions of Pauline's position and the anxieties of the children in her 1928 novel, she never recognizes the reprehensible oversimplification in her own racial politics—the hatred of "nigger society" and "dirty Jews." (Not even Morton Fullerton's argument against "the cultivation of such weeds as Antisemitism" [*Problems of Power*, 101] could persuade Wharton otherwise.)

These novels of cultural and reproductive politics affirm the "inner life" usually associated with Wharton's purposes. The following chapter, "The Advance Men and Edith Wharton: The Public Relations of Writing," shows Wharton's turn inward to the spiritual possibilities of the "inner life" in this social atmosphere of universal simplification. At no other time during or after World War I is Wharton so focused on her personal, i.e., financial, problems and the aesthetics of pleasing a popular audience obsessed with what advertisements and popular culture had to offer. In the context of her struggle to meet the demands of popular culture, she takes on the next stage of the reproductive debate: companionate marriage. Controversy over divorce and birth control raged in the twenties and thirties. Companionate marriage advocates argued for greater accessibility of birth-control information and divorce by mutual consent. Ernest Groves's *The Marriage Crisis* represented the problem as one of sex and passion, "sex-expression" being the necessary corollary to the twenties obsession with "self-expression." Arguing in 1928 that "Marriage faces a crisis and birth control is largely responsible" (46), Groves suggested that "regulating sex behavior" is the antidote to excessive self-expressions of youth and their pleasure-seeking habits. The family suffers in companionate marriage, so he argues, because companionate marriage means "arrested family" (54). Moreover, experimental marriage "will be driven by the consequences of its policy to legalize abortion," as Groves claims Russia has done (119–20). Groves concludes with a call to aesthetic experience as a support to married life: "Matrimony flowers best when deeply-rooted" (242).

Wharton dismisses these organic metaphors for marriage in her Vance Weston novels, *Hudson River Bracketed* (1929) and *The Gods Arrive* (1932). The social regulation of family life and the regulation of sexual desire are issues central to this pair of novels, since both issues arise from the impulse toward individualism and self-expression at the expense of social responsibility. How far Wharton is willing to go toward legislating that morality, and in effect politicizing aesthetics, is the topic of my next chapter.

4

The Advance Men and Edith Wharton: The Public Relations of Writing

As Wharton writes to her friend Elisina Tyler on 1 January 1930: "I am overwhelmed by what you say of 'Hudson Riv.' After allowing for all the indulgence of affection, there seems so much more praise than the book deserves—yet I *wd* rather hear it of this than any other I have written. It is a theme that I have carried in my mind for years, & that Walter [Berry] was always urging me to use; indeed I had begun it before the war, but in our own milieu, & the setting of my own youth. After the war it took me long to re-think it & transpose it into the crude terms of modern America; & I am happy to find that my readers think I have succeeded" (Lewis and Lewis 525). Wharton's translation of her story into the "crude terms of modern America" allows her a range of cultural critique that she did not imagine in her earlier fiction. The argument that follows situates Wharton's 1929 *Hudson River Bracketed* and its sequel, *The Gods Arrive* (1932), in the context of modernism, and at the intersection of the rise of department store commercialism with the concomitant emergence of free love bohemianism, the novels' two tropes for cultural disintegration. These novels, I contend, are less an "argument with America" in the twenties, a decade with which Wharton was notoriously disenchanted, than they are an engagement of cultural dialogics dramatizing how the new advertising culture had its roots in middle-class artistic and sexual experimentation. In doing so, Wharton links bohemian oppositionalism with New York as a land of desire, represented here in the new cult of celebrity and personality. While her audience sought perpetual gratification, Wharton advocated the satisfactions of the "inner life."

If writers such as Sinclair Lewis, Fitzgerald, and Loos, among others, made their reputations by confronting twenties and thirties culture head-on, Wharton portrays how social politics transforms the inner life, examining the more or less private drama of achieving an ethical position. Few of her contemporaries were as involved in setting such a specific agenda for negotiating radical change and social assimilation. In this regard, *Hudson River Bracketed* and *The Gods Arrive* represent her most critical positions with regard to the new American mass culture, whether the targets of her reproach are revivalists such as Billy Sunday and New Thought curists like Elizabeth Towne, the Pulitzer ("Pulsifer") Prize committees, or the "crude terms of modern America" in general. These novels take to task the whole range of her annoyances, from neurasthenics to anarchists, and in the process demonstrate Wharton's discomfort with both high modernism, in writers like James Joyce and Virginia Woolf, and technological modernity, in advance men, advertising, and production-line culture. Rather than being reactionary in their politics, these books—Wharton's last completed novels—are much less strident than *French Ways and Their Meaning,* where American popular culture—the "movie" and the music hall—is the locus of her attack (68). In these last novels, Wharton envisions a much more complex theory of culture than she has ever created before. *Hudson River Bracketed* fuses these various concerns in a sustained look at advertising, modern art and society, and business. *The Gods Arrive* turns to a more intimate critique of the bohemian challenge, encoded in free love and artist life, and demystifies the business-as-usual of gender politics under capitalism.

Perhaps we can tell more about Wharton's state of mind, however, after she finished the Vance Weston series and embarked on her last novel, *The Buccaneers.* To her friend Edward Sheldon in 1936 (2 November), she confesses her despair over a world so changed that no readers could be interested in the life of private motive and public meaning which she had always valued and from which she made her living (Lilly Library). Out of nostalgia for the quieter times when her writing was more in vogue, Wharton contrasts her fiction of the "inner life" against the current popularity of novels of propaganda.

As clear as Wharton's targets are in these novels, she does not finally embrace "the quieter universe" for which she had once intended her fiction. In fact, the contradictions of twenties life propel her writing, forcing her to come to terms with modernity, especially the spectacle of advertising, commerce, and market relations. The "inner life"—as it was for Wharton, as it is for Vance, her artist-hero—needs exactly the stimuli of passion, crisis, and intellectual challenge to vitalize it.

As early as 1919 and the publication of *French Ways and Their Meaning*, Wharton had expressed her frustration with American taste. Using the simile she later gives Newland Archer to condemn May Welland's enforced naivete in *Age of Innocence*, Wharton questions whether some races are born as "irremediably blind as Kentucky cave-fishes" (52). Wharton complains that America's post-war failure, in business as in education, is the new tendency toward the "short-cut," contending that Americans, unlike the French, want to commodify their learning into knowledge that "can be bottled, pickled and absorbed" quickly (55). Her fears for the predigested American culture first emerge in her criticism of America's new reading practices, which seem to deliver no more than gossip "and nothing more nourishing than . . . hanging about the store, the bar and the street-corner" (69). Recognizing that America's "get-rich-quick" possibilities may provide more leisure and, therefore, more time for culture (72), she also predicts that those virtues may just as easily celebrate individual wealth and crowd out anything else. Despite her reservations, Wharton stopped short of endorsing the problematic solution of social control and engineering as solutions to the problem of taste. Yet Wharton's question persisted: How could she write her own version of reform novels for this popular culture and still circumnavigate the trends in American taste? How could one continue to write when one needed to protect oneself from public outcry and enjoy the financial benefits of good public relations?

Social Engineering and Social Realism

There may be tons of dynamite in the race question.
—E. A. Ross in "The Firing Line in Sociology" (19 February 1928)

As the previous chapters show, the conjunction of eugenics and nativism in late nineteenth- and early twentieth-century American culture led to the rise of new social sciences, and ushered into American letters an unprecedented view of social and somatic progress. As a result, these sciences also heralded a new vision of modern America that both accommodated and promoted early eugenics arguments, nativist sentiments like 100% Americanism and anti-hyphenates, and eventually the Immigration Restriction Acts of 1921 and 1924.[1] "Social engineering" was quite literally the conclusion many social scientists offered, with many American realists adopting this set of purposes as their directive and objective. The concurrent rise of eugenics movements, as well as their relation to nativ-

ist and racist sentiments underwriting the emergence of various fraternal
organizations (which had their origins in anti-immigration crusades), the
second wave of the Ku Klux Klan, family studies research (such as H. H.
Goddard's famous study of the Kallikaks, in which he argued that feeblemindedness could be found mostly among the insane and the criminal),
and Margaret Sanger's birth control crusade (later aligned with the major eugenicist arguments) also influenced Wharton's fiction, from *Summer* onward, especially her last two completed novels, devoted to the
career of writer Vance Weston and his literary projects.[2] Concerned as
these novels were about fiction's purpose, they were particularly ani-
mated by social questions about the abilities of working-class and un-
cultured peoples—the masses—to "think beyond themselves."

E. A. Ross, a professor of sociology, had already formulated his major
ideas about "race suicide" in *The Old World in the New*.[3] Ross's various
writings on "race minds" (ca. 1914), "Christian Education and Social
Control" (1921), feeblemindedness and degeneration (1931), birth control (1934), and "The Comparative Value of Races" (no date), all demonstrate his major contributions to eugenics and nativist thought. No Social
Darwinist, Ross argued throughout his tenure at the University of Wisconsin from 1906 through 1937 that the culture needed a rationally
engineered plan for social growth; "My own confidence in science has
not in the least made me a 'Social Darwinist'" ("Christian Education and
Social Control," reel 32, 22 Nov. 1921). Only through social engineering
would we avoid the "social war" that was promised by the organizing of
the working class into soviets and then into a republic (for Ross, this
defined "bolshevism"). Like Wharton in *The Mother's Recompense*, Ross
railed against the outrages of modern life, but for different reasons. Ross
saw films as especially culpable, inspiring in youth a taste for untrammeled sex-expression, what his friend Charlotte Perkins Gilman called
"going native" with "women of frankly lower race" (Gilman 1931, 121–
22). As Ross argues in "What the Films Are Doing to Young America," a
movie "ravels out what has been knit up with such care"—the sexual
repression of the Puritanical culture (2). He fears that young people, like
the Polynesians described by Mead and Malinowski, give themselves too
freely to love. In his view, "such erotic absorption as prevails among the
people of the South Seas who can gain their living by catching fish and
gathering bread-fruit, might be very dangerous in a populous society like
ours where strenuous devotion to the job or to preparation for the job is
a *sine qua non* of success. One can hardly imagine much great achievement in a society whose young people gave themselves up to the pursuit
of love" (reel 33, p. 4). Ross's imagination of beneficent social engineer-

ing for the success of the white race dovetails with Charlotte Perkins Gilman's fantasy of the disaster that would ensue were Nordic Protestants to submit to sex indulgence and sex parasitism. For them, the goal of education is not the habit-bound, self-adjusting individual. Rather, as Ross states in "How Can Education be Made to Promote Socialized Character?": "We wish to create the self-critical self-adjusting individual who has formed the habit of breaking all habits" (reel 32, p. 1).

A generation of American writers from the teens through the thirties saw their objective as instructing readers in this kind of social and self-discipline. American literature of these decades addresses in various detail the complex challenge of modernity, sounded in the call issuing from various quarters to control the "lower" orders and "baser" passions.[4] Gilman, who was sociologist, economist, and novelist, wrote with the explicit purpose of promoting race hygiene and social engineering. As we have seen in Chapter Three, Atherton also joined this novelistic bandwagon when, in the novel *Black Oxen,* she became the literary advocate of the Steinach Treatment, a procedure designed to rejuvenate the most eugenically fit of white Anglo-Saxon Americans through the use of X-rays.

The controversy over eugenics policies declined in the late twenties, and the attention shifted from birth control to intense debates about the morality of companionate marriage and the availability of divorce. Ross's and Gilman's mutually reinforcing views suggest the parameters of a larger debate over the premises of social engineering: namely, "the manageability of social change" in the face of greater individual self- and sex-expression (McClymer 46). This discussion came to a head in 1927, with the publication of Judge Ben Lindsey's advocacy of "Companionate Marriage." His controversial stance galvanized the forces both for and against the issues surrounding social control: on the one hand, the eugenicists with their nativist and antiradical conservatism; on the other, those social critics who believed that legislating private morality would lead to authoritarian politics. Ross articulates the former position in "Are We Headed for Degeneration?" written in the late 1930s, sustaining an argument that runs throughout his twenties writings: "As a body our Elite contributes nothing to the growth of our people; it all comes from the undistinguished. The outstanding achievers—say, 1 in a thousand—are not leaving enough children to fill their shoes. It is doubtful if even our best endowed twentieth are doing it! The cause is not celibacy—we are more married now than ever before—but birth control in marriage" (reel 32, pp. 5–6). In meditating on the success of his 1901 study, *Social Control,* Ross entertained the criticism that the psychology behind social engineering was "antiquated." That psychology, as he recognized, belonged to the late nineties, before Freud, Jung, Adler and Pavlov had made their mark. "Such psychological terms as *drive, complex, conditioned response, stereotype, projection,* [and] *identification. . . .* were yet to be minted. The term *personality* lacked much of the content it has today . . ." (reel 33, p. 5).

When Wharton takes up the issue of social control and the invention of the twentieth-century psychology of personality, as she does in *Hudson River Bracketed* and *The Gods Arrive,* she shows how the post-Freudian artistic personality complicates cultural notions of social conditioning. Despite her well-known conservatism and off-hand racism, with references to the lowbrow "Poles and Dagoes" in *Hudson River Bracketed* (41), Wharton campaigned for a mediation or negotiation of private morality with social good, a tendency we have seen that leaves her in the same vexed relation to modern culture, but as a less authoritarian advocate than some of her fellow intellectuals were, like Gilman and even Loos.

Yet Wharton found herself vexed by crude modern America, so much so that these novels may seem like personal tirades. Often taken as Wharton's "me-books" about the trials of her own artistic genius, *Hudson River Bracketed* and *The Gods Arrive* are more explicitly concerned with the social and financial world of American business than with representing an alienated artist-hero. Both of these novels contemplate the fate of artistic "genius" in the face of a changing literary readership. Frenside, the novel's literary critic, evaluates Vance's potential for Halo Tarrant (who will become Vance's lover in the second of these two novels): "If he goes on retailing the successive chapters of his own history, as they happen to him, they'll be raw autobiography, or essays disguised as novels; but not real novels." Wharton continues, "It was his conviction that the 'me-book,' as he called it, however brilliant was at best sporadic, with little reproductive power" (GA 220–21). Vance experiences the social pressures of artistic celebrityhood, where art is made and marketed to a "big reading public . . . fed up with descriptions of corrupt society people, like there was a demand for in the East" (257). So writes Mrs. Weston to her son, reminding him of the Midwestern taste for "pure manly stories." Like Wharton herself, Vance cannot lift the "yoke" of material concerns; that is, the need to publish to survive in "the world of food, clothes, salary, sickness or health, prosperity or failure, mothers-in-law or boarding houses" (HRB 253). Vance's Grandma Scrimser "could not understand why a successful novelist, who knew all the publishers and critics in New York, shouldn't be making a big income . . ." (HRB 441).

Hudson River Bracketed chronicles the financial and artistic progress of Vance Weston, a novice writer who signs a bad contract forbidding him to write for any magazine other than *The New Hour;* another bad contract, his precipitous marriage to a young woman, Laura Lou, with whom he is infatuated, seems to seal his destiny as a hunger-artist. This infatuation soon gives way to a deeper attachment—more intellectual, even literary—to Halo Tarrant, who is married to Vance's editor Lewis Tarrant at *The New Hour.* Laura Lou's death at the end of *Hudson River Bracketed* frees Vance, if not Halo, from a miserable marriage. When Vance and Halo go off to Europe in *The Gods Arrive* to test a trial marriage, he soon tires of her companionship, too, and pursues an old love, Floss Delaney, with whom he had his first sexual encounter in Illinois. Bored by his intellectual pretensions, Floss throws him off and Vance eventually returns to Halo, who is pregnant with their child. The sequel ends when Halo welcomes Vance back, not as a spouse but as another child to care for.

At the same time that culture was stressing personality and self-fulfillment in New Thought and mind cure, Wharton's novels countered by stressing exactly what critics have assumed she forgot: the demands of the material world, the "cruelty of social conditions" (HRB 389). Rather than indulge in an elitist view, she was acutely aware of the American hypocrisy about success as being, at once, the ultimate goal and a source of general cultural ambivalence, often a source of disgust. Vance's changing plans for his novel exemplify this ambivalence, but also speak to the marketing of novels and novelists as celebrities. Vance begins writing *Loot*, based on the "tumult of life and wealth and energy" he finds in New York (HRB 153). On his second round to New York, he wants to start from scratch and write from experience, not from his exuberance about his initial vision of New York. When he first conceives of writing for a living, his goal is self-expression, and it was Laura Lou who first sparked his vision of writing as career. His financial obligations now temper his approach: "The new tale was different," Halo notices, "less vehement, less emotional, above all less personal" (HRB 220). In the publishing world, "me-books" touted individual genius but seemed self-indulgent to Wharton and her crowd, a quality Wharton abhorred in *Ulysses* (Lewis and Lewis 461).

Hudson River Bracketed often follows the rhetoric of a catalogue, as if all the critic of culture had to do was cast her eye on the panoply of social and political excesses and vulgarities. The novel reflects her chaotic responses—ambivalent, often overwhelmed—to twenties culture and the host of new influences: the Yiddish Theatre, the rise of the Harlem

Renaissance she has already denounced in the mid-twenties, comparisons
to Joyce and Dreiser and their "elephant[ine]" novels (379). In contemplating his second novel, to be called "Loot," Vance thinks in language
reminiscent of Wharton's letter about Van Vechten and his focus on
Harlem life: "The public was fed up with skyscrapers and niggers and
bootleggers and actresses. Fed up equally with Harlem and the opera,
with Greenwich Village and the plutocrats. What they wanted was something refined—something to appeal to the heart" (398). Perhaps these
were wish-dreams on Wharton's part; she wanted something "beyond"
all of the current fads she lists only to attack. Vowing to write a Great
American novel—like Anita Loos's *Gentlemen Prefer Blondes*—Vance
mouths these frustrations with cultural obsessions, to offset these fads
and right the wrongs of mass-produced culture.

The Twenties and the Cult of Genius, the Individual, and Self-Expression

Social engineering of the kind suggested by both British and American
eugenics movements followed from the belief in Aryan superiority and
American exceptionalism, and became the watchword of the twenties.
When the academy welcomed the social sciences as academic disciplines,
the arts, too, were adapting the views of social science as the impetus for
a new mode of writing fiction. The values of individual genius and the
virtues of self-expression were no more celebrated than in the twenties
when advice from social activists like Gilman to write "with a purpose"
rather than for celebrity fell on deaf ears (1990, 121). Instead, the faith in
technological progress moved many to believe that history could be controlled, that social laws could be discovered through logical positivism.
Such self-help thinking, according to sociologist Dorothy Ross, led to
movements trying to harness individual energy for social progress and
individual enlightenment: the evangelism of big-time operators like Billy
Sunday; the advertising of Bruce Barton and associates, preaching the
self-promotion of self-made men; self-improvement tracts like "How to
Win and Hold Love" and "Game of Life and How to Play It"; the writing
of sentimental fictionists like Kathleen Norris, whose eighty-some-odd
novels, including *Mother* (1911), trace the possibilities of love and maternity in the midst of the new ethics.[5]

Moreover, the culture's new enthusiasm for advertising—for products
and for the self—was linked with the celebration of individual genius. At
the very moment when large numbers of individuals were being social-

ized into mass culture, the glorification of individual genius was a contradictory cultural ideal. How could the artist play to the masses yet retain a sense of America's particular exceptionality? Wharton writes this conflict into her novels, especially when Vance worries about being either a non-entity or an individual genius in a culture where such genius must be marketed by publishers like Dreck (whose name derives from the Yiddish word for crap): Vance's novel "*Instead* was only forty-five thousand words long, and Mr. Dreck [the publisher] told Vance he didn't know a meaner length. He'd rather have an elephant to handle like *Ulysses* or *American Tragedy,* than a mouthful like that. When readers have paid their money they like to sit down to a square meal. An oyster cocktail won't satisfy 'em. They want their money's worth; and that's at least a hundred thousand [words]" (379). Wharton bristled at such measures, even as she was forced to consider them for her own work given her declining investments and uncertain finances.

Human nature may not have changed, for Wharton, in or around December 1920 (as it had for Virginia Woolf in 1910), but culture did. Novelists from Fitzgerald to Atherton, from Hemingway to Loos, all showed that the "Reign of Youth" (as Atherton termed it in *Black Oxen*) had taken hold over mass culture. While many theorists write about the feminization of mass culture or of mass culture as other, for Wharton the rise in mass culture was generational. Thus, even more crucial to Wharton's sensibility was the transition from her intense focus on kinship taboos (such as in *The Age of Innocence* in 1920) to her realization—later in the decade—that a new authority was no longer to be found in the family but in youth. Mass culture may have been something Wharton feared, not so much because of its class and gender affiliations, but because it signalled the end of her generation and the rise of another literary era. After World War I, she may have been able to pretend, feted as she was, that her generation still held sway, but by the end of the decade the illusion would no longer obtain.

By all accounts, modern consumerism gained its ascendancy in the twenties. Writers no less distinguished than Wharton had to figure out a new way of maintaining their "authenticity" while dealing with consumer culture and being mass-marketed in huge department stores like the one Wharton depicts in *Hudson River Bracketed.* Wharton's account of the Department Store corresponds to what William Leach describes, in *Land of Desire,* as the New Thought pragmatism. This was "the American conviction that people could shape their own destinies and find total happiness. . . . Mind curers looked outward, opening 'the self' completely to what they perceived to be the 'full abundance of the universe'" (227). These new abundance theories, as we have seen in *The Mother's Recompense,* supported the values of the new business culture, a realm of attainable—and standardized—desires. Wharton had already criticized this standardization in earlier novels, but her target in this novel was surer. As Leach suggests, the new advertising sought "to put people in touch with commercial institutions that, in turn, would convert them all into standardized consumers with low intensities of desires" (240). These desires were soon to be translated into the cruder terms of mass consumption and mass leisure (see Leach 372), so that self-expression (like sex-expression) would be part and parcel of this abundance theory. As we have seen, if Wharton hated most forms of mass culture—flapperhood, flicks, drugs, commodification—she also found ways of incorporating the cultural rhetoric of commodities in her fiction. She had to: her competition was legion in the pseudo-gratifications of evangelism, Mary Baker Eddy's "inner light," and more popular authors, like Atherton and Loos, who could—and did—make Wharton's "inner life" fiction look obsolete. Wharton may have celebrated Anita Loos, but she also feared her popularity. Citing *Blondes* as "the great American novel," Wharton also wants "to know if there are—or will be—others and if you know the young woman [Anita Loos], who must be a genius" (cited in Carey 108). Wharton had written this on a postcard to Frank Crowninshield, who forwarded the note to Loos with the following: "[Wharton] is getting very fussy and peculiar as she grows older, but still has a streak of humanity, kindness, humor, and love left in her" (Carey 108; R. W. B. Lewis 1975, 468).

Hudson River Bracketed challenges such ever-ascending middle-class aspirations, like discovering one's genius and banking on self-improvement, rooted as they were in the culture of advertising and mass production. Vance's father names his son after a real estate development, "Advance" (also the name of an actual Indiana town involved in Klan activities), a gesture precisely representing the Midwest provincialism that Vance rejects.[6] Here Wharton herself gets a bad rap from literary historian Frederick Hoffman, professor at the Universities of Wisconsin and Chicago, who finds her distaste for Midwestern life inexcusable: "It is not only that she considered the Midwest tedious, unmannerly, vulgar; she did not know it at all and created a fantasy of 'what it seemed,' which was more improbable than any parody of an imitation of a Sinclair Lewis novel. . . . The forces that, in her opinion, were destroying the society she respected seemed always to have come nakedly from the Midwest, where apparently all commercial drives, all cultural stupidity, existed in a pure, abstract form, waiting merely the impetus to move them eastward"

(332). This overstatement is useful, but inaccurate given the circumstance that Wharton's criticisms of American culture are actually more national than regional ones. After all, Vance's middle-class Midwesternism is set against his adventures in New York, and Wharton is just as critical of the pretensions prevailing there. Vance's arid marriage to the young beauty, Laura Lou, is juxtaposed against the arid intellectualism in the marriage between New Yorkers Lewis and Halo Tarrant. While Halo is searching for authentic experience and authentic literary talent, her husband is trying to balance his own economic and intellectual interests. Vance sometimes distinguishes the two, sometimes conflates them: "These easy affable people could talk—did talk—about everything! Everything, that is, but the exclusively local matters which had formed the staple of the only conversation Vance had ever heard. What they talked of was simply *all the rest*; and he could see that they did it without the least intention of showing-off, the least consciousness that their scope was wider than other people's—did it naturally, carelessly, just as his mother talked about electric cookers, his father about local real estate, Mrs. Tracy about Laura Lou's school pictures and Upton's job at the nursery" (118). Wharton's novels show the extremes of culture—the Midwestern philistinism versus New York dilettantism—and show each to be as bad as the other.

Hudson River Bracketed begins by mocking the idealism of individualism at the same time that it denounces promiscuous reformism (6). Consider how Wharton describes Vance Weston's invention of a new religion to counteract the "religion of business" in the twenties (42). Weston's philosophy, based on the vaguest Emersonian transcendentalism, searches for god within the self. Even his grandmother warns him. Be careful, she says, "how you're mystical. . . . time and again I've known that to end in a baby" (8). And it does. Weston's vision also shores up the cult of sacralized individualism Wharton finds so disturbing in the twenties. Like Sinclair Lewis, she saw individualism as being at odds with reformism, given that American reformism saw the individual funneled into mass movements and what Lewis called, in a 20 June 1931 letter to Wharton, "undigested chunks of theorizing" (Lilly Library). However, American reformism seemed to be undertaken in the name of individualism, where an illusion of choice and democracy substituted for the real thing. Somewhere in between Emersonian individualism and rampant reform lies Wharton's vision of community, and that community seems ever more possible to create. Although she often points to Vance's father's business practices (27), the exposure of corruption is at the periphery of her fiction, never at its center, since she sees individual betrayal as far more appropriate than political corruption as the subject of fiction.

She still means to distinguish herself from muckraking, even though she may personally feel that "the U.S. gov't is a stupid task-master, which is worse than (& results in) being a hard one" (to Elisina Tyler, 12 March 1928), but she rarely lets such explicitly political remarks enter her fiction.

While this particular social critique is marginal, her portrait of the artistic genius here and in *The Gods Arrive* is meant to expose the political—and personal—limits of genius. The emphasis in the 1920s on "self-expression" combined genius and individualism, which the citizen was enjoined to support for the good of the nation, but in making genius democratic through popular calls for self-expression, Wharton saw it as becoming still another buyable commodity. She worries over this to the degree that she must enter this market and write another kind of fiction— more popular, less contentious or argumentative, as Ammons rightly suggests—though she distrusts *in toto* the market economy of publishing. In this way, the truly modern aspect of American literary modernism, for Wharton, is that it was yet another occasion for deploying advertising strategies and marketplace techniques.

Her novel is not only a critique of the American soil of genius, but also its marketing of what she had called in *Twilight Sleep* the new "League For Discovering Genius" (226). Halo Spear (later Tarrant) first instructs Vance in Coleridge and in culture; his culture has come only in the "mutilated"— academic—form of college textbooks (64). For Vance, "unusable reality" such as class distinctions (92) are the material facts of everyday life; he rejects the prosaic world of experience and lives in his invented world of poetry. He sees Halo Spear as pure intellect, remarking on her "exquisite participation" in his genius when he reads her his manuscript, "Instead," a short book different from the "incoherence and brutality" brought out by Vance's publishers (377). Laura Lou's death results in some part, however, from a failure of Vance's attention to material existence. Had he not had his own literary work, Vance "would have borrowed a revolver and made an end. . . . All the wild currents and whirlpools of critical opinion in New York had shaken his faith in himself; not in his powers of exposition and expression, . . . but in his choice of a theme, a point of view, what the politicians called a 'platform.' It had never before occurred to him that the artist needed any" (374). The novel observes Vance's platform as writer, from his Midwest beginnings in Advance to his metropolitan career with the *New Hour* in a career that preserves his "genius" at the cost of his wife, a turn of events even grossly ironic.

As always, the intersection between economics and the psychological dynamics of marriage disturbed Wharton, a tension leading her to endorse the notion of trial and companionate marriages: "Most husbands seemed to their wives like harmless lunatics (when it wasn't the other way around, or perhaps reciprocal)" (330). Later, she describes Halo's marriage to Tarrant as "a mist of illusion" or a "chained" existence (337). Tarrant pays off Halo's family's debts; Halo's "links" of the chain are her repayment: "He wanted her; she suited him; he had bought her" (337). Wharton leans toward this progressive idea—trial marriage—since it is based on what she describes as "fervid intellectual communion" (342). Vance can't relinquish Laura Lou or the "primitive [domestic] craving" she represents for him (411). Not surprisingly, marriage metaphors come from the vocabulary of the prison: "gaoler" (414); "handcuffed and chained" (423). Within a year, Vance is distressed by this "enforced" yoking: "What sense was there in living in one room with an idle child-less woman whom he had long since forgotten though she was always there?" (411).

As it had for Kate Clephane in *The Mother's Recompense* and for Pauline Manford in *Twilight Sleep,* Vance's sexual and intellectual confusion marks this novel's psychological and economic dilemma. In one crucial scene where Vance confesses his passion for Halo just as Halo cautions patience, Wharton includes Vance's thoughts in parenthetical asides: "(You had to be everlastingly promising things to women . . . even with your life blood running out of you, they'd make you promise. . . .)" (424). While Vance seems to distinguish Halo from other women, he collapses that distinction, focusing instead on his anguish. Vance's desire for intellectual companionship may be central to *Hudson River Bracketed,* but *The Gods Arrive* studies the failure of Vance and Halo's trial marriage. This trial ends in Halo's pregnancy and in the return to a conventional relationship, a source of ambivalence for Wharton since it means Halo is reduced simply to taking care of her husband-to-be Vance.

To critique this celebration of inner genius, the novel is set against a background of self-help books, what were then popular as "conduct of life" manuals. Gospels of self-expression and advertising such as Bruce Barton's *More Power to You* (1917), C. Espey's *Popular You,* and Orrison Swett Marden's series on love valued being good to oneself, achievement, and "making life a masterpiece," all aims that conflicted with Wharton's more stoical, less aggrandizing claims for the "inner life." She denounces Halo's parents as "tired reformers" (179) and Vance's Grandmother as an "inspirational faddist" (187). Yet Wharton could no longer ignore that readers bought these books by the millions. When Vance's old friend Bunty Hayes, now a department store mogul, gives him an advance to work in the publicity department of his "Storecraft," Wharton mocks the prevailing attitude about art: "Fellows who knew how to sling words were what they were after, Hayes continued; many of the literary people didn't seem to realize yet that writing a good advertisement was just as much of an art as turning out *Paradise Lost* or *Gentlemen Prefer Blondes*" (510). By collapsing literature with mass market fiction, and advertising and artistic expression, Bunty Hayes sums up the ethos of the twenties: all expression—artistic, sexual, and commercial—has been levelled out by the rising middle class, their tastes and their ambitions. Accounting for this new audience, Wharton was not shy about her own advertising, but she reveals here the way the new commercialism deprecates her craft, since her artist-hero must "sling words" himself in this market.

Wharton, the New Evangelism, and Advertising Culture

Mr. Sunday knoweth well,
　　Where dwelleth hopes and fear.
He knoweth where to bat for smiles,
　　And where to punch for tears.
He knoweth WHO is WHO and where,
　　The crowds he swayeth well,
But he's really at his best,
　　When he gives the Germans hell.
　　　　—Emma T. Martin (in Bauman, 385)

In Chapter Two, we saw how the threat of bolshevism affected the politics of writers like Loos, Atherton, and Wharton. The force of the red scare was linked to the psychological fear of failure, a "psychic projection" according to Hoffman's cultural history of the twenties (311). Reputations for being self-made men and incentives for self-promotion were meant to keep the reds at bay, but these very "solutions" to the bolshevik threat made writers like Wharton skeptical. Rather than develop hyperconscious advertising techniques to counter the radical effects of bolshevization and the red scare, Wharton invested in other alternatives to Atherton's social comedy and Loos's satire: Wharton wrote serious social critique. As she had predicted in 1919, "get-rich-quick" schemes would promote mass culture and "get-educated-quick" schemes, both of which would leave Americans in worse straits. Intellectual decline and regression, she found, were far worse threats than the bolsheviks.[7]

By her own account, Wharton transforms these cultural issues into the "crude," dramatic terms of "modern America" with which her hero must contend.[8] It was a telling coincidence, then, when Sunday, Andrew Carnegie, and Judge Ben Lindsey (who wrote the book *Companionate Marriage* with Wainwright Evans) were tied in the 1914 *American Magazine* poll nominating the "greatest man in the United States" (McLoughlin 49). As crucial background figures, both Sunday and Lindsey exhibit traces of Wharton's beginning this novel before World War I. Then it would have been up to the minute, for Sunday represented for her the forces of a levelling reformism, while Lindsey's battles with the Ku Klux Klan and his advocacy for birth control (in the Family Court of Denver over which he presided) suggested America's needs for an expansive grasp of private morality and individual judgment.

Lindsey's reformism relied on tolerance; Sunday's evangelism, on intolerance. These two famous figures embody these extremes, and the impact of their work will shape my reading of the novels. The two were both self-made men, but of different stripes entirely. One was conservative, the other liberal; both had major influence as representative men in the twenties. The preacher Sunday denounced bolshevism: "No damnable anarchistic bunch like that would ever march down the streets of my town shouting the praises of Russia and spewing out their propaganda. So help me God, I would line them up before a firing squad and ship all that were left over out of the country" (qtd. in Calkins 297). The judge, on the other hand, was linked to bolshevism. H. L. Mencken, however, refuted this charge: "Dr. Lindsey does not advocate abortion, and neither does anyone else save a few frantic Bolsheviki" in a 1928 issue of *American Mercury* (126). Billy Sunday represents, as much as anyone could, the Midwest influence that Wharton is accused of decrying in *Hudson River Bracketed*. Lindsey's arguments for "companionate marriage" perhaps best represent the influence of the modern city and erotic companionship in *The Gods Arrive*.

Billy Sunday's preaching to a gullible America provoked Wharton's resentment. While Sinclair Lewis's satire of Sunday in *Babbitt* as "Mike Monday . . . , the distinguished evangelist, the best-known Protestant pontiff in America" (83) is vitriolic, Wharton's attack is more subtle, but just as caustic. She enclosed a copy of an article on Billy Sunday, from the 22 January 1934 *New York Herald,* in one of her letters to Royall Tyler. The article probably jogged her memory of Sunday's proselytizing for US entrance into WWI: he had argued early for America's "Preparations" and a call to arms (Furnas 107–8). Yet Wharton may have feared that in America all things were becoming too equal. When President Wilson appointed George Creel to manage the internal propaganda and public relations for the war, Creel turned to a wide variety of sources for his PR. As Furnas observes, "The cultural range of Creel's efforts ran from Edith Wharton's ladylike but cogent magazine pieces about visiting the Western Front to the slaverings of Billy Sunday briefing Divinity on behalf of the U.S. House of Representatives" (232).

While before the war "advance men"—minions who whipped up excitement—were only associated with evangelism, Wharton sees how such "crude terms" of appropriation apply to *Hudson River Bracketed*. Whether or not Wharton appreciated Sunday's technique, she seems to have studied it, adapting Sunday's strategies to those of her businessman Bunty Hayes. Sunday's anti-immigrationist, Klannish sentiments piqued both her interest and her anger, and while Wharton may not discuss evangelism per se, she locates the roots of modern business culture in this mass-movement of Christianity, transformed as it was by the shock therapy that evangelism provided. Wharton characterizes this example of twenties success in Bunty Hayes, her foil for Vance Weston. No one understood better than Sunday—and eventually Wharton came to terms with it, too—the need for big-scale self-advertising. Sunday's reliance on advance men to drum up business for his "hitting the trail" religious campaigns were accompanied by the quick erection of huge tabernacle buildings to serve during the eight-week (average) stays in cities targeted for Sunday's revivals.[9]

Sunday's first job as an advance man for a Midwest evangelist, J. Wilbur Chapman, was to prepare for the urban evangelist by going to communities "in advance" to rent halls and advertise, to orchestrate the business of urban revivalism (Furnas 108). Sunday's sensationalism dovetailed nicely with the conversion of American religions into prosperous financial affairs: "Outlandish stunts were sometimes employed during Sunday's early years of prominence. . . . In Fairfield, Iowa, for example, in 1907, Sunday found his tabernacle about half empty. He promptly exploited his reputation as a star baseball player by organizing the town's shopkeepers into two baseball teams. . . . The revivalist put on his old uniform and played for both teams" (Weeks 31). So canny was his knack, McLoughlin notes, that by 1918, Sunday amassed millions in his soul-saving business.

The different senses of the term "advance" (as prepayment, progress, advertising—all embodied in the artist-hero Vance) suggest just how much—consciously or not—Wharton derived from the rise of public relations, New Thought philosophies, and advertising in the twenties. So close was this identification that Wharton first associates Bunty with baseball (Billy Sunday first played with the Chicago White Stockings), then with alcohol and women—all of which were part of Sunday's past, as noted in Ellis, Dorsett, and McLoughlin. When Bunty Hayes reappears in the novel after his first drunken round at the baseball game where he had first met Vance, he is a barker for a sightseeing tour in a rubberneck car. Bunty then becomes a professional buyer and ad man. Later, he capitalizes on the showman's instinct in his business, as Billy Sunday had in evangelism, by creating "Storecraft" (reminiscent of Klankraft, as the Ku Klux Klan used to be called), an example of Bunty's religion of business—and for Vance (another Advance man) an example of the "moral apathy" of the country (410). "Storecraft" is Bunty's Department Store, whose motto is "Supplies Taste and Saves Money," and sells everything from household goods to "Tomorrowist" art (404). Bunty Hayes does not work for religious evangelism, but for his own economic advancement; the "advance" men before the war—like Billy Sunday—are transposed (to revise Wharton's 1 January 1930 letter [Lewis and Lewis 525]) into the crude modernized ad men of the late twenties. In the midst of a sightseeing speech which Bunty Hayes gives while Vance and Laura Lou (who will become the artist's bride even though she is engaged at the moment to Hayes) are reacquainted after a three-year separation, Hayes claims that an old family mansion will be turned into "a twenty-five-million-dollar skyscraper of fifty stories, with roof gymnasium, cabaret terrace, New Thought church and airplane landing . . ." (196). As Wharton has it, New Thought accompanies the advance of New Money, a new degraded system of ethics and intimacy. Bunty Hayes is an evangelist of commodities, employing what he knows about spectacle and audience to make a success of his department store-cum-New Thought temple called "Storecraft."

Even Grandma Scrimser is not safe from Bunty's evangelism, since he markets her brand of spiritualism in "The Seekers" (440). One of the first of Bunty's pamphlets for Storecraft advertises Grandma's religion. Although Vance is disgusted, he overcomes it because he needs Bunty's money: "He had spent an hour with 'Storecraft's' publicity agent, and besides the money his pockets were bulging with models of advertisements—'blurbs' and puffs of every conceivable sort, from an advertisement of silk stockings or face cream, or 'Storecraft's' insurance policies, to circulars and prospectuses featuring the lecture tours managed by 'Storecraft's' Arts and Letters Department. In the bunch, as Vance glanced over them, he found his grandmother's advance circular . . ." (510). Vance is reduced to the humiliation of asking Bunty for a job in Storecraft's advertising department, a gesture that registers the decline of his moral as well as aesthetic values. Even the crude religious terms of

Billy Sunday's work seem preferable to the commodification of art, fiction, and culture in Bunty Hayes's monolithic "Storecraft"—an emporium where one could even buy a bust of the author Vance Weston. Bunty Hayes's "Storecraft" is the site of the "Tomorrowists" show, surely Wharton's allusion to the "Futurists" of the fascist Italy she hated and whose propaganda she could spot in American culture.

The effect Vance strives for in his book is the same "emotional surrender" that Grandma Scrimser elicits from her audience (439). While Wharton is at pains to show how much she distrusted the commodification of art, and distances her artist-hero from the spiritual faddists of New Thought and evangelists like Ella Wheeler Wilcox—author of *Poems of Power* and precursor to the Mother of New Thought, Elizabeth Towne (see *Twilight Sleep,* 140)—Vance's is a case in point about how difficult it is to remove art from the public, commercial sphere. His most recent attempt to write a novel is on the subject of spiritual starvation, a topic he sees as an antidote (much as Wharton saw her novels) to the "intellectual laziness" of his Grandmother's spiritual healing (488, 496). His book, to be called *Magic,* would banish the indignities against aesthetics that such men as Bunty Hayes brought about in their desire only and always to expand the marketplace. In order to market fiction in this day and age, Vance complains, one had to be "a combination of Sinclair Lewis, Kathleen Norris, and Mrs. Eddy" (512).

Why does Wharton class Mary Baker Eddy with Kathleen Norris and Sinclair Lewis? They all catered to popular taste, and they all knew how, regardless of the form, to advertise their work to make a profit.[10] For Wharton, "Mrs. Eddy" and her cult of Christian Scientists solved the ideological purposes of bringing public relations and evangelism together. New Thought (most popular after World War I) and Christian Science depended on the tricks of advertising and mail-order to sell salvation (see William Leach 314). No wonder, then, that Wharton's nagging concerns in *The Mother's Recompense* and *Twilight Sleep* were constellated in making sense of advances, advance men, and the advertising of such diverse products as evangelical Christianity, art, and politics.

Yet Wharton's distrust of business mentality is neither unremitting nor unsympathetic. What redeems Bunty is his loyalty and affection, particularly when Bunty appears at Laura Lou's deathbed. Bunty had loved Laura Lou, and his presence at her death suggests how he doubles for Vance. His candid desire for success, moreover, is at least preferable to Vance's self-deception. Vance is numb and cannot take care of himself or Laura Lou. Bunty steps in and oversees the fire, the nursing, and the doctors, and Bunty is the one most affected by her death. Without excusing the artist, Wharton speculates on Vance's inability to deal with the real world and with real people: "He wondered if at crucial moments the same veil of unreality would always fall between himself and the soul nearest him, if the creator of imaginary beings must always feel alone among the real ones" (536). This last sentence of the novel is an indictment of the cult of genius which Vance had entered: he wraps that veil of unreality around him in order to keep himself unsullied by the world of work and everyday desire. Wharton has no sympathy with Vance's isolation or alienation; at this moment her sympathy is all with Bunty, who is more comprehending than Vance: "Hayes put out one of his short thick hands and [drew] down the lids over Laura Lou's eyes. Then [Vance] saw him walk out of the room, very stiffly, with short uneven steps" (524). Like John Marcher witnessing a solitary mourner's intense grief at the grave next to May Bartram's in Henry James's "Beast in the Jungle," Vance Weston sees what real grief might have been. In living as an uncompromising artist, he misses what he might have had.

Art as intensified genius: the new religion Vance invented is really not new at all and serves later to buttress his erotic domination of Halo. Vance believes in the myth of genius, the romantic illusion of the artist's essential loneliness. In condescending to Halo and treating her as the child-wife he once saw in Laura Lou, Vance reestablishes the very terms his new companionate marriage was supposed to undo. In fact, companionate marriage had already piqued Wharton's interest. As early as *The Age of Innocence,* Wharton had been planning a project concerning companionate marriage. As Alan Price explains, one of Wharton's three original plans for the earlier novel was to have Newland and Ellen engage in a trial marriage (see Price 24). She abandons that plan but recovers it for *Glimpses of the Moon* and, twelve years later, for *The Gods Arrive.* That novel begins with Vance Weston and the undivorced Halo Tarrant's cruise to Europe, where they will begin their companionate living. Wharton glosses over their pasts, including the news of Vance's father's financial recovery and a real-estate boom in Crampton, one of Wharton's broadly ironic Midwest geographical creations. With his father's financial rise, Vance can afford to travel in the literary circles of Europe— bohemian, gipsylike—without the financial worries that plagued him in the first novel. Grandma Scrimser has given up evangelizing Fifth Avenue, and the family now awaits Vance's best-seller—which will be published as the critically acclaimed but idiosyncratic "The Puritan in Spain." Wharton is out to show how the mystification of genius leads to ignorance of the material world, and that this material knowledge is something from which the novelist could no longer afford to shrink.

The Debate over Companionate Marriage

Rubber has revolutionized morals.

—Judge Lindsey, in *Companionate Marriage*

Advertising in the 1920s made it incumbent on the woman of the house both to uphold her traditional moral influence and to demonstrate the new companionate comradeship Wharton outlined so clearly in *Hudson River Bracketed*. With this directive in mind, Wharton shifts the second novel's interest from Vance, the artist-hero, to Halo, the erotic companion. Described as a "problem" novel in 1932, *The Gods Arrive* tackles the "marriage question." Despite Vance's failure to sustain the experiment, trial marriage intrigues Wharton for many reasons, not the least of which was its seeming opposition to the middle-class norms she had scrutinized in *Hudson River Bracketed*. The novel shows how attempts at both social control of the masses—through marriage and divorce laws—and resistance in bohemian living are frustrated by the workings of personal, mostly sexual desire. As Wharton well knew, such passions could not easily be engineered.

Like Billy Sunday's evangelism in the teens and twenties, Judge Ben Lindsey's arguments for companionate marriage dominated the cultural debate of the late twenties. If one attack on Lindsey called him a bolshevik, others sidestepped that issue to link him with the "social philosophy of Karl Marx" and "modern neopagan culture" (*The Commonweal*, 25 March 1931). The *Catholic World* enlisted popular authors like Kathleen Norris to denounce sex reform and call for "good mothers" and the repression of sex "appetites" (June 1928, 258–59). Journals like *The Forum* published confessions—"We Try Trial Marriage"—denouncing their failure (84 [November 1930]: 272–76). In 1928, Bertrand Russell defended Lindsey's proposals as "conservative, not subversive" (*The Forum* 84: 7). In addition, a certain Dr. Herman Rubin argued in his *Eugenics and Sex Harmony* (1943) that "sooner or later, as Judge Ben Lindsay [*sic*] has suggested, consideration of [sexual promiscuity and the rise in divorce] is certain to modify our present accepted ethical and moral standards. We are in an age of transition. Old values are being revaluated. We are openly discussing questions of paramount scientific import, which, but a few years ago, were taboo" (144). Almost all of her critics say that Wharton failed in these novels insofar as she abandoned the social and aesthetic goals of her earlier, successful novels. However, her success in the late fictions is the untangling of the various controversies having to do with the regulation of private life that the Vance Weston novels particularize.

The plot of *The Gods Arrive* mirrored the great issue of the day—trial marriage, what Billy Sunday likened to "barnyard marriage." Sunday's rival as a moral arbiter of American culture, Judge Lindsey, argued against marriage as a lifelong prison sentence (Furnas 403). Drawing on the work of such sex reformers as Bertrand Russell, Bronislaw Malinowski, and Havelock Ellis, Lindsey proselytized for marriage with legalized birth control in order to allow couples the financial and emotional freedom in their first years together and, if failing, mutually agreed-upon divorce (Lindsey 279). His 1927 *Companionate Marriage* suggests that marriage should go hand-in-hand with the scientific birth control information that the Comstock Law had made illegal. Lindsey's campaign sought to legitimize Sanger's birth-control program and to advance eugenics (232, 237). A "companionate marriage," unlike a "family marriage," was childless by choice, through "bootleg birth control" or abortion, the latter a practice fairly widespread and even condoned, Lindsey contends, by the Klan (229–30). This bootleg birth control preserves the Klan's fundamentalist intentions to keep "America . . . for White, Nordic, Blond, Protestant, One Hundred Per Centers" (229). Most important for the terms of my argument, Lindsey had read Wharton's *Age of Innocence* and envisions the present age as sexually experienced, but without effective birth control. He can see only a "blend of tragedy and comedy" in the present age of sexual folly. "What an indictment of that dead and gone social period which Mrs. Wharton has felicitously called 'The Age of Innocence,' and whose walking ghost still haunts us here even amid the clangs and alarums of Science" (7). According to Lindsey, *Gentlemen Prefer Blondes* does another form of cultural work in convincing one young would-be flapper to "gild" her hair (167).

Lindsey's 1931 essay entitled "The Promise and Peril of the New Freedom" urges Americans to accept a realistic attitude toward sex and sex relations, thereby making "American tragedies" like Dreiser's obsolete (cited in Schmalhausen 447). He argues for birth control and sex education, citing his interviews with college students as evidence of the widespread trend toward premarital sex. As he writes, "Reproduction of the species, once [sex's] sole function, is now generally recognised as a secondary purpose. Unquestionably the chief value of erotic passion under present forms of civilisation is the contribution that its satisfaction makes to health and emotional stability with a resulting stimulus to the higher creative faculty" (454). Lindsey contends that economic conditions and progress from "a rural frontier America" to modern culture must include an alternative to the "old morality and the old family" (453). Thus, he describes the "revolt of women against the brutalities of ceaseless breeding," a revolt in support of racial progress and happiness (453). His claim that erotic passion plays a far greater role in civilized life reinforces what Wharton would have read in Malinowski or in Havelock Ellis, one of the "breathless" reads of the day, as Wharton says in *The Gods Arrive* (46).

The idea of companionate marriage contests the patriarchal directive to conquer business, audiences, and women. The "experimental male," as Lindsey calls him, looks for a mate, and this mate must have access to birth control and, failing that, abortion, which he predicts to be no less than a million and as high as three million throughout the country (in Schmalhausen 455–56, 465–66). Only through equality between men and women would the "new morality" take hold, but Lindsey knows that the woman who experiments "in any but the most superficial way . . . must . . . pay the penalty" (459). Two kinds of marriages, companionate and procreative—the former for sexual relations and the latter for family ones—would eliminate the "obscene divorce system" by which Halo suffers under Tarrant's refusal and her own reluctance to go to Reno. Without perjury or collusion, no divorce was possible, even by mutual consent. In Lindsey's words: "The real American Tragedy is that the great majority of our girls and young women are being denied these desires and wishes closest to their hearts by a reactionary ecclesiasticism and legalism and their superstition, greed, and ignorance" (465). Dreiser's novel of a young woman murdered as a result of a pregnancy becomes a caution against the too rigid control of youthful sexuality.

The nature of the opposition Lindsey met is important, since he was not only removed from his judgeship in Denver and threatened by the KKK, but was also attacked by scores of critics, including H. L. Mencken. Mencken did not agree that altering marriage laws would reduce human unhappiness at all, believing as he did that the estate of human beings is to be unhappy. Yet he challenges American hypocrisy, greeting Lindsey's ideas in his 1928 *American Mercury* review of *Companionate Marriage*:

> The ideas in this tract, when Judge Lindsey first expressed them on the stump, instantly aroused the indignation of the rev. clergy, and in consequence they have been so furiously denounced and so gaudily distorted that the reader who examines them will probably be greatly astonished by their moderation. For what the learned jurist advocates is really nothing to bulge the eye, even of Mr. Babbitt. . . . He does

not, in fact, advocate the sad slavery known as free love, nor does he even advocate trial marriage. (126)

Lindsey's position rests on how unaffordable children are when two people start out. Also, like Wharton, he resists the legislation of private choice:

> Happily for the American people, and for the future of Marriage and Divorce in this country, Congress has so far stubbornly resisted all efforts to persuade it to pass a federal law for the regulation of Marriage and Divorce.
>
> I say "happily" because I am one of those who profoundly distrust the intent and purpose that have inspired the proposed legislation. I think the underlying intent of it is restrictive and meddlesome; that it is plausible but unsound; and that its real, unacknowledged purpose is to thwart certain vast social changes which are now in the making and which should have the right of way. (1927, 370)

As with eugenics, so with marriage and divorce. Wharton, like Lindsey, everywhere suggests the unpredictability of human motives and the impossibility of legislating morality. Wharton's novel is pitted against those reactionary forces in society, especially as they inhibit women's sexual choices and desires, though it stops short of endorsing Lindsey's desire for "an increased birth rate among our cultured classes" (465).[11] Her ambivalence is less about experimentation, with which she herself was familiar, and more about the rationalization of eugenic control over sexuality, a control she feared would validate fascism.

Five years before Judge Lindsey wrote *Companionate Marriage*, Wharton suggested its benefits and limits in *Glimpses of the Moon* (1922). *Glimpses* predicts what Judge Lindsey sees as the virtues of companionate marriage: testing out conjugal relations without children before the commitment to procreate, which Wharton satirized as early as *Custom of the Country* (1913). In this novel, Susy Branch and Nick Lansing agree to marry provisionally, until something better might interest either of them, such as richer spouses or more fruitful connections. As companions, they form a "partnership for . . . mutual advantage" (49), and their partnership allows them the benefit of wedding gifts and checks—however long they may last. When their moral dilemmas over their support by rich friends come between them, Susy and Nick part, but they are brought together again by their mutual desire and by Susy's transformation as "temporary mother" in charge of the Fulmer children (296). Wharton's novel ends nostalgically, ambivalently, parodying the couple's inability to reconcile their "moral contempt" (166) for the world they had grown up in and their attachments to "money, luxury, fashion, pleasure" (134), to which both are held hostage. The conflict over such renunciation marks Wharton's twenties fiction, especially *The Mother's Recompense,* a tendency, I will argue, she will only put to rest after the Vance Weston novels.

Like Lindsey, Wharton indicts the hypocrisy of American divorce proceedings. Rather than divorce by mutual consent, Nick must first pretend to go off with another woman, a trick that winds up causing Susy pain and embarrassment before they eventually reconcile. By the end, *Glimpses of the Moon* celebrates domesticity and maternity at the same time that it confirms the argument for companionate marriage, a childless marriage where birth control has allowed the couple to come to a temperamental and economic negotiation of their independent needs. Sentimental and melodramatic as the ending of *Glimpses of the Moon* is, its gentle mockery of Nick and Susy's reunion anticipates Wharton's concerns about the legislation of divorce and marriage laws in the twenties, what she saw as the increasing regulation of the individual by the state. In short, the companionate marriage issue generated two separate obsessions for Wharton: marriage as an outdated institution and the revision of marriage as business partnership.

The debate about companionate marriage was inextricable from the welter of other current issues Wharton also addresses: abortion, reproductive rights, sex reform, and twilight sleep. In *Hudson River Bracketed,* Vance and Laura Lou's marriage embodies the kind of relationship that might go wrong, since it lacks any lasting passion. Vance struggles with the difference between his affection for Laura Lou, a compassionate affiliation, and his passion for Halo: "For Laura Lou seemed to belong equally to his body and soul—it was only his intelligence that she left unsatisfied. Into the world of his mind, with its consuming curiosities, its fervid joys, she would never enter—would never even discover that it existed. . . . He had never known that kind of companionship, had just guessed at it through the groping wonder of his first talks with Halo Spear, when every word she spoke was a clue to new discoveries" (322). In *The Gods Arrive,* Vance and Halo's trial marriage fails, until Halo gets pregnant. Halo's pregnancy virtually seals their relation, creating what Lindsey would call a "family marriage." Quite conventionally, the novel tests Vance's commitment to the Mother (Halo) and his erotic muse (Floss Delaney) by having Vance choose between them, since the two roles—mother and erotic companion—could not yet be merged and still sustain the twentieth-century economy of heterosexual relations.

The Gods Arrive and Trial Marriage

Give All to Love

. . . Though thou loved her as thyself,
  As a self of purer clay,
  Though her parting dims the day,
  Stealing grace from all alive;
  Heartily know,
  When half-gods go,
The gods arrive.

—R. W. Emerson

The Gods Arrive takes up where *Hudson River Bracketed* leaves off: with Halo and Vance in a trial marriage, the kind denounced in the above-mentioned editorial, "We Try Trial Marriage." "We had learned," Helen Conway concludes, "that the way to liberty is not always by non-conformity to the accepted order. . . . I do not think individual happiness can be achieved by an arrangement which attempts to defy the existing order with impunity. It now seems to me that there would be so much more freedom in marriage" (276). Despite such counterarguments, Wharton's novel gives trial marriage a try, yet that effort is more Halo's story than Vance's, concerning as it does Halo's search for happiness: "What happiness could equal that of a woman permitted to serve the genius while she adored the man" (GA 29). Halo Tarrant runs away from her self-centered husband in order to join her lover and "comrade": in doing so, "she found herself a new woman in a new world . . ." (10). Book One begins with Halo Tarrant's and Vance Weston's "experiment," while the two of them run away from family to a bohemian life in Spain, where Halo is "cut" by a Marquesa who refuses to acknowledge Halo's relation to Vance. Lewis Tarrant's refusal to grant Halo a divorce complicates her social position. When Vance finishes his new book, they decide to travel to France, where Halo is cut again by a New York society matron, Mrs. Glaisher.

While Halo experiences anxiety about her marital status, Vance undergoes similar crises about aesthetics. He deplores the vacuity of Fifth Avenue patrons like Mrs. Glaisher and detests even more her hypocrisy, such as her queries about the "naughty things" in his second novel, "The Puritan in Spain" (130). Book Three sees Vance and Halo settled in Oubli-sur-Mer; at Nice, Vance meets his old flame, Floss Delaney (with "her small imperial head, the low brow, the heavily-modelled lids and mouth") whose father had made big money in a real estate deal in Euphoria (217). Floss's "low brow" provides a sharp contrast to Halo's highbrow culture, and Vance finds himself caught between his attraction to Halo's intellect and the allure of "going native" with Floss. As her father describes her to Vance, "There's nothing on God's earth as undemocratic as a good-looking American girl" (228). Again, Halo is cut by one of the local families when they discover she is not married to Weston; in fact, they blame her, ridiculously, for their son's suicide. Under these pressures—Halo's increasing alienation and Vance's restless passion for Floss Delaney—she and Vance split in the penultimate book; Book V brings them back together only after Vance realizes that his last novel, "Colossus," is a failure—too trendy to be of any critical value—and that he needs Halo's steady, nurturing influence.

As members of what E. A. Ross would call the "elite," Vance and Halo represent the struggle to harness their passions for the good of the race. Halo dismisses the moral arguments about marriage by thinking that "in such a heaven as ours there's no marrying or giving in marriage" (33). Yet early on in their experiment, Halo realizes that she's to be the "peg to hang a book on" (36), an expediency of no lasting value to Vance. Forgetting Halo's earlier relation as his muse, Vance is easily seduced by the intellectual glibness of his new friend Alders, the "scholar gypsy" (45), a new bohemian with old social values: he won't take Halo to meet his salon hostess, the Marquesa, since Vance and Halo aren't married. Vance responds to Halo's objection by warning her not to "fetishize" marriage (54). Her initial desire to give Vance "intellectual companionship and spiritual sympathy" pales next to the slight she is given (57). However, Halo's struggle is between conventional morality and trial marriage, intellectual commitment and sexual inequality: "Free love, [she] found, was not the simple experiment she had imagined" (82).

Although Halo's mother considered herself a New York bohemian, she bristles at Halo's decision to leave her husband for Vance:

> Mrs. Spear had specialized in receiving "odd" people at a time when New York was still shy of them. She had welcomed at her house foreign celebrities travelling with ladies unprovided with a marriage certificate, and had been equally hospitable to certain compatriots who had broken their marriage tie

when such breaks were a cause of scandal. But though she sympathized with "self-expression," and the mystical duty to "live one's life," and had championed the first adventurers in the new morality, she had never expected any one belonging to her to join that band of heroes. (31)

Part of the psychoanalytic jargon of the day, "self-expression" also means a commitment to creativity that is a transgression against the church, the law, and even social custom.[12]

Sexual and artistic self-expression are Wharton's two concerns here, insofar as they signify what she ambivalently calls the "new culture" of modernism (75). But self-expression proves short-lived, for Halo soon sees that her lover is void of "any trace of that impatience to express himself which had been his torment and rapture when she had first known him" (62). Wharton's several references to Havelock Ellis in these novels suggest how attuned she was to the new discourses of the sexologists, especially those arguing for the compatibility of artistic and sexual expression. According to Nina Miller in "The Bonds of Free Love," "sexology popularized psychoanalysis. . . . Village bohemia was allied with the conservatism of sexology in important ways, not least in its heterosexism" (39). "Free love" became a signal of "bohemian subcultural identity," an identity predicated on "rebellion against bourgeois society [that] had its roots in the Romantic and American literary traditions and was, consequently, integral to a long-standing paradigm of artistic identity" (53). By linking the artist-hero to the bohemian sex-expression of "free love," Wharton shows the disastrous effects of the trial marriage upon her alternate heroine, Halo Spear-Tarrant. Freedom for the male artist comes at the expense of the woman who sacrifices her life for his genius. She identifies herself with him, only to find that their "crazy experiment" is not enough to sustain her (358).

The crux of the novel, then, is Halo's and Vance's attempt at bucking the social values and restrictions of conventional marriage. Nevertheless, Halo discovers that "the coast of Bohemia might be pleasant to land on for a picnic, yet the interior of the country prove disappointing . . . She knew it was not based on moral scruples (morally speaking the business was still a labyrinth to her) but on a sort of inherited dislike of being unclassified, and out of the social picture" (82). At a time when companionate marriage and birth control dominate discussion, Wharton works through her heroine's ambivalence about free love. Trial marriage leaves Halo unanchored, while "almost all the young men of the group stood in the same unfettered relation to one or more young women" (82).

Refusing to pass judgment on free love even as she explores its gendered politics, Wharton laments its exclusion of women by dramatizing Halo's "outsider" status (82). "She had wanted Bohemianism on her own terms, as a momentary contrast to convention" (83), but that desire for oppositionalism proves to be bankrupt, for the "laws" of bohemianism are no less "irksome" than those of convention and no less grounded in heterosexual privilege. As Nina Miller explains, "The telos of a free love career was often to 'settle down' after a period of exploration (not unlike the logic of the conventional culture's 'companionate' marriage). . . . Nevertheless, the bohemian ideology of personal liberation was perceived by its practitioners as a serious and coherent critique of bourgeois society and its oppression of women. Such a perception depended to a significant extent upon a powerful rhetorical mechanism by which bohemian ideology could be simultaneously elevated above and masked in its complicity with existing social relations" (41). Wharton's goal has been to disarticulate ideological schemes from their intimate, emotional results: "The new generation argued that it was easier to separate if you were married, since divorce formalities were easier than a sentimental break" (GA 83). Unsentimental in her view of these rhetorical mechanisms, Wharton shows Vance's bohemian flashes—impulsively leaving Halo to be alone in order to create and then following Floss Delaney wherever she turns up—to be only another version of the rationalizations for the heterosexual privileges men have always enjoyed in society.

Wharton's irritation with free love, anarchy, and bohemianism is much less political (and much less politically reactionary) than it is a highly sensitive reading of these movements' gendered—and nativist—effects. While Wharton had intermittently assailed these movements in earlier novels, it is only after examining the gendered exclusions of eugenics, parental responsibility, and divorce that she can turn to a sustained look at the limits of free love and bohemianism. While her characters find passion in the work they do in the name of bohemian principles (one sells censored books in an out-of-the-way book-shop, and Halo's brother plans a musical spectacle, "Factories," "to be expressed entirely in terms of modern industrialism, with racing motors, aeroplanes and sub-marines as the protagonists" [86]), Halo cannot find fulfillment in being Vance's lover because Wharton cannot imagine that sexual submission—especially in the name of bohemian revolt—can ever be fully gratifying.

Halo suffers throughout *The Gods Arrive* from a systematic social exclusion—"cutting," in the day's terminology—as a result of the scandal of her leaving Lewis Tarrant for Vance Weston. Halo's brother tells her that all the other young bohemians are waiting to "have" her once

Vance "chucks" her (95). His "comrades" were waiting, she imagines, for their chance at her (103), though all along she realizes that she is too conventional to be a "poet's love" (102). When Halo realizes that she is neither Vance's intellectual comrade (383) nor the inspiration for his erotic passion, she assumes the only role left: the Mother. Moreover, the insubstantiality of bohemian life gives way to the settled heterosexuality of the most conventional, reproductive couple. Bohemian relations result in the infantilization of the artist-hero, Vance, at the hands of the increasingly more-maternal Halo.

Thus Wharton reveals the results of mastery, domination, self-promotion: Vance "was not particularly interested in the idea of being interviewed or reviewed. From the outset of his literary career he had been unusually indifferent to the notoriety attained by personal intervention. . . . It was not that Vance was indifferent to success, but because its achievement seemed to him so entirely independent of self-advertising" (170–71). Halo worships Vance's creative genius and submits to his will, while she suffers from anxieties over her undivorced state and hence her insecurity with Vance. At the heart of this insecurity is her conviction that she should be Vance's "comrade," when all around her she finds the pressure to conform: "Women who cast in their lot with great men, with geniuses, even with the brilliant dreamers whose dreams never take shape, should be armed against emotional storms and terrors. Over and over again she told herself that her joys were worth the pain, that the pain was part of the rapture; but such theories shrivelled to nothing in the terror that had threatened her very life. . . . Everybody was reduced to the same abject level by the big primitive passions, love and jealousy and hunger . . ." (149). Her conflict is predicated on her past independence and her current dependence, a tension she cannot maintain. Halo submits, but in terror of losing Vance; he dominates, but in fear of causing her pain. Her pain, however, reinforces his sense of genius, thereby reinforcing the cycle of dependency and erotic domination. In doing so, they lose the mutuality on which companionate relations are founded. Trial marriage fails, but not because of Wharton's old-fashioned morality; it fails because it obscures the compulsory mothering of geniuses in which men and women may be said to collaborate.

In asserting his genius and will, Vance aggressively destroys Halo's comradeship, so that her collaboration with his genius changes into the most traditional caretaking: she finds her calling to be painting, decorating, and typing, as opposed to reading and editing his works, the collaborative function the couple earlier imagined as the raison d'être of their bohemian experiment. Vance keeps his writing from her, fearing her disapproval but also celebrating his independence while negating hers. Her will subsumed in his, Halo can no longer serve as Vance's intimate critic or comrade, and so he requires the vague praise and resisting readings of his male friends. Her identification with and submission to Vance's genius only hasten the end of their relation. No self can "give all to love," Emerson's imperative. One's erotic or intellectual domination of the other negates passion and companionship, two of Wharton's ultimate values.

Jessica Benjamin's *The Bonds of Love* argues that capitalist culture is predicated on this linear movement from dependence to independence, exemplified in what the twenties perceived as "self-made men" (49). Similarly, *The Gods Arrive* enacts that drama: whereas Halo aspires to a mutuality with Vance, he cannot maintain that balance between separation and union. Rather, he runs from his domination over Halo, whom he had used as an "ear to listen, not as an intelligence to criticize" (333) and submits himself to Floss Delaney's playful erotic attentions. As Benjamin has it, the "satisfaction [that] is sought and found in submission" provides the key to erotic domination and submission (55). Submission to an idealized figure—which Halo sees in Vance—is the key to pain and pleasure in erotic relations, especially given Vance's "unwilling subjection" to Floss (260): "Intelligent though Halo was, could he hope to make her understand that a man may love one woman with all his soul while he is perishing for the nearness of another?" (261). Such self-serving rationalization invites more of Wharton's scorn to the extent that Halo's worship of Vance is another sign of the misguided and distorting idealization of male genius. *The Gods Arrive* argues against the middle-class self-promoting, self-deluding literary world that Wharton came to resent, an artistic world that celebrated the infantilized genius of artists like Gratz Blemer, once the writer of "robust and patient realism," now grown old and materialistic (389–91).

Perhaps the real struggle belongs to Halo, who must define herself outside of the dominant middle-class categories as wife, mistress, lover, even as Vance shores up these same middle-class categories in his life and in his fiction. His discussions about art with his friend, the suicide Chris Churley, are telling because Vance embodies the narcissistic denial of intellectual comradeship that Wharton feared in the new generation, as Anne Clephane of *The Mother's Recompense* earlier exemplified. Churley remarks: "I believe the novelist's richest stuff is in the middle class, because it lies where its name says, exactly in the middle, and reaches out so excitedly and unexpectedly in both directions. . . ." Vance agrees: "But no one wants to admit belonging to it, because we all do . . ." (176).

Halo's sacrifice, therefore, bolsters his power and his sense of transcendence over the middle class, his fear of being a "nonentity" (328). She takes refuge in his power, disenfranchised as she is from her old station in life as Mrs. Lewis Tarrant. Like Tarrant before him, Vance cannot recognize Halo's talents except as they reflect his own. In erotically and intellectually submitting to Vance's self-made manhood, Halo achieves only a circumscribed access not to a master but to one who writes, as Vance does, masterpieces like "Colossus."[13] Yet ironically, Wharton's sympathy is all with Halo when Halo returns, alone and pregnant, to her inherited home at the Willows.

Recuperating from Grandma Scrimser's death and then his own illness, Vance has his own metaphoric lying-in period in Belair, Wisconsin. His transformation in Belair is represented as a rebirth, only he— suffering from a "touch of pneumonia"—is now a bit of an infant: "His legs still rambled away from him like a baby's when he attempted his daily walk . . ." (412). After months of communing with nature, he returns for nostalgic inspiration to Paul's Landing, where *Hudson River Bracketed* began and where, once again, he runs into Halo. She welcomes Vance back, symbolically as her second child, into her care: "But then I shall have two children to take care of instead of one!" (432). This rebirth only confirms the sexual economy of the novel: schemes like bohemian life and trial marriage rely on maternal ideology and the maintenance of heterosexual norms. Although he doesn't yet want to return to Halo, unsure of himself and unsure of his feelings for Floss, he submits.

Probably the bleakest ending in Wharton's late fiction, the conclusion of *The Gods Arrive* suggests that trial marriage fails because of the conventionality of a culture that glorifies male literary genius, a sense of individuation vitalizing the demand to cross social boundaries. Yet, in the end, Vance opts for a domesticity whose promise of tranquility is everything bohemianism worked to oppose: "Marriage and a home; normal conditions; that was what he craved and needed. And Floss Delaney seemed to personify the strong emotional stimulant on which his intellectual life must feed. Intellectual comradeship between lovers was unattainable; that was not the service women could render to men" (382–83). The ending of *The Gods Arrive* sees Halo assume the maternal impulse to nurture Vance, as Halo becomes one of "The Mothers." Yet rather than celebrate the maternal,[14] Halo's compensatory fantasy of mothering the child and Vance, as in *Summer* and *The Mother's Recompense,* prompts a sustained critique of a terrible backsliding in egalitarian "comradeship."

Immersed as she may be in modernity's claims upon the author,

Wharton is writing against modernism, against the new styles of Hemingway, Joyce, and Woolf. We find interspersed in these pages Wharton's anti-stream-of-consciousness rhetoric, which she includes out of her impatience with being compared too often to Virginia Woolf. She rejects the attention to the "exploration of the subliminal" advocated in Vance's literary circles, "as if the highest imaginative art consisted in decomposing [man] into his constituent atoms" (GA 112). Wharton shows how closely aligned these aesthetic and moral contradictions and anxieties are for her. As we have seen, Vance is no sympathetic figure; he remains unsentimentalized in these two novels of the artistic spirit. Wharton's focus on the maternal is another way of registering cultural pressures, her way of negotiating the various urgencies of "self-expression," advertising, and free love. Always complicated, Wharton's response to reproductive and racial crises—whether in terms of the twilight sleep controversy, the eugenics craze of the preceding decade, or the cries for racial purity in Hitler's Germany—suggests the vexed intricacies of women's position.

In "Roman Fever," the subject of the next chapter, she returns to the fantasy of maternal compensation but still clings to some features of her eugenics preoccupation. Grace Ansley's maternal blood, not Delphin Slade's genetic heritage, is responsible for their daughter's "brilliant" flights of bravado. The debate over maternal heredity is the crucial factor in the next generation, a vestige of the eugenics thinking Wharton had dismissed more consciously in the twenties. The influence of the maternal, at this stage of Wharton's career, remains important, even if it does not redeem the social ideals of her youth. Instead, the social values surrounding the cult of the mother reveal to Wharton otherwise veiled prejudices of the 1930s and, in so doing, point to the turmoil to come.

5

"Roman Fever": A Rune of History

Isn't it awful to have the world at the mercy of two madmen?
    —Wharton to Elisina Tyler, 16 September 1935 (Lilly Library)

Jokes, as Wharton tells them, can be as aggressive as they are subtle. Consider the jokes Wharton and her friend Louis Bromfield used to share; Bromfield sends her two "banker" jokes in 1934 (January 18, Lilly Library). The second one goes as follows:

> And then there is the other story about the two men who met for the first time in the ten years since they were at college together. One said to the other "Well Jim, what are you doing now?" Jim turned away and with bowed head, murmured, "I'm a banker but don't tell my mother. She thinks I'm playing the piano in a brothel."

Given Wharton's financial worries in the thirties, it is not difficult to guess the source of her aggression against bankers and tax-assessors (whom she identifies as the "Dark Divinities" in a letter to Elisina Tyler, 2 September 1935, Lilly Library). But the first of Bromfield's jokes, which she repeats to Royall Tyler, is curious in its anxious mixture of a personal and social sense of change, for it is connected with her money worries and the joke's explicit racism (11 February 1934): "There was a terrible scandal in Connecticut last week. A white girl married a banker" (Lewis and Lewis 573). For Wharton, bankers—once the safest members of genteel society—are now associated with the turbulent underworld of culture: blacks, Jews, brothels, and bolsheviks. "Whiteness," similarly, once associated for Wharton with cultural authority and security, was threatened. The joke disrupts Wharton's usual cliche of approval, as it appears in the example from *Hudson River Bracketed*, "Well, that's white of you" (128), or in this description of the American sense of French patriotism: "I tell you, they're white! And they're fighting as only people can who feel that way about mothers and babies" (*The Marne*, 99). As she had explained in *French Ways and Their Meaning* (1919), Wharton argues for the fundamental resemblance of American and French cultures, if one "dig[s] down to the deep faiths and principles from which every race draws its enduring life to find how like in fundamental things" France and America are as races (16–17). This well-known expression is telling for Wharton, given her perception of the Harlem threat and of the Depression, which ushered in her own financial woes. What does it mean, then, for Wharton to develop an "inner life" based on racial hierarchies and cliches? How does the culture she disparages around her merely make explicit the change in values she, like many people, once associated with "whiteness"?

Perhaps because of an obsession with her own finances and perhaps because of race blindness, Wharton elides the racial prejudice of the joke (which may itself be the target of the joke) and focuses instead on its nativist sentiment. Denouncing American hypocrisy in this way, Wharton exhibits a rare touch of patriotism: "There is too much sour-grapes for my taste in the present American attitude. The time to denounce the bankers was when we were all feeding off their goldplate; not now! At present they have not only my sympathy but my preference. They are the last representatives of our native industries" (11 February 1934 to Royall Tyler, Lilly Library). We may not think much of Bromfield's jokes, but Wharton took them seriously enough to respond to them. In the letter to Royall Tyler, Wharton glosses the joke by redirecting the aggression implied in it. Her anger is not against bankers but against the "raving chaos" of American culture, (20 September 1933 to Elisina Tyler, Lilly Library), hostile as it seemed to be to her tales "designed for a quieter universe." Despite her sense of the American chaos, she spares bankers from the blame.

As we have seen in relation to her arguments against eugenics, Wharton was loathe to blame any scapegoat. Her own financial affairs are especially shaky at this time; her friends, herself, and especially Minnie (her sister-in-law) lost money in real estate investments, and Wharton is more distressed than ever about money and its relation to artistic genius. She writes, she says, for money; at least, she admits to her financial distress in the thirties—"I *must*, at last, get to work on a novel again, if only for the basest pecuniary reasons" (21 March 1934 to Royall Tyler, Lilly Library). While in her earlier correspondence she freely discusses payment and terms, her 1930s letters are explicit about her money needs and worries.

In writing one of her most biting short stories, "Roman Fever," Wharton reveals the same sort of aggressive humor that her jokes had. Only this time Wharton confronts her terror of the growing fascism in Europe. R. W. B. Lewis's biography mentions the story as a masterpiece of "rhetorical coherence," but he insists that in writing it Wharton was "undistracted" by news from Europe of a "terrible revolution . . . at hand" (1975, 527). He suggests that the pervading tone of calm and repose in the 1934 short story, originally part of the collection *The World Over*, underscores her virtual mastery of history—of Wharton's own past, particularly the question of her paternity, and of the history of the species represented by the Roman ruins. "Roman Fever," however, more fundamentally addresses the connections among origins, persecution, and sexual violence—Rome being a powerful site of such primal violence. Her story interrogates society's periodic demand for an ultimate return to origins: whether it be racial purification or sexual housekeeping. Lewis writes that the possibility of Wharton's illegitimacy "must have edged its way into Mrs. Wharton's mind over the years that followed [1908–9: the years in which the rumor began]. . . . The situation of Grace Ansley's whole lifetime is revealed in a single phrase, and just possibly, with all obliqueness, one phase of Edith Wharton's situation as well" (1968, xxv). Yet the question of race and origin, which is central to "Roman Fever," also invokes the moment of history—the "terrible revolution" brewing in Europe (see Letter 2, Lilly Library).[1]

Many critics would agree with Lewis about Wharton's apolitical, "serene," and "new state of being" in the thirties (1975, 524). Cynthia Griffin Wolff does not deal with Wharton's politics at all, while, at worst, other critics limit their political analysis by labeling her an anti-Semite. Cynthia Ozick writes that Edith Wharton was compliant in the face of her friend Paul Bourget's openly-declared anti-Semitism (293). In *The Jew in American Literature*, Sol Liptzin's citation of Wharton's caricature of the "bounder Jew" as an example of her anti-Semitism (154) typifies the usual objections. Wharton's name also appears as evidence of a general cultural anti-Semitism in Florence Kiper Frank's 1930 *Bookman* essay, "The Presentment of the Jew in American Fiction," and more recently in Michael N. Dobkowski's "American Anti-Semitism." At best, Wharton is considered a social critic with her own ideological blindspots, with racism and anti-Semitism notably among them.

Aug. 19. 34

PAVILLON COLOMBE
St BRICE-SOUS-FORÊT (S&O)
TÉLÉPHONE: St BRICE-SOUS-FORÊT, 12

Dearest Elisina — On my way home
the other day I dropped, I forget in what
church, a passing tribute to St Antoine —
& on arriving at Colombe I found
Linky's harness awaiting me; or rather,
it came up the following morning on
my breakfast-tray! All my gratitude
to my saint & to his executive — yourself. I suppose I whisked the harness
out of the car when I leapt out at Francey.

        Thank you also for Hitler. I am
keeping him for a quiet hour after
my guests are gone (the Nicholsons.) Last
week we had a super-celestial day at
Chartres, & tomorrow we are going on a
two days' giro, to Provins, Sens, Troyes, &c.
They are so intensely appreciative that it
is a joy to take them about; & Hitler will

Letter from Edith Wharton to Elisina Tyler about reading Hitler (19 August 1934).
Reprinted by permission of the Lilly Library, Indiana University, Bloomington, IN.

148

seem a blasphemy against all this beauty.

Mme Gillet telephoned me the day
before yesterday that the Journal had
sent Gillet back to Berlin —to see the
plébiscite, I suppose. I wonder if they
will let him in, after his admirable
article in the Rev. des deux Mondes?

Even little Lyrey has been to Berlin!
He's coming in today to tell us all about it—
bringing the curator of Mediaeval art
from the Metropolitan. Do you know him?

Greetings to all Antigny, including the Bills, who are due today, are
they not? I wish I cd look in on you—

Yr aff'y Edith

If the most cited example of her anti-Semitism is Simon Rosedale, the "glossy Jew" in *The House of Mirth*, recall that even Rosedale is not completely dismissed; in Chapter Six of Book Two, Wharton has Rosedale take on the "paternal rôle" with Carry Fisher's child: Lily "could not but notice a quality of homely goodness in his advances to the child" (250). The same chapter casts Carry in the maternal role, providing a counterpart to Lily's new view of Rosedale. Rosedale not only becomes more like Carry, the most solicitous figure for Lily's welfare besides Gerty, but he also serves as Lily's foil: "Little by little, circumstances were breaking down her dislike for Rosedale. The dislike, indeed, still subsisted, but it was penetrated here and there by the perception of mitigating qualities in him: of a certain gross kindliness, a rather helpless fidelity of sentiment, which seemed to be struggling through the hard surface of his material ambitions" (299–300). Lily's view of Rosedale changes when she recognizes his sensitivity, his "gross kindliness." Her "old standard of values" has changed, as has her anti-Semitism. Yet whether Lily's change in attitude here mitigates for us the charge of anti-Semitism against Wharton is not the crucial issue.

What is at issue is the tendency to read characters as the reinforcement of cultural stereotypes. If anything, Wharton was keenly aware of these stereotypes, as her jokes about bankers suggest, and she challenged the political construction of caricatures throughout her fiction of the twenties. Reading these stereotypes as an endorsement of certain racial or class politics has led many to reject Wharton's late fictions as conservative, but Wharton's views on cultural and racial politics and "race hygiene," as eugenics was called, do not necessarily coincide with her characters' views. And as we have seen in at least one late novel, *Twilight Sleep*, Wharton refuses us the vantage point of one character's perspective. In fact, she denies us the narcissistic pleasure of identification by forcing us to see subjectivity as fragmented, to see as subjects without the grounding of "selves." Wharton does not align her authorial voice with those of her characters, as I see it, but orchestrates the cultural contradictions she foregrounds through narrative voices. In order to illuminate the writer's politics, we need to look in other, less stereotypical places.

Charting the ideological shift in her work shows that "Roman Fever," for instance, responds to a reactionary political climate, demonstrating an anti-reactionary thrust to Wharton's fiction that counters the critical conception of her as apolitical or politically naive. In the 1930s political climate, she notices the authoritarian powers at work, and her fiction addresses this political trajectory, just as she had earlier addressed "Fordian culture" in *Twilight Sleep*. The stakes in such a critical endeavor are high: Wharton attempts to interpret a reactionary social climate for the popular audience and, therefore, to teach her readers to be skeptical of the rhetoric of racial and cultural purity. To describe this attempt, I would like now to move from scientific eugenics to a reading of Wharton's discursive style. I am not attempting to uncover cultural or historical references, but to theorize the cultural impact of air-wave and journalistic rhetoric upon the imagination of Wharton as social critic. The traces of a changing and horrifying political climate are etched in Wharton's fiction, and highlighting those traces brings their mark to the surface.

Before I turn to "Roman Fever" (written in the midst of Mussolini's and Hitler's rise to power), I want to provide some sense of the things Wharton would have been hearing about social politics during the thirties. Lewis claims that she listened to Hitler's rhetoric over her wireless. In her own words, she was appalled by his "angry screams and accusations of cowardice against any one who loves peace and beauty better than a general massacre," no less than she was by Italy's acceptance of fascism and the earlier rise of Mussolini (1975, 505). Lewis writes that Wharton "reserved her harshest words for Hitler." This is, however, Lewis's only major reference to the politics that inform Wharton's time.

Wharton sets this tale of two women, of motherhood and illegitimacy, in the context of Rome in the 1930s and against the backdrop of Mussolini's fascist control over maternity. As Victoria de Grazia argues in *How Fascism Ruled Women*, there was a "deep conflict within the fascist state between the demands of modernity and the desire to reimpose traditional authority" by relegating women to the role of wives and mothers (2). As one of fascism's mottos had it, "War is to man what motherhood is to women" (Sarti 187). While in the twenties, Mussolini led the charge against bolshevism; in the thirties, he marshalled his forces against racial amalgamation, using the "Jewish question" as a means of bolstering his ties with Germany's anti-Semitic campaign. Thus the debate over racial purity was ignited in Italy, although Mussolini had earlier rejected theories of "pure" races and superior stock. According to de Grazia, "Insofar as ethnic diversity and female emancipation were identified as obstacles to success, biological politics was easily fused with antifeminism and anti-Semitism" (4). In the early years of his rule, Mussolini wanted more babies, regardless of the genetic stock.

While Wharton's characters are Americans visiting in Rome, their situation only serves to highlight the growing fascist biological politics emerging in what de Grazia calls "eugenics, Italian style" (52), a "cult of fertility" designed to eliminate the signs of any illegitimate sexuality from public life coupled with the maternalist politics of the state (44, 72). That Grace Ansley's only fear over her illegitimate pregnancy is the charge of unrespectability, not fascist discipline and punishment, puts in relief the totalitarian control exerted over Italian women's lives.

Early 1933 seemed to be a turning point toward more anti-Semitic attacks, when, in fact, the European middle-class objected to "visible" attacks on Jews in their neighborhoods (Koonz 3–17). A "legal" boycott on Jewish businesses was called in Germany on 1 April 1933 (it was called off after twenty-four hours). Shortly after this highly publicized incident, Edith Wharton wrote to her friend Gaillard Lapsley with the exclamation: "Oh, & how I want to talk to you about Roosevelt, Hitler, & that awful Moscow business, which I no longer find myself able to read—" (15 April 1933, Beinecke Library). Instead of turning her face to the wall when it comes to politics, here (and elsewhere) she seems to have the political situation much on her mind. I read her claims as ironic ones in her 3 June 1935 letter to Royal Cortissoz, her friend and the art critic for the New York *Herald Tribune:* "I have not met anyone in France who is alarmed for the future, as far as one's own personal welfare is concerned; but politically, it does not look brilliant at present; nor does ours at home, either. So perhaps we had better turn to the Titians and the Giorgione, and try to forget it all" (Beinecke Library). She did not forget, however. Her act of remembering is inscribed in her late fictions.

The Law of the Father and Racial Purity

Wharton's story investigates a general force operating in culture—call it fascism, patriarchy, or discipline and repression. Wharton sees cultural origins as fictive rather than mythic and explores the danger of ignoring the difference. As Frank Kermode writes, "We have to distinguish between myths and fictions. Fictions can degenerate into myths whenever they are not consciously held to be fictive. In this sense anti-Semitism is a degenerate fiction, a myth. . . . Myths are the agents of stability, fictions the agents of change" (39). Wharton's "Roman Fever" acts as an agent of change insofar as it identifies how the sexual aggression in this story reflects the pervasive dissolution Wharton identifies in the culture. Her late fictions, from *The Mother's Recompense* to "Roman Fever," concern sexual violence, perhaps the only generic and thematic form which her more general preoccupation with civilization could take.

Wharton's story about procreation and history generates two discourses which she finds perversely intertwined. Her story goes as follows:

two middle-aged women meet again, accidentally, in Rome after many years and after much personal history, in a place where they had a shared history. They contemplate vaguely the Roman vista and the numerous ironies that emerge at their having been brought together once again at the scene of destruction—the Roman Forum—leaning as if at the limit of some terrible drama threatening to take both of them into its oblivion. Both had been teenagers here, and both had found husbands here. Both women have daughters, both of whom are marriageable and on a double-date; however, Alida envies Grace's daughter Barbara for her brilliance while her daughter, Jenny, "made youth and prettiness seem as safe as their absence" (14). Their conversation leads to a reopening of old wounds, rivalry, renewed violence, and a series of revelations. Twenty-five years before, Alida Slade had forged a letter to Grace Ansley in the name of Alida's future husband, Delphin Slade, in order to get rid of Grace, who she knew was also in love with her husband-to-be. The letter sets up a rendezvous between Grace and Delphin in the Colosseum, though of course Delphin, according to Alida's plan, would not be there. That Alida says she knew Grace would not die of "Roman fever," even though she sends her friend to the Colosseum in the cold night air, does not diminish the essential violence of that letter. In a moment of forced contrition, Alida is willing to grant Grace this one possession—a memory—since Alida eventually married the man both of them loved and bore Delphin's legitimate child. Alida says Grace had nothing but a phony letter, while for twenty-five years she herself had Delphin, his money, his name, and his child. Grace retorts with the most effective comeback possible: the fact that she had Delphin's illegitimate child, Barbara.

Thus, the story has a surprise ending: a specific hierarchical relation is reestablished between the two women in a story that begins, in the first paragraph, in a vague darkness: "From the table at which they had been lunching two American ladies of ripe but well-cared-for middle age moved across the lofty terrace of the Roman restaurant and, leaning on its parapet, looked first at each other, and then down on the outspread glories of the Palatine and the Forum, with the same expression of vague but benevolent approval" (9). As this opening suggests, the women remain content in their ignorance of events, which each of the widows has kept secret these twenty-five years. The story, then, like a Greek ritual tragedy, moves gradually toward anagnorisis. What has brought these women here to battle for social position and authority?

The first paragraph, again, helps to suggest an answer. As they survey the Palatine Hill, these women have "a vague and benevolent approval" of these ruins, a site that not only represents great triumph but also vast decay, death, and destruction (9). If their mien is "vague," they must have temporarily forgotten whatever it is that might prevent their look of benevolence. And since they look benevolently at each other, then that forgetting also includes the repression of their shared history. The task of the narrative is to remember in an explicit way. What Eric Sundquist suggests about Hawthorne in his critical study, *Home as Found,* may be true of Wharton as well: "'remembrance' is often literally that: one re-members what has been dis-membered, reconstructs what has been shattered, and atones for what has been ruined or murdered" (91). In the act of writing, we re-member what has been dis-membered through experience; Wharton's storytelling here is an act of piecing together the histories of these women competing for Delphin Slade and for authority. Wharton's task is to remember the function of these Roman ruins both as a symbol of Western civilization's origins and as a place where young American women go to make love. The history of Roman treachery is repeated in a pale and humorous parody.[2]

Consider the story of Great Aunt Harriet, a story that Grace Ansley first told to Alida when they were girls: Great Aunt Harriet seems to have committed "fratricide," as it were, by sending her rivalrous sister to her death of Roman fever. Now we also see that the story itself—a cautionary tale—has a specific function for different sets of women. As Mrs. Slade explains: "What different things Rome stands for to each generation of travellers. To our grandmothers, Roman fever; to our mothers, sentimental dangers—and how we used to be guarded!—to our daughters, no more dangers than the middle of Main Street. They don't know it—but how much they're missing!" (15). For the mothers of Grace Ansley and Alida Slade, the tale functions to frighten the girls, to prevent them from going out and catching Roman fever or, what might be worse, going out and catching a Roman—or being caught by one. Grace Ansley uses this story in another way: since Roman fever no longer exists, the ruins seem to have been overrun with tenacious lovers. In other words, when Grace narrated the story of Aunt Harriet to Alida, she was attempting to warn her symbolically; the story, thus, is an apotropaic, a warning. However, when Alida reminds Grace that Grace had used the same warning against her, Alida is invoking that dangerous, destructive situation again, as well as the power of the maternal. Alida means this memory to be a taunt since she believes Grace had been cheated, thwarted. Thwarted from what? From exercising her will in the only way women are allowed: reproductive choice.

The letter that Alida forges, too, has a similar place and function in the story, precisely because Alida seems to have cleverly turned the story against Grace. The same story has several different narrative uses depending on the situation: in the first instance, the story is intended to discipline daughters. In the second instance, the story is used as a vehicle for Grace's aggression against her rival, Alida. In the third instance, the story is reappropriated by Alida in order to thwart—if not kill—her rival. In short, their storytelling on the terrace after dusk recalls the various levels of treachery that belong to Rome's history writ small. In any case, Alida writes fiction, the letter, which, given its context, has a powerful effect. She usurps Delphin's voice—that, too, is a kind of violence against herself and Grace—in order to trick her rival. And the trick would have been perfect had Grace not answered the letter to a willing Delphin. But that is precisely what a rival cannot imagine, the reciprocity of the act, a reply or counterthrust, the ultimate act of re-membering what had been dis-membered by the letter. Alida was too clever, perhaps. The counterthrust comes, then, years later when Grace has found a context within which to reply: "I had Barbara" (24). And at this point, we understand the nature of the displaced rivalry between the daughters, Babs and Jenny, who engage in the same kind of rivalry for a suitor in Europe.

Why women are moved to behave in this way is Wharton's recurring question in her late fiction. Since the entirety of the story plays itself out against the backdrop of "the great accumulated wreckage of passion and splendour" (17) in Rome, I am suggesting that Wharton means to put into some relation the fortunes of civilizations and the fortunes of these two families, the Slades and the Ansleys. The story insists, first of all, that our own myth of origin—from which we get all of our founding or inaugurating force, our authority—is inherently arbitrary. Like the stories we tell about ourselves, the foundations of civilization are always at risk, unsettled, in transition. Wharton's fiction, therefore, participates in a (destructive) process of demystification: both women believe their own inaugural myths about their daughters. Alida believes that her daughter is the only offspring of the man she loved. Grace believes that Delphin initiated the events that would result in the birth of Babs, that he "loved" Grace. Both are wrong about the order of things, and Wharton uncovers a profound emptiness at the heart of history since chance seems to rule. Wharton's art disturbs the powers that benefit from the insistence on propriety and respectability as conservative forces. The rub is that conservative powers sustain themselves in the very events that threaten them.

When the two women stare down at the Palatine, Mrs. Slade claims it to be the "most beautiful view in the world" (10). Mrs. Ansley replies that it will always be "'to me' . . . with so slight a stress on the 'me' that Mrs.

Slade, though she noticed it, wondered if it were not merely accidental, like the random underlinings of old-fashioned letter-writers" (10). That she wonders but dismisses Mrs. Ansley's stress or emphasis on "me" suggests that she does not really read their situation accurately. She is far more interested in her own pronouncements than in dialogue. What is more, Mrs. Ansley recognizes that there is an essential ignorance about each other and their own daughters: "I've come to the conclusion that I don't in the least know what [our daughters] are. . . . And perhaps we didn't know much more about each other" (11).

Although they "reflected how little they knew each other," those reflections do not stop them from creating necessary fictions about the other: "Each one, of course, had a label ready to attach to the other's name; Mrs. Delphin Slade, for instance, would have told herself, or any one who asked her, that Mrs. Horace Ansley, twenty-five years ago, had been exquisitely lovely—no, you wouldn't believe it, would you? . . . Good-looking, irreproachable, exemplary" (12). That respectability, however, conceals the very disorder that gives respectability rational motivation. Mrs. Ansley manipulates appearances so that no one suspects that her exemplary marriage conceals an illegitimate child. Until the moment of the story's events, Mrs. Ansley behaves as a sort of sexual fugitive, which demonstrates the degree that she has internalized the social norms she eventually renounces. Even a moment of confession such as the last line in the story does not correct Grace's pretense of twenty-five years.

Indeed, after the deaths of Horace Ansley and Delphin Slade, Mrs. Slade especially feels the loss of her social status: "Being *the* Slade's widow was a dullish business. . . . In living up to such a husband all her faculties had been engaged" (13). From the time Mrs. Slade appropriates Delphin's voice in the letter she writes to Grace, she does not escape inscription into a world that makes her a social appendage to her husband. Such a state of affairs virtually assures that Alida's social and mental development would remain profoundly limited. What Mrs. Slade intuits is Mrs. Ansley's pity for her: "Mrs. Ansley had always been rather sorry for her . . ." (14). Thus, the women continue in this round of petty suspicion and judgment: "So these two ladies visualized each other, each through the wrong end of her little telescope" (14). Which is to say, both Mrs. Slade and Mrs. Ansley see a reduced version of the other and of their social situations. In this limited vision, then, they do not see that their violence to each other belongs, as Wharton suggests, to the violence women have engaged in to force a place for themselves in society, a violence resident at the center of Western civilization. The surprise of the story demonstrates how hopelessly enmeshed they are in the fictions about women's place, the fictions their mothers told, the one that Great Aunt Harriet enacted when she arranged for the death of her sister, her rival.

The "Memento Mori" which they face in Rome is not some abstract principle or historical ruin for these women, but the "rune," the sign, of their own deaths—acted out so long ago when they each warned the other about Roman fever. Right now, however, Alida Slade is consumed with envy because she imagines that Babs, Grace's daughter, is "out to catch that young aviator—the one who's a Marchese. . . . And Jenny has no chance beside her. I know that too. I wonder if that's why Grace Ansley likes the two girls to go everywhere together?" (16). In other words, Mrs. Slade still continues to think of marriage in terms of social hierarchy, just as she had thought about her own marriage to Delphin as the mark of social superiority over her rival. Although she notices that Roman fever has changed over the years, and the girls are no longer in danger of catching malaria, she does not notice that her account of Babs and Jenny—as rivals for the same man—dooms the daughter to repeat her own history. In fact, the widows compete once again in marrying their daughters off. Furthermore, Mrs. Slade envies Grace Ansley her brilliant daughter: "Mrs. Slade broke off this prophetic flight with a recoil of self-disgust. There was no one of whom she had less right to think unkindly than of Grace Ansley. Would she never cure herself of envying her? Perhaps she had begun too long ago" (17). History does not change for either Mrs. Slade or Mrs. Ansley. Why envy? Mrs. Ansley had posed a sexual threat to Mrs. Slade, and sexual threats for Wharton's characters invite violent retributions.

What is strange about the story is that Mrs. Slade realizes she hates and envies Mrs. Ansley but cannot pinpoint the source of her "exasperation" (18). She badgers Grace Ansley with reminders of her sight-seeing in the Colosseum, the sight-seeing she believes resulted in her "illness." All that Mrs. Ansley can gracefully reply is that "prudent girls aren't always prudent" (19). Once again, Mrs. Slade fails as a successful reader of the runes of her own personal history. She does not interpret any of Grace Ansley's statements, but merely takes them at face value, just as she had—years ago—failed to anticipate Grace's response to Delphin's letter. Mrs. Slade explains her part in the scheme to get rid of Mrs. Ansley, but her wrath and exasperation disappear immediately: "She wondered why she had ever thought there would be any satisfaction in inflicting so purposeless a wound on her friend. But she had to justify herself" (21). Neither Mrs. Slade nor Mrs. Ansley can keep herself in check any longer after so long a silence. Hence, in their discussion, they let loose with what Wharton herself calls "violence." Although Alida realizes somehow that her aggression is misdirected, she is powerless to control it.

After Grace "recovers" from Roman fever, her mother quickly marries her off to Horace Ansley, a move Alida interprets as pique, committed so as "to be able to say you'd got ahead of Delphin and me. Girls have such silly reasons for doing the most serious things" (23). Here, above all, Alida trivializes Grace's quick marriage to Horace, not realizing that the celerity of the courtship was to avoid a scandal. This passage highlights the sense of fragility and emptiness of human institutions even as it suggests the circumscription of women's identities in a patriarchal order, since Alida interprets marriage as just another mode of competition. She can only see the competition as an instance of jealousy; passion does not even come into the picture for her because her rivalry drowns out all other emotions.

What Mrs. Slade suspects is the dissolution of distinctions between Mrs. Ansley and herself—a fearful symmetry between the women, making each one socially interchangeable as a prospective wife for Delphin Slade. Alida must get rid of Grace for a while in order to secure Delphin's affection. Her fear is that Delphin does not see a difference between them, and what difference he does see is in Grace's favor. Ironically, both women see their origins in Delphin, the originator of the rivalry. For Delphin, it seems, one woman is as good as another; it depends on the rivalry between the women, therefore, to determine who gets the community "prize," the husband.

Significantly, during all those years of marital comfort, Alida stares out the window in surveillance of her rival. "When the drawing-room curtains in No. 20 East 73rd Street were renewed, No. 23, across the way, was always aware of it. And of all the movings, buyings, travels, anniversaries, illnesses—the tame chronicle of an estimable pair. Little of it escaped Mrs. Slade" (12). She even jokes about Mrs. Ansley, when the Slades are about to move to Wall Street: "I'd rather live opposite a speakeasy for a change; at least one might see it raided" (12). This joke reveals Alida's fear of what is kept repressed in her opposition to Mrs. Ansley.

And it is this repressed joke that these women must confront in the restaurant looking over the Palatine. The joke results from Grace Ansley's uncanny ability to manipulate signs, to "signify herself" as an utterly respectable woman when we come to know that this respectability is a sham. When Alida finally confronts Grace with the forgery of the letter, Grace retaliates by rejecting her role as representation of the respectable. Alida has always existed as sign, as wife and widow to Delphin

Slade. Grace Ansley now forces her to see the tension between herself as sign and as a subject responsible for her own determination. She makes Alida feel other to herself by tearing away the veil over Babs's paternity. Alida had always wondered "how two such exemplary characters as [Grace] and Horace had managed to produce" an offspring as "dynamic" as Babs (16–17). Once Alida discovers that Babs is the product of Grace and Delphin's union in Rome, she realizes that Grace has become a mysterious quantity, not the other—the woman as sign—that she had so long believed. In contrast, Alida's usurpation of Delphin's power—his voice—is a ruse, a result of the competition forced upon women as a means of escaping their identical status as signs.

Elizabeth Allen writes that, in the nineteenth century, "women represent the culture of America, its social relations, its customs, its manners, its forms. They carry on the appearances of life which can flourish only when some civilisation has been attained. As American women, they must both signify the degree to which America is different and changing (free and easy, democratic, spontaneous, young, rich, etc.) and the very constants of life, the customs and forms" (19). If women as signs represent American culture, then Grace Ansley's gesture can only mean that her character rejects domestic harmony and opts, instead, for the scene of destruction, the scene of confrontation with the other (Alida Slade) who represents the repressions of a patriarchal culture that has infected them (like the fever itself). By throwing the whole notion of paternity in doubt, and therefore throwing her daughter's name up for grabs, she displaces herself as sign of American culture and becomes the signifier of the disruption of the proper name, of paternity, of patriarchal order in general. History as Wharton plays it out thus becomes a scene of destruction of the patriarchal codes by which women are conventionally signified. If the proper name, the Name-of-the-Father, is an attempt to introduce order into an inherently unstable field of social relations, then Grace Ansley's final gesture in the story invites the whirlwind. The setting of the story itself—the site of Roman dissolution—bequeaths, as it were, the legacy of corruption against which social law is meant to legislate.

Grace shows the law of culture, in this case the father's law to which Alida clings, to be suspect and arbitrary, but all the more powerful because it is enforced. Grace refuses to signify the "truth" of American culture (whatever that truth happens to be): its moral rectitude, its vague link with a superior cultural heritage. Instead, her confession opens up the question of the patriarchal law, forcing us to see the Roman ruins as more than just an occasion for unreflective congeniality. As Jane Gallop, after Lacan, explains:

The legal assignation of a Father's Name to a child is meant to
call a halt to uncertainty about the identity of the father. If
the mother's femininity (both her sexuality and her untrust-
worthiness) were affirmed, the Name-of-the-Father would always be in doubt, always be subject to the question of the
mother's morality. Thus the Name-of-the-Father must be ar-
bitrarily and absolutely imposed, thereby instituting the reign
of patriarchal law. (39)

In her claim that she "had Barbara," then, Grace threatens the symbolic
order of society by exposing the arbitrary assumption Alida makes about
Babs's father, not to mention the assumption about Grace's respectability.

Here is Wharton's strongest doubt about origins and respectability.
The Other must be invented in order to establish the boundaries of the
self as subject. That is how Mrs. Slade imagines Mrs. Ansley—as the
other who poses a threat and at the same time constitutes self-consciousness. But her triumph is only made possible by entering the conflict in the
first place and defeating her "friend," another woman, after both husbands are dead. Similarly, Grace undermines the Name-of-the-Father
with her claim to "immorality" in which she authors a notion of herself
for Alida, even though this gesture merely follows a long conformity to
patriarchal law. In this way, she disrupts the dream of power Alida has
had. "Paternity cannot be perceived, proven, known with certainty; it
must be instituted by judgement of the mother's word" (Gallop 47). Even
the suggestion of a mother's infidelity, Gallop goes on to argue, calls into
question the Name-of-the-Father since "the woman's presumed honour"
is the most reinforced cultural assumption (Gallop 48). In this case, Alida
reproduces that chivalry in presuming Grace's honor, thereby reproducing the law of culture, the father's law.

Grace and Horace "produce" in Babs a sign that does not signify the
sexual union of Grace and Horace: it can be no representation or reproduction of their union. Rather, it is a misrepresentation, a simulacrum,
the reading of which threatens Alida's own comprehension of herself as
social sign. Grace does not cause Alida's lifetime anxiety; rather, Alida's
assumptions about her place in the social hierarchy produce her anxiety,
an anxiety that in any case does not end with marriage to the man she
desires, which is the purported end to the sexual-social exchange. Alida
doubts the mark of privilege that marriage (the proper name) has given
her as Mr. Slade's wife. She has taken this privilege up to now as "natural" rather than as an ambiguous sign of her own uncertain status. And
with these doubts, Wharton calls the "ruins of history" into question

and unveils history as a "rune"—a sign of doubt—which demands re-interpretation.

Wharton's short story reproduces, at the level of form, the metaphor of the inverted telescope that describes the vision of the two women: it reduces the social landscape many times over and thereby participates in the scene of destruction. As Lewis suggests, the story assiduously re-presses the rancorous events of its history—the European wars—in order to focus on a specific micro-conflict taking place between two well-to-do women at the end of their active social lives; in this social context their husbands' deaths, in effect, kill them, too. But even in this forgetting, the destructive character emerges, for forgetting clears the way for new orders and new possibilities. Grace Ansley appears to represent, against the life-denying investment in conventional norms that Alida Slade has made, a kind of life principle. She condemns the past, the tradition that has imprisoned her under the Name-of-the-Father, in order to live, to assert her own life-making principle: "I had Barbara." Just so, Wharton attempts to write a past after the fact from which culture might originate, against that origin which has given it its form in traditional culture.

All along, Alida has assumed Grace to be an exemplary figure, even boring in her moral rectitude. However, Grace's final speech dashes this assumption on at least two levels. First, it proves wrong, in essence, Alida's reduction of Grace's character, a reduction sanctioned by the cultural norms that would reward such respectable behavior. Second, it reveals the grounds of this assumption, the unwavering belief in patri-archal authority and feminine compliance, to be empty, as fragmented as the Roman ruins themselves.

Despite Grace's transgression early in life, and despite the eventual emergence of this secret after a long silence, her society's capacity to conserve itself in the face of dissolution remains powerful. At the very least, Wharton's story accounts for the pragmatic costs of conserving a surface structure of social relations, a structure that ultimately conceals unstable ground. Cultural origins prove to be the stuff of fiction.

Elements of Social Change

What keeps readers from seeing the nature of Wharton's critique may be interpreted as the result of a violent repression, perhaps even into the unconscious, that drives her into inexplicitness, even virtual silence about Hitler's rise to power. Wharton deserves, however, much more credit as an acute observer and ironist in her contemporary scene than we have yet given. On the question of Edith Wharton's social politics, a passage from Horkheimer and Adorno's "Elements of Anti-Semitism" in the *Dialectic of Enlightenment* seems illuminating. Written in 1944, Horkheimer and Adorno's work can illuminate Wharton's story and the culture in which "Roman Fever" was produced. Horkheimer and Adorno propose that the general symbolic order cannot be separated into components such as anti-Semitism, antifeminism, racism. These prejudices are all of a piece called force. And it is this force—the negative or destructive character, as Walter Benjamin called it—which Wharton isolates in her story. Horkheimer and Adorno write that race

> is not a naturally specific characteristic, as the folk mystics would have it. It is a reduction to the natural, to sheer force, to that stubborn particularity which in the status quo constitutes the generality. Today race has become the self-assertion of the bourgeois individual integrated within a barbaric collective. . . . The persecution of the Jews, like any other form of persecution, is inseparable from that system of order. However successfully it may at times be concealed, force is the essential nature of this order—and we are witnessing its naked truth today. (169–70)

Horkheimer and Adorno speculate on the social schema necessary to produce what looks to them like ritual murder, a powerful structure against which men and women have no resources for resistance. The opportunity to express repressed anger "does not help men but panders to their urge to destroy" (170). This anger leads to a ritual sacrifice of the other, not because the other is guilty, but because of his or her sacrificial vulnerability. Horkheimer and Adorno detail a rhetoric of motives for force and violence:

> Attacking or defending blindly, the persecutor and his victim belong to the same sphere of evil. . . . Anti-Semitism is a deeply imprinted schema, a ritual of civilization; the pogroms are the true ritual murders. They demonstrate the impotence of sense, significance, and ultimately of truth—which might hold them within bounds. The idle occupation of killing confirms the stubbornness of the life to which one has to conform, and to resign oneself. (171)

This ritual of hatred is played out in "Roman Fever": Mrs. Slade resigns herself to the law of culture, and Mrs. Ansley, already a transgressor against the law of morality dominant at the time, pretends invisibility and respectability. But Mrs. Slade's hatred of the life she leads is translated into her competition and hatred of Mrs. Ansley—a deflected anger from their profound (if also repressed) discomfort with the reactionary force against them. Wharton's story turns on the hatred Mrs. Slade feels for Mrs. Ansley. As Horkheimer and Adorno put it in general terms: "The hatred felt by the led, who can never be satisfied economically or sexually, knows no bounds. Their hatred cannot be worked off because it can never be fulfilled. . . . True, personal anger in the civilized man is roused by the constraining situation: by the anger of the tormentor and of the tormented, who are indistinguishable in their grimace" (171, 182). In "Roman Fever," Mrs. Slade's long-repressed anger is roused by being Delphin Slade's widow (a dull, confining business), and the anger of the tormented—Mrs. Ansley's—is roused by her rival's underestimation of her resistance.

Mrs. Slade's problem is a false projection onto the other, her victim, whom she wants to reduce to an object of hatred (a hatred of a bourgeois respectability that has kept her dominated by Delphin Slade and the social world he represents). In Horkheimer and Adorno's words, she clings to her "own paranoia by participating in the collective form, and clings passionately to the objectivized, collective and confirmed forms of delusion" (197). As Martin Jay explains, paranoia is no longer personal but politicized, part of a cultural and political unconscious. Jay notes: "For Horkheimer and Adorno, then, perhaps the ultimate source of anti-Semitism and its functional equivalents is the rage against the nonidentical that characterizes the totalistic dominating impulse of western civilization" (98–99). Mrs. Slade refuses to think through to the source of her hatred for Mrs. Ansley. She does not want to acknowledge that her paranoia over Mrs. Ansley's smile and offhand comments emerges from her own resistance to the social law she is compelled to follow. Wharton demonstrates the lack of self-examination at the heart of all social relations—between the anti-Semites and the Jews, and between these two little women here—Mrs. Slade and Mrs. Ansley, looking at each other through the wrong end of their telescopes.

For Wharton, Alida Slade's attack on difference amounts to an attack on the cultural ideology (of difference) she values. "The anger against all that is different" is at the root of Wharton's story, just as it is at the root of anti-Semitism as formulated by Horkheimer and Adorno (207). Grace's attack on Alida's shabby morality does not change either the morality or its products in the social relations articulated by Wharton's story. We might assume, without confirmation from the narrative, that Babs will get her mate and the rigid hierarchical relations that produced the mothers' histories will continue for another generation to come. Still, life outside the text—the only life that counts—is always open to question, and we can see the dangerous, destructive potential of Wharton's fiction if we understand the text to be a kind of symbolic hand-grenade. The story does not disrupt social relations themselves so much as it undermines the supposed ground of those relations. Without investing in some purely imaginary space of freedom, we are compelled to confront the historical circumstances of our choices.

In the eleventh of his "Theses on Feuerbach," Marx created a practical philosophy with the imperative to change, not merely interpret, the world. Wharton's fiction implicitly responds to this imperative to change. I suggest that we cannot accept at face value Wharton's pronouncements about her turning her back on politics. She deserves credit for articulating the destructive character of misogyny that led all too quickly to what she saw in 1933, as she writes in a 20 September letter to Gaillard Lapsley, as a "world . . . whizzing down so crazily to the everlasting abyss" (Beinecke Library).

6

"Edith Agonistes"

Poor Billy Carlton's taste for cocaine was as nothing to mine for your conversation . . .
—Wharton to Gaillard Lapsley, 21 May 1920 (Beinecke Library)

Wharton's ability to "think against herself," to resist all of her conservative impulses, is revealed nowhere more clearly than in her ironic confession of an "addiction" to intellectual exchange. She likens her need for that stimulation to an acquaintance's addiction to cocaine, a very popular drug during the twenties. Indeed, Wharton's craving for intelligent conversation with her cohort of friends increased in the twenties and thirties, when both her money and her mobility decreased. As she reports in her autobiography, *A Backward Glance* (1933), Wharton loved to be among her intimate friends more than anything else in her life. By the thirties, when many of her companions, like Henry James and Walter Berry, had died, and when her longtime maid, Catharine Gross, had spent her last years growing increasingly feeble and senile, Wharton's signature on a 25 May 1937 letter, "Edith Agonistes," was a telling phrase for her sense of a lonely struggle (see Letter 3, Lilly Library). While Wharton and her friends had once confronted a disintegrating culture and an increasing cultural conservatism, she now imagines that she fights, like Samson, alone and figuratively in the dark. With characteristic self-parody, this letter's sign-off humor suggests, in 1937, Wharton's both ironic and sympathetic stance toward the issues that had engaged her ever since her 1917 *Summer*. Irony and sympathy characterized the twin features of her imagination throughout her career and, in her loneliness, they also marked her response to a world irrevocably changed.

Both her Pulitzer-Prize winning *Age of Innocence* and her last novel, *The Buccaneers*, unfinished at the time of her death, converge on the political issues of assimilation and social exclusion. In the 1920 novel, Wharton figures these "trends" in the presence of the gipsy-like Ellen Olenska, whose associations with the foreign are treated as a perceived threat to American social standards. By her last work, published post-humously in 1938 with a Note by Lapsley explaining Wharton's progress on the novel, the racial and class amalgamation that dominated the previous generation—sounded in the fears of degeneration by sociologists such as Edward A. Ross—is figured as a comedic cultural invasion, when two American families "invade" London aristocracy as the "buccaneers" of Wharton's title. Both of these novels are historical romances, representing Wharton's fantasy of cultural history and crystallizing anxieties of dangerous social trends and foreign ideas. In the seventeen years between them, as we have seen in *The Mother's Recompense, Twilight Sleep, The Children,* and "Roman Fever," Wharton argued more strenuously than ever that the international audience she envisioned for her novels—American, French, and British readers—had less to fear from foreign intruders and their alien ideas or from indigenous "cultural invasions" like bohemianism and sexual revolutions than it did from internalized fears and projections of dominance over others. *The Buccaneers,* then, establishes the limits of dominance and ascertains the value of cultural assimilation.

We might remember here Wharton's "lesson" in *The Mother's Recompense,* concerning Kate Clephane's desire to transcend the past even as the novel confirms that the past cannot be transcended. Like Alice Haskett-Varick-Waythorn in "The Other Two," Kate Clephane cannot shed her past the way a man, like Chris Fenno—Kate's old lover, can and does. The new America of the twenties holds out this false utopia of new tolerance, while Wharton's novel refuses the terms by which such a new tolerance could help her heroine Kate create a new identity. For Wharton, identities are predicated on past actions and decisions, just as they are on traditional class and race categories. The novel is at once both sympathetic to the new spirit of tolerance and its loosening hold on the social scene and, at the same time, is deeply split, especially with respect to the threat of unchecked sexual desires, in which Wharton sees social anarchy such as the kind she envisioned in the Harlem Renaissance.

Wharton's ambivalence about heredity, race, and personal change is revealed in these character studies. This ambivalence is especially apparent in the fear of exposure Wharton plots as the novel's theme. Chris's fear of exposure is intertwined with Kate's fear of her past sexual relation with Chris. Yet, as we have seen, only when Kate realizes that a black woman, Phemia, might guess Kate's secret does Wharton reveal the limits of the "new tolerance." To Kate's amazement, Phemia informs Kate's daughter Anne about her mother's furtive visit to Chris in Baltimore. That revelation sets the second half of the narrative going, since Anne's discovery of her mother's interference causes her to break with her mother and reconcile with Chris. The novel turns on the fear of exposure and revelation—and, what is worse for Kate, exposure because of a black woman, a maid. Here Wharton's repressed racial unconscious returns with a vengeance.

In the bleak light of this subsequent novel, it is interesting that *The Age of Innocence* invokes the familiar and often-repeated fears that Americans needed in order to hold the line against both immigrants and their influence.[1] The kind of anti-social behavior associated with the "lower" cultures of Eastern Europeans could be discovered in Ellen's refusal to return to her husband and in the inherited madness of the Chivers family, two examples of the ways in which the popular belief in Darwinian and neo-Lamarckian theories about instinct and heredity made familial aberrations all the more threatening as a sign of the danger within rather than outside the family. The fear of hereditary madness reinforced the greater modern inclination for social engineering and control. As Carl Degler notes, "Charles Loring Brace in his influential book *The Dangerous Classes of New York and Twenty Years' Work Among Them,* published in 1872, warned that the pathological character traits of drunken or criminal parents might well be inherited by their offspring. Medical men, Brace pointed out, were convinced that children could inherit insanity, criminal habits, and even a tendency toward prostitution" (35). Julius Beaufort—also a foreigner—commits bank default, thereby reinforcing the popular sense of crime as hereditary. That Ellen seems to be able to associate with foreigners and with radicals, like her bohemian neighbor Ned Winsett, suggests just how potentially contaminating such associations were understood to be. Reading Ellen through Mary Douglas's anthropology, Judith Fryer argues in *Felicitous Space* that Ellen's danger arises from her potentially polluting presence (Fryer 138–39). Her presence portends a sexual transgression, further complicated by a symbolic alliance with her Eastern European married name as well as her mixing with other bohemians.

Elizabeth Ammons's claims in *Edith Wharton's Argument with America* are important in this respect, contending as she does that Wharton focused on motherhood—and The Mothers—as women's ways to establish authority in light of increased attention to cultural purity through

CHATEAU DE GRÉGY
☎ 85 BRIE-COMTE-ROBERT
SEINE ET MARNE

May 25. (1937)

Tuesday.

Dearest Elisina,

Only a brief scribble to thank you for your welcoming letter to Claude. Your speed telegram (that night to Rome came first on my list.) + 1st letter of the 21st, addressed here, which came the day of Saturday. Claire, invited to another tea, trip that I sha see letter, I'd able to write a little low excitedly, but as that does not seem so bright, I will just scribble a few words on this —

and can manage to catch up with a little of that out Venetians — front. You think, what of Copy of — I'd arrived there, bewildering, unable to see anything! Borne can keep to to of Peter —

& devoted

Edith Forster

Long I don't Elisina Sunburn
cd. write special letter, this!)

thanks for all your sympathy,
Mary Wemyss's death is a real
blow, Frank. Crozoli,
As for Crozoli's
— !

Letter from Edith "Agonistes" Wharton to Elisina Tyler (25 May 1937), on folded stationary. Reprinted by permission of the Lilly Library, Indiana University, Bloomington, IN.

maternal (genetic) influence. Ammons writes: "[Wharton's] new argument is fundamentally emotional and conservative and says that women must sublimate their desires for freedom to the higher duty of serving their families and the culture as mothers" (185). Ammons sees this move as "reactionary" and faults the writer for not creating "fully dimensioned" mothers and instead imagining "maternal characters to argue a thesis about American culture" (186). In a time when American societies offered women political propaganda about motherhood, however, it is possible to say that Wharton offered her own. Referring to Bachofen's *Das Mutterrecht* ("The Mother Right") as Wharton's source, Ammons concludes that the matriarchal theories of the nineteenth century shape Wharton's sense of mothering and power (192). Yet we know that Wharton came to distrust those matriarchal theories which were the very same as had fueled the totalitarian eugenic politics she most feared. Wharton trained her hatred of radicalism in general and bolshevism in particular on such domestic policies, and she also denounces American anti-foreign activity for its ritualistic and totemic bloodshed. In fact, Wharton discredited this vision of cultural formation in favor of a sociological one, a vision meant to defeat the rising tide of xenophobia, immigration restriction, and 100%-Americanism as social bywords.

As Claudia Koonz argues in "Genocide and Eugenics," the prevailing sentiment after World War I was inspired by the wide support for the 1926 law stipulating forced sterilization laws: "Oliver Wendell Holmes wrote the majority decision—declaring that after so many of the nation's finest had sacrificed their lives in World War I, it would not represent a great sacrifice if the least qualified gave up their potential to reproduce" (156). Such a bio-political dimension of modern science was central to the theory behind Nazism in particular, and modern culture in general. Marked by instability in established religious, familial, and communal life, the culture sought radical bio-political solutions, like sterilization of the "unfit," while growing nostalgic for the past. Wharton's solutions, however, did not take a reactionary form. Instead, she tried to divest authoritative mass-produced culture of its alienating control over individuals. Whether the threat was a standardized beauty (as it was in *The Children*) or the more blatant class argument for twilight sleep and eugenic legislation, Wharton blasted the simplification in such measures and the state regulation of the individual. As Nancy Stepan and Sander Gilman argue in "Appropriating the Idioms of Science: The Rejection of Scientific Racism," the rhetorical power of late nineteenth-century science rested in its claims of objectivity, neutrality, and universality; in order to present an intellectual resistance to these claims, one had to appropriate scientific idioms to subvert them. "From 1870 to 1920, science became more specialized and authoritative as a cultural resource and language of interpretation. . . . The outcome was a narrowing of the cultural space within which, and the cultural forms by which, the claims of biological determinism could be effectively challenged" (80). In *The Age of Innocence,* Wharton begins to revise the ethical and political claims of the new sciences and their explanatory force. In doing so, she posits fiction's moral force against the determinism of science by subverting science's own terms and theories. In taking up the contradictions of human nature, she suggested that desire is more variegated than the movements for birth control, marriage, or family studies policy were allowing for.

Ultimately, Wharton sought to unravel the implicit ties between the early twentieth-century campaign for racial purity and the cult of feminine purity she herself inherited as a legacy of nineteenth-century domestic life. Almost every Wharton novel of the twenties centers on divorce (engineered by a New Woman), with divorce serving as Wharton's dominant trope for the disruption of the bourgeois family. Unlike contemporary writers such as Charlotte Perkins Gilman and Gertrude Atherton, Wharton resisted the call of eugenics schemes as a bulwark against changes in the social "trend."[2]

Appearing in 1920, the year that saw a great wave of anti-foreign incidents culminating in the second wave of the KKK and the Anti-Immigration Act of 1924, but set in the 1870s, Wharton's *Age of Innocence* links two central preoccupations, women's purity and hereditary purity—concerns that come unnervingly together in the person of Ellen Olenska. What critics have called May Wellandism is less nostalgia for the cult of true womanhood and more the fantasy of women's freedom from such demands. Throughout the novel, Wharton links Ellen to the fears of racial impurity and even to the anti-immigrationist sentiment contemporaneous to this novel. May Welland, on the other hand, is associated with a no less disquieting social blindness. Newland Archer contemplates May's ambiguous "abysmal purity" (7) and what marriage to "that terrifying product of the social system he belonged to and believed in" might mean: "the young girl who knew nothing and expected everything, looked back at him like a stranger through May Welland's familiar features; and once more it was borne in on him that marriage was not the safe anchorage he had been taught to think, but a voyage on uncharted seas" (43). As much as anything, Archer's "readings in anthropology" affect his view of this situation (69). Indeed, the 1870s witnessed a passion for social science, especially anthropology, matched only in Wharton's time by the twenties' consequent fascination for the primitive.

The anthropology that people would have been reading in the 1870s was hereditarianist in kind, drawing on theories of instinct to describe human nature, and Archer himself is learning to see the world through his new anthropological framework.

Marriage becomes more complicated for Archer precisely because he interprets it as a ritual function, exorcising impure and threatening social elements. Newland's rumored adultery with Ellen is also much more complex than it appears, in that, for him, their love affair threatens the ritual transmission of American cultural values. The anxiety over foreign contamination and amalgamation guarantees the ritual exclusion of Ellen from the family. Not only is she married to a foreigner, but she is also likened to gipsies and aligned with Mediterranean stock, and with an Eastern European stock as embodied in the Polish Count Olenski.

Archer's worry merely renders small the novel's claims about intermarriage and how its dangers clarify the perceived threat to cultural transmission: the Albany Chiverses had "insanity recurring in every second generation" (10) and Ellen Olenska's Uncle Thorley Chivers dies in a madhouse (60). The lessons of intermarriage and eugenics are clear: marriage is much less an affair of the heart and more a social cement, one which could be used to yield "blameless stock" (12). The "family," as the critical backdrop of Wharton's novel, is something to be investigated and guarded to preserve its purity. When Newland Archer's mother worries that the "trend" was changing Old New York, she sees it embodied not only in Ellen's bohemianism but also in that professor of archeology, Emerson Sillerton, a member of "a venerable and venerated family tree" (219). Mrs. Welland especially objects to the professor's giving a party for a "black man," but it is impossible to tell whether she objects to the guest of honor or the party's timing, since the party coincides with Julia Mingott's *thé dansant* (220). For the Wellands, blacks appear only as a supply of house servants in St. Augustine or as Mrs. Mingott's maid. Mrs. Welland expects the professor to know that her *kind* does not mix socially in the black man's society: "No one in the Mingott set could understand why Amy Sillerton had submitted so tamely to the eccentricities of a husband who filled the house with long-haired men and short-haired women, and, when he traveled, took her to explore tombs in Yucatan instead of going to Paris or Italy. But there they were, set in their ways, and apparently unaware that they were different from other people" (220).

At every turn, Wharton parodies the good breeding of her characters, whose genetic lines are assumed to assure "congenital" supremacy. When describing Lawrence Lefferts, she trivializes the character traits phrenology was once assumed to reveal: "One had only to look at him, from the slant of his bald forehead and the curve of his beautiful fair moustache to the long patent-leather feet at the other end of his lean and elegant person, to feel that the knowledge of 'form' must be congenital in any one who knew how to wear such good clothes so carelessly and carry such height with so much lounging grace" (8). With little more than a knowledge of form to promote himself, Lefferts gossips and snipes. Personal qualities seemed to have been purged from the leisure classes, and Archer wonders about May whether "'niceness' carried to that supreme degree were only a negation, the curtain dropped before an emptiness?" (211). Repeating a fear she had first expressed in *French Ways and Their Meaning,* Wharton has Archer liken May Welland to the Kentucky cavefish, blind and able only to "look out blankly at blankness" (83). In this way, Archer comes to realize that the good breeding he once believed in is little more than "factitious purity" (46).

Arguably the most famous passage from *The Age of Innocence,* as I have suggested in the Introduction, concerns the "arbitrary signs" of the "hieroglyphic world" Wharton depicts. Following that passage is another which suggests how anthropology, one of the new social sciences popularized in the late nineteenth century, had begun to influence "advanced culture": one of those arbitrary signs is Mrs. Welland's "air of having had her hand forced [in the announcement of her daughter's engagement], quite as, in the books on Primitive Man that people of advanced culture were beginning to read, the savage bride is dragged with shrieks from her parents' tent" (45). Books about Primitive Man were the rage; they kindled in Wharton the sense that the line between primitive and advanced was as arbitrary, but no less powerful, than any other sign in culture. Preserved in the rite of marriage is the "elaborate system of mystification" Newland Archer recognizes as cultural lore about the exchange of the young girl in marriage, which is the subject of at least one of Malinowski's books and of several other contemporaneous anthropological texts, and of the new sexology that Havelock Ellis and Sam Schmalhausen codified. Here Archer fears that May cannot survive in his world, since social purity demands that women become blind to passion and that the power of "insight" be bred out of them (83).

To this extent the commonly-held functionalist view of the family as regulatory force is the object of Wharton's criticism. The family's irregularities and permutations interested the writer as important human and familial variations. In this regard, a key word in *The Age of Innocence* is "bohemianism" with which Ellen is associated: even as a child she is dressed as a "gipsy foundling" instead of in black American mourning clothes for her parents (60); she is linked to the "gipsy-looking people" Wharton had first discussed in Charity's lineage in *Summer*. Katherine Joslin reads "the Bohemian Peril" embodied in Ellen as a threat to Old New York and to Newland, since bohemia is "a world of independent ideas and artistic expression" (Joslin 106–7). Yet the reference to the bohemian in this novel is not to the artistic world of the 1920s but to the influx of Bohemian immigrants of the 1870s. The "Bohemian" in the novel refers first to the largely peasant immigrants from Eastern Europe, not the few spirited inhabitants of the social and sexual enclaves of New York. This confusion may well be deliberate, significantly so because it illustrates the connections Wharton makes between European immigration and the artistic and intellectual freedom that followed. Reading the "Bohemian" in the novel simply as a sexual threat, then, ignores the 1870s anthropological influence. That Wharton creates an amalgam of 1870s and 1920s cultures is telling: the bohemian life represented a threat to culture not because of its sexual permissiveness per se but because of what it suggested about heredity and radical thought. Remember that the "Bohemian" is associated with Mediterranean stock: Marchioness Manson's Spanish shawls, Nastasia's Sicilian accent and "swarthy foreign-looking" demeanor (70), and Ned Winsett's radical intellectualism are all distrusted as expressions of inferior ancestry compared to Nordic roots, not to mention the failed European revolutions of 1848–49: "Archer, who dressed in the evening because he thought it cleaner and more comfortable to do so, and who had never stopped to consider that cleanliness and comfort are two of the costliest items in a modest budget, regarded Winsett's attitude as part of the boring 'Bohemian' pose that always made fashionable people who changed their clothes without talking about it, and were not forever harping on the number of servants one kept, seem so much simpler and less self-conscious than the others. Nevertheless, he was always stimulated by Winsett . . ." (124). Winsett's greatest wish is to emigrate, and he addresses his radical bent to a sympathetic but ironic Archer: "You'll never amount to anything, any of you, till you roll up your sleeves and get right down into the muck" (126). Winsett implies that Archer might end up like the social gadfly Larry Lefferts, shallow and smug, unless he commits himself to radical change, namely politics. Where Winsett fails, Ellen succeeds in compelling Archer to be "once more conscious of the curious way in which she reversed his values" (104).

Ned Winsett lives in the same bohemian neighborhood as Ellen, which Ellen's family dislikes. It was "not the peril but the poverty" to which her family objected, the relative squalor of "a 'Bohemian' quarter given over to 'people who wrote'" (104). "People who wrote" as the neighborhood's principle of inclusion suggests that intellect and inclination, and temperament and talent, would presumably distinguish who belonged and who didn't much better than heredity or money—and this was a situation not to be abided. Yet its poverty is explicitly linked to a self-consciousness, to the extent that writing and privation were closely associated with peril, both in politics and waning culture. Wharton is quick to undermine this danger, however, since Winsett's and Ellen's lives are intertwined by an act of kindness Ellen does for Ned's little boy, whose leg she bandages when she sees him hurt in the street outside her house. Here Ellen's foreign threat is domesticated by one democratic act of kindness. The subtler impact of the scene is also part of Wharton's strategy: the maternal instinct, seen as a universal trait binding all women together, served to show how all women held the same values of family and home that Americans did. By appealing to a kind of universal motherhood, Ellen Olenska—"bare-headed, carrying [the son] in her arms, with his knee all beautifully bandaged, and . . . so sympathetic and beautiful"—represents the "better" sort of immigrant, the maternal symbol of the universal family (123).

Or does she? This image of Ellen is almost immediately reversed when she appears out of the "armor" ladies usually wore in the evening. Wharton's ambivalence about Ellen is never so clear as when Ellen appears as the Venus in Furs, the figure for whom Leopold von Sacher-Masoch named his 1870 novel. Wharton's depiction of Ellen's attire—"heedless of tradition"—closely recalls Sacher-Masoch's icon of masochism: "But Madame Olenska . . . was attired in a long robe of red velvet bordered about the chin and down the front with glossy black fur. Archer remembered, on his last visit to Paris, seeing a portrait by the new painter, Carolus Duran, whose pictures were the sensation of the Salon, in which the lady wore one of these bold sheath-like robes with her chin nestling in fur. There was something perverse and provocative in the notion of fur worn in the evening in a heated drawing room, and in the combination of a muffled throat and bare arms; but the effect was undeniably pleasing" (105–6). Sacher-Masoch's hero Severin, who becomes the love slave of the masochist Wanda in the 1870 novel, feels the same about seeing his mistress draped in furs: at various points, Severin (whom Wanda renames Gregor) associates the furs with cruelty, despotism, and tyranny (108). Their symbolic meaning is tied to masochistic love, as Severin declares: "I have repeatedly told you that suffering has a peculiar attraction for me. Nothing can intensify my passion more than tyranny, cruelty, and especially the faithlessness of a beautiful woman" (75).

Why does Wharton identify her heroine with the sensational confessions of the masochist? One could argue that she merely employs this reference as a cultural marker for the historical setting, just as she refers to *Middlemarch* and books by Herbert Spencer and Alphonse Daudet (Archer's impatiently awaited books from London) to give her novel the social texture that the realist novel required. Yet the comparison is more deliberate since the novel concerns Ellen's erotic control over Archer, with one lover as the hammer, the other as the anvil, as Sacher-Masoch has it. Drawing as it does on the contemporaneous images of sadomasochism, Ellen's appearance as the Venus in Furs gives the lie to Wharton's ironic title, "age of innocence," since the age was not innocent but embroiled in new sexological debates about sadomasochism and perversion. The "age" of the novel is not innocent; rather, it is the "age" that lost the struggle to preserve innocence and that set in motion the corruptions to come. In this context, Wharton's matriarch, Catherine the Great, the nickname of old Catherine Mingott, is also ironic: as Sacher-Masoch, among others, suggests, she was history's first sadist. The heroine of *Venus in Furs,* Wanda, instructs her slave Severin about the moral of his punishment: "I may confess to you that I loved you deeply. You yourself, however, stifled my love by your fantastic devotion and your insane passion. From the moment that you became my slave, I knew it would be impossible for you ever to become my husband . . ." (238). Ellen's lesson to Archer is no different: Archer is willing to abandon himself to his ideal of Ellen, without making her his equal. He wants to be her slave, to be dominated by her worldliness. Archer's abjection at Ellen's hands supplants the fantasy of cultural purity underwriting the age's pretense of innocence and taste, in a novel where divorce and default are the most popular topics of conversation.

If passion is instinctual and inherited, as some sociologists argued, then those who would give themselves over to it—like Ellen and like Archer—must be disciplined from within the familial ranks. May's pregnancy proves to be just such a retaliatory function, reining in Archer just as he is about to stray. May prematurely assures Ellen that the Newland Archers are about to have a baby, an announcement that in clinching Ellen's allegiance to familial order proves to be an internally motivated regulation by the family. As a weapon against Ellen, May's intimation of her pregnancy takes on an unethical cast; in miniature, this act harbingers the state regulation of families through eugenics, which was portentous for Wharton. Nevertheless, that Newland and May's three children are studies in human variation and heredity—Mary and Bill like their mother, but Dallas ready to marry the exiled Julius Beaufort's daughter, Fanny—suggests that these human variations are necessary to revitalize culture and to establish "more tolerant views. There was good in the new order too" (349), Archer reflects.

At the end of the novel, Archer contemplates the scientific changes of technological modernity in this new order: "There would one day be a tunnel under the Hudson through which the trains of the Pennsylvania railway would run straight into New York. They were of the brotherhood of visionaries who likewise predicted the building of ships that would cross the Atlantic in five days, the invention of a flying machine, lighting by electricity, telephonic communication without wires, and other Arabian Night marvels" (284). He conjectures that these modern inventions would propel changes in social behavior and compel human adaptability to them. Yet Wharton represents the antimodern impulse, too, in *The Age of Innocence,* in a group whose nostalgia for simpler, less self-conscious life leads them to recreate it. A brotherhood of visionaries, Dr. Carver's Community offered spiritual antidotes to the general fears of a disintegrating society. While Archer fosters his alienation as his refuge from Family, Carver's meetings try to combat such feelings in their outward search for meaning and simplification of life. At the same time, one response to the new anthropology is suggested by the vague transcendentalism of Dr. Carver's "Valley of Love Community," his theories of "Direct Contact," and his "Inner Thought" meetings (158–60, 184, 208). These are antidotes to the general sense of cultural decline the Wellands name the "trend." But they are also, as Jackson Lears suggests, ballast for antimodernism. For Lears these communities arose in opposition to the new ethnic and class-divided laborer societies in urban centers. What the "overcivilized bourgeoisie" needed was a self-improvement community of their own, derived from the Protestant evangelical tradition and with a certain antimodern appeal (see Lears 1981, 71–73).

Even so, Wharton distances herself—and Archer—from these radical antimodernists in that she returns to Ned Winsett's claim for sustained, however tentative, political engagement. Archer's own refusal as a "gentleman" to enter politics early in life is drawn from his indifference to collective politics and a belief—as his above rumination suggests—in technological and scientific progress. That he later enters politics under the mentorship of Teddy Roosevelt suggests how shaken his vision of innocence has been. For Archer, the new society has courage, but he has no conviction in it: "The young men nowadays were emancipating themselves from the law and business and taking up all sorts of new things. If they were not absorbed in state politics or municipal reform, the chances were that they were going in for Central American archaeology" (345).

Once again, South America serves as Wharton's dystopia of political evasion, as it had in *The Reef* and *The Children* in particular.

The contradiction between Wharton's professed interest in the new anthropology and her hatred of the so-called primitive such as Harlem life—or, here, her scorn for antimodern primitives—cannot be over-emphasized. She writes approvingly of the discoveries of anthropology at the same time that she relegates blacks to "the local African supply" of servants (143). Franz Boas's 1911 *The Mind of Primitive Man* changed social science in its insistence on the complexity of the "primitive," argu-ing for the equality of mind between primitive and civilized—a tack Wharton also seems to take in *The Age of Innocence* by showing how primitive the rituals of bloodshedding, potlatch, and fetishism were in New York society. On the other hand, while Wharton launches an attack on the neo-primitivism of the Simple Lifers in Dr. Carver's communities and brotherhoods, she objects to the representation of the primitive as Van Vechten celebrates it in *Nigger Heaven,* since its simplifications seem to her to glorify primitive over civilized consciousness. Wharton knew that civilization could not return to such profound "innocence," and saw in the worship of the primitive in modern jazz the same distorted and misguided resistances to the enervation and commercialization of mod-ern life that she did in Carver's Valley of Love Communities. The way to salvation and happiness, for Wharton, led through the much more com-plex terrain of cultural contradictions, by embracing the ambivalence that was so much a part of modern life for her. To see the "beyondness of things" (137), as her heroine Nan St. George in *The Buccaneers* later expresses it, was the goal of the "inner life" and the focus of Wharton's last novel (see Hoffman 269).

Wharton's Last Novel

In *The Buccaneers,* Wharton writes another historical romance, a genre that allows her, as it had in *The Age of Innocence,* to treat aristocratic manners and xenophobic thinking in a setting more comfortable and comical than a novel set in the turbulent present of the thirties. The novel follows the vicissitudes of 1870s fashionable society, along with the fates of two families whose beautiful but undisciplined daughters fail to make social connections in New York. Their failure induces the governess, Laura Testvalley, to take her charge, Nan St. George, and her older sister Virginia, and Lizzy Elmsworth on a "buccaneering" voyage in England, where the governess can oversee their social success. The St. George girls—Virginia and Annabel, or Nan—marry English aristocrats, the handsome Lord Seadown and the dour Duke of Tintagel, respectively. Yet their "buccaneering" success does not result in happy marriages, and Nan's developing consciousness of her misery is the primary focus of the last third of the novel.[3]

Readers know that Wharton's marriage plots do not hinge on the success or failure of the individual, but on the entire class and racial heritage of the eligible suitors and women "out" in society. Conchita Closson's engagement to Lord Richard Marable sparks the first scandal of the novel. Conchita's mother enters fashionable Saratoga society under the supervision of Mrs. St. George and Mrs. Elmsworth, two of the more established visitors at the summer resort. Attached to one of New York's new moneyed men, Mrs. Closson is a Brazilian divorcee who may or may not be black (her daughter's skin is "dark") and who may or may not be actually married. When the Closson daughter, Conchita, is engaged to Lord Richard Marable, who is vacationing in Saratoga with his Brazilian friend, Teddy de Santos-Dios, all the "anguished mother" of the British groom can do is contact Laura Testvalley to ask the crucial question: "Is she black?" (91–92). Variously referred to as "dark" or "brown," with her Italian blood marking her as foreign, the governess Laura Testvalley herself is a mixture of Italian and British blood, a relation to Gabriel Rossetti, uniting the Italian Testavaglias with "exiled revolutionaries and antipapists, producing sons who were artists and agnostics, and daughters who were evangelicals of the strictest pattern, and governesses in the highest families" (40). However, *The Buccaneers* has a markedly different tone than the foreboding *Summer,* which exploits a similar fear of intermarriage between North Dormer and the Mountain, the high and low cultures. In the twenty years between the novels, Wharton transforms the terrors of cultural amalgamation from a drama into a satire. While, in 1917, intermarriage among classes proved the stuff of serious debate, by the thirties it recedes but does not disappear as one of the world's problems; Mussolini and Hitler were threatening a much greater solution to the apparent decline of the West. The ominous tone of *Summer* becomes a parodic one in *The Buccaneers* in order to suggest the magnitude of political problems greater than intermarriage.

Juxtaposed against English manners, the "unknown ground of American customs" is the subject of this novel, yet Wharton's treatment has changed significantly since *The Age of Innocence,* becoming more sympathetic in this final work. The upheaval of culture creates the possibility, if not the fact, that a "black" Brazilian woman could marry an English Lord. In the same vein, the Dowager Duchess, the Duke's mother, considers the heroine of the novel, poetic Nan, uncivilized: "To all his people it was as if Ushant [the Duke of Tintagel] had married a savage . . ." (309). After an argument with her husband, Nan miscarries her first baby and, afterward, fails to produce an heir to the Tintagel line since she refuses sexual relations with him: "He, the Duke of Tintagel, wanted a son, he had a right to expect a son, he would have had a son, if this woman's criminal folly had not destroyed his hopes . . ." (259). She breaks with the Duke over his refusal to reform his tenants' village, their badly drained cottages and their infected milk. While she is ignorant of "organized beneficence," she resists his "manifold inhibitions" and his stubborn suppression of reform: "I tell you I don't want a child if he's to be brought up with such ideas, if he's to be taught, as you have been, that it's right and natural to live in a palace with fifty servants, and not care for the people who are slaving for him . . ." (254–55).

Nan St. George is dissatisfied with the parties and games which satiate her sister and their friends. After her marriage, she is even more disgruntled with life as a Duchess under the young Duke's diffident command. She grows estranged from her husband, decides to leave him and, with the help of Laura Testvalley, runs off with Guy Thwarte, whom she had briefly met before he left to make his fortune in Brazil. Although Wharton did not finish the novel, her plan for its conclusion suggests this ending: Laura Testvalley is compromised by the scandal, and her lover, Sir Helmsley Thwarte, "breaks with her, and the great old adventuress, seeing love, deep and abiding love, triumph for the first time in her career, helps Nan to join her lover, who has been ordered to South Africa, and then goes back alone to old age and poverty" (358–59).

None of this would be unusual in a marriage plot, except that Wharton takes great pains to link Laura Testvalley to the Italian revolution—the Risorgimento, in which her grandfather was a "fomenter of insurrections"—in 1848 (40).[4] The novel gives us a clue to Wharton's attitude toward cultural assimilation, since Laura Testvalley is the pivotal figure on whom Nan St. George's future depends. In characteristic fashion, Wharton transforms that radical spirit into a psychological trait associated with Laura's heredity. Laura Testvalley is connected through familial heritage to "revolutionary radicalism," a heritage from which she derives the courage to help Nan escape from the petty tyrannies of her marriage. The three main characters, then, are linked by their association with foreignness and adventure, transgression and revolution. Once again, Wharton sends her troubled hero to South America, only this hero, unlike the bachelors Martin Boyne in *The Children* and George Darrow in *The Reef,* finally returns to his home in England. As Gloria

Erlich astutely observes, "Any form of contact with Brazil seems to un-ravel Anglo-Saxon inhibitions and liberate the instincts. The experience of working on a Brazilian plantation loosens up the social behavior of several of the young men. The most unashamedly sensuous of the 'bucca-neering' girls, Conchita de Santos-Dios (but known by her step-father's name, Closson) comes from Brazil" (160).

In fact, off-stage as it were, Guy Thwarte had been married to a young Brazilian woman, Paquita; she dies, but not before he realizes that he had made a mistake in trying to "strip his mind of conventions and face the hard reality underneath. It was inconceivable to him now that, in the first months of his marriage, he had actually dreamed of severing all ties with home, and beginning life anew as a Brazilian mine-owner" (269). Even though Guy Thwarte, flexible as he may be, cannot imagine absolute assimilation into Brazilian culture any more than he can forget the con-ventions and the reality of his attachment to the conservative values of his father's England, Wharton suggests that the amalgamation of cul-tures—the English and Brazilian or the American and the British—leads to a more passionate, less reactionary society.

If Brazil is one source of trouble to established English manners, the English also find fault in "exaggerated" American customs and promis-cuous manners. Confusing the Virigina Reel with an old dance "the Wild Indians" had once taught the Americans, the British matrons at the new Duke and Duchess's hunting party decry what they see as the end of tradition. At the piano sits Lord Brightlingsea, and Sir Helmsely Thwarte, as the Dowager Duchess remarks, sits nearby "clapping his hands and stamping his sound foot in time with Lady Dick's Negro chant—they said it was Negro. All so very unusual, especially when associated with Christmas. . . . Usually that noisy sort of singing was left to the waits, wasn't it? But under this new rule the Dowager's enquiring eye-glass was really a window opening into an unknown world—a world in whose reality she could not bring herself to believe" (278). The Negro chant and "nigger-minstrel shows" (243), the attendants and the waits, the black Brazilians, the brown Italian governess, the savage Americans—all of these are part of Wharton's comedy of assimilation into fashionable London society.

The "transatlantic invaders" have brought with them a vast array of cultural entertainments which offend the hierarchy of value the English aristocracy had established. Negro chants and savage dances (the Vir-ginia reel, where reversing one's partner is considered the height of "in-delicacy") are the topics of the Dowager Duchess's conversation with her British friends, who discuss racial mixing and transatlantic crossings in

English and American intermarriages. Their fear of cultural disintegration is displaced onto the rites and customs of the American buccaneers. In polite society, even the tormented mother of Lord Richard Marable, Lady Brightlingsea, can only muster the timid, but oft-repeated question "Is she black?" about her new daughter-in-law, Conchita. Yet the repressed fears of miscegenation and of mixing cultures are symbolically displaced, only to appear in the novel's repetition of various transgressions against English custom. The historical novel, thus, treats these fears in repressed but repeated reminders of the foreignness of Brazilians, Italians, and Americans on the British scene.

The Negro chants and "nigger-minstrel" show which the Americans and Brazilians introduce to British society are the critical points of entry into the ways in which customs and rituals displace the discussions of the fears absorbing the novel's historical and social scene. In a sense, those preoccupations were still central in 1937, since the rise of Nazism and fascism made the question of social origins controversial again. In a letter to his son in Brazil, Sir Helmsley Thwarte writes of the "subversive times" when "the American backwoodsman and his females" seem to be colonizing Britain and the aristocracy loses its "importance as custodians of historical tradition and of high (if narrow) social standards" (230–32). His letter continues: "When Lady Brightlingsea heard of Dick Marable's engagement to the Brazilian beauty she cabled to the St. Georges' governess: 'Is she black?' . . . Their bewilderment is so great that, when one of the girls spoke of archery clubs being fashionable in the States, somebody blurted out: 'I suppose the Indians taught you?'" (233–34).

These "subversive times" that the father documents for his son— including the pivotal question of the novel, "Is she black?"—are crystallized in the minstrel shows the buccaneering girls imitate for their British aristocratic society. As Conchita explains to one of the American buccaneer girls, "The men are blissfully happy in a house where nobody chaperons them, and they can smoke in every room, and gaze at you and Virginia [St. George], and laugh at my jokes, and join in my nigger songs. . . . If we stick to the rules of the game, and don't play any low-down tricks on each other . . . we'll have all London in our pocket next year" (158). Hers is the strategy of the adventuress, employing the "con game," as Eric Lott terms it, of blackface minstrelsy to disguise her purposes (Lott 1992, 44). Later in the novel, after Virginia's marriage to Lord Seadown, "Lady Seadown was said to be getting up an amateur nigger-minstrel performance for the Christmas party at Allfriars, and as for the wild games introduced into country-house parties, there was no denying that, even after a hard day's hunting or shooting, they could tear the men from their after-dinner torpor" (243). In both cases, the Negro songs and performances are associated with the repressed and then unleashed passions of British men, who are attracted to the variously black, brown, and savage women from Brazil, Italy, and America.

As Lott suggests about the history of blackface minstrelsy, a carnivalesque performance that obscured its relation to slavery by "pretending that slavery was amusing, right, and natural" (23), the pleasure of the performance was linked to the abandoning of "the normally repressive boundaries of bodily orifices [so that] the white subject could transform fantasies of racial assault and subversion into riotous pleasure, turn insurrection and intermixture into harmless fun—though the outlines of the fun disclose its troubled sources. . . . This, of course, was neither the first nor the last time an ambivalent white male attraction to blacks, (self-) degradation, and infantile pleasure were conjoined by way of an imaginary racial Other" (31–32). The two most aristocratic men—Lord Brightlingsea and Helmsley Thwarte—are also attracted, but eventually repress, their desires for the society of Conchita Closson and Laura Testvalley, the black and brown women of this novel, suspending their conscious allegiance to, as Thwarte puts it in his letter to his son Guy, "duty," "tribal loyalty," and protecting "social origins" (230–32). Instead, they "go native"[5] in enjoying the minstrel and Negro songs, the displaced desire for transgression with "foreign" women sublimated by the fun of indulging in what they consider "savage" American customs. As Lott suggests, "an aura of illicit sexuality—nineteenth-century observers called it 'vulgarity'—shadowed the most chaste of minstrel shows. From the start it appeared that a sort of generalized illicitness was indeed one of minstrelsy's main objectives" (25). Unlike the Duke of Tintagel who, as his young American wife Nan says, "hates anything foreign" (285), the other men contain their desires through the displaced symbolic fulfillment of Negro songs, chants, minstrel shows and, of course, Conchita's jokes. They can ambivalently indulge in foreign pleasures at the same time that Helmsley reinforces his "tribal duty" to British Dukes and Duchesses. When he foregoes marriage to Laura Testvalley because of her complicity in the scandal, he is finally asserting his loyalty to ancestral British social and racial norms.

While the minstrel show had as its objective the staging of racial boundaries (see Lott 27), Wharton invokes that history to perform the opposite function in this novel: the English aristocracy and gentry cannot hold the line against the American invaders. The invocation of the American racial other, the Negro, leads the British to contemplate a whole legion of others against whom they must defend themselves and their traditions: Brazilian and Latin American invaders, in the person of Conchita Closson Marable; Italian revolutionaries, such as the Rossettis and the passionate governess Laura Testvalley; and the savage Americans, whose most naive representative, Nan, proves to be much more intractable than any of the others.

The minstrel show, Wharton's trope for black culture, allows the temporary, carnivalesque abandonment of high and low cultural distinctions. Nevertheless, Wharton is split about this cultural form, as she had been about other forms of authentic and inauthentic "folk" culture and mass-produced art. It is, after all, the "foreign" women who introduce the Negro songs and sexual laxity into London society, as if these buccaneering women need to shore up their own cultural superiority by invoking slavery and racial superiority. Losing ground themselves in English society, they must constantly amuse and thus establish their own cultural value by raising the specter of racism implicit in the minstrel show. There is no indication that Wharton was aware of her own "racial unconscious," as Eric Lott terms the repressed anxieties about the color line invoked in the minstrel show. In fact, the minstrel show creates in Sir Helmsley Thwarte a greater consciousness that he must defend "social origins" against the invaders from America: "My poor friend Blanche [Tintagel, the Dowager Duchess] would faint if she knew that I had actually ventured to imagine what an England without Dukes might be, perhaps may soon be; but she would be restored to her senses if she knew that, after weighing the evidence for and against, I have decided that, having been afflicted with Dukes, we'd better keep 'em" (232). The minstrel show unconsciously raises the stakes of the American invasion from the matter of social class to one of racial amalgamation. What Wharton only hesitantly, often ambiguously, broached in *The Age of Innocence* gets a braver treatment in this novel.

As Wharton's late novels show, the very invocation of these color and culture lines suggests the anxieties and instabilities of hierarchical structures of privilege. Wharton's last finished pages are telling in that they seem to document the British resignation to American "breezy independence": "The free and easy Americanism of this little band of invaders had taken the world of fashion by storm, and Hector Robinson [a Conservative member of Parliament married to Lizzy Elmsworth, one of the original American buccaneers] was too alert not to have noted the renovation of the social atmosphere. 'Wherever the men are amused, fashion is bound to follow,' was one of Lizzy's axioms; and certainly, from their future sovereign to his most newly knighted subject, the men *were* amused in Mayfair's American drawing-rooms" (355). This is the least threatening of all the cultural amalgamations that the mix of Brazilians, Americans, Italians, and British portends. These last words of this unfinished novel suggest a possible change of heart and a new tolerance for the "new America" that Wharton was not capable of in *The Mother's Recompense*. As she writes to Elisina Tyler in the thirties, it seemed "strange to hold one's head up again when one's country is spoken of" (n.d., Lilly Library). Yet she does not celebrate the antihierarchical, carnivalesque minstrel-show performances by Conchita or Virginia, whose acts neither liberate nor radicalize the English. Rather, Wharton creates an amalgam of the stiff British aristocracy and the rowdy American buccaneer.

That is, Wharton divides her characters into three categories: first, the sympathetic ones who reveal their passions directly, as Guy Thwarte, Nan St. George, and Laura Testvalley do; second, the ambivalent ones who channel their frustrations and aggressions into symbolic rituals of London society, such as Virginia St. George and Helmsley Thwarte, along with other fashionable society-mongers; and third, the most unsympathetic of Wharton's characters, those who repress all of their passions, such as the Duke of Tintagel, who "dissects" and "dismembers" clocks for entertainment and his mother, who gardens "with a guilty fervour" (311, 322). Clocks and gardens are the operative metaphors these two use to contain the threat of foreignness. For instance, the Duke's mother warns him that "women are not quite as simple as clocks" (245). Nan's fantasy about social reform makes her more sympathetic than her sororal cohort or her clock-winding, hot-house-gardening relatives. In fact, when Ushant tries to strike a sexual bargain with Nan, offering her the money she requested to pay off Conchita's debts, Nan refuses, using the proposition to break for good with her husband. Neither the mother nor the son has the means to express the "storm of unaccustomed emotion" that Nan visits upon them (330).

While the "middle" category provides Wharton with her social satire and comedy of manners, the last category represents the most dangerous type, since their repressed desire returns in the wish to dominate others. Repressed desire proves to be dangerous to those who attempt to control or deny it. Both the Duke of Tintagel and his mother the Dowager Duchess think Nan should be "shield[ed] from every contact with life," and the Duke admits to marrying her "to form her" (227, 245). But her sympathy—and our readerly identification—is directed at those three characters who have made early romantic mistakes. First, Laura's early entanglement with Lord Richard Marable was a "fugitive adventure" (60) that had been short and secret. Second, Guy Thwarte's impulsive Brazilian tie was, as one British character remarked, "an unfortunate marriage . . .—but luckily the young woman died . . . leaving him a fortune'" (338). Finally, Nan's naive acceptance of the dull Duke's marriage offer crystallizes Wharton's change in attitude about transgression. If once such transgressions embarrassed or irritated her, here she is even sympathetic.

Such activities as cardplaying, dancing, and chanting allow the characters a symbolic lexicon by which repressed passions are channeled. The real fears of insurrection and revolution, figured in the novel as the repressed histories of America and Italy, are recast as fears of cultural trends and new indelicacies. Cardplaying expresses the general displacement of sexual transgression onto gaming and gambling, a stylizing of bluffing, bidding, and trumping. As Lily Bart and Kate Clephane had done before her, Virginia St. George plays for high stakes, and, at the end of the cardplaying scene, Virginia is forced by Lady Churt, Seadown's lover, to announce her engagement. Similarly, dancing the Virginia reel is one of the leisure activities of high society, but it, too, evokes passions that cannot be repressed. The dance brings together Nan and Guy; after the reel is over, Nan confesses her marital unhappiness to Guy. Yet the refusal to speak about these "trends," as Newland Archer's mother had called them in *The Age of Innocence,* leads to repressed terror and anxious projection. Just as Wharton had expressed her fear that the "world [is] at the mercy of two madmen" (16 September 1935, Lilly Library), so does the novel reveal the spectacle of symbolic aggression to which intolerance of any kind of cultural or racial difference gives rise. By 1937, too many people had come to identify their well-being through the very real aggressions that Hitler and Mussolini directed.

If *The Buccaneers* gives us two choices, between duty or obligation to nativist and nationalist thinking *or* transgression against tradition, Wharton finally opts for transgression, although it is associated with all her misgivings about the sexual promiscuity of the flapper and the financial insecurity of gambling, not to mention novel-writing. *The Buccaneers* is not, as Ammons contends, a novel that "suggests that the aging author was treating herself to a respite from her struggles with post-war problems" (196); rather, the novel is the culmination of her thinking through those problems, to what her character Nan called "the beyondness of things," that gives us a last vision of her faith in passion and commitment. Wharton's strategy all along has been to change the terms of our sympathetic identifications, compelling us to side with women who have constricted or conflicted choices. In doing so, she shows us that obstructed passion returns, as the repressed always does, in devastating ways.

Wharton's Spiritual Link

Wharton's war work and her charities are often cited when critics discuss her social philanthropy. Her commitment to war-relief charities is well-documented by R.W. B. Lewis and Alan Price, among others, including Wharton's editing of the *Book of the Homeless* to raise money, establishing relief charities for orphans and displaced Americans and Belgians. In Nan, Wharton gives us a woman most like herself before World War I, in the course of which she had learned independence, beneficence, and tolerance. Yet, Wharton is best known not for her charities, but for her mastery of the symbolic vocabulary of social gestures, rituals, and manners. Curiously, in many of her private letters written in the thirties, Wharton's relation to her pet Pekingese Linky functions as the symbolic exchanges and acts of a cultural negotiation—cardplaying, singing, and dancing—do in her novels. While Wharton criticizes the symbolic playing out of repressions in gambling, minstrel-shows, flapperism, drugging and dancing, she is never ambivalent about her sentimental investment in pets. Loving dogs, for Wharton, is a sign of civilization and sophistication, since caring for pets means respecting the difference between human and animal worlds. In his "Personal Memories of Edith Wharton," Bill Tyler writes that he came to know Wharton "maturely only in the last eight years of her life, between 1929 and 1937." His parents had been friends with Wharton since 1912, and their friendship was cemented by Bill's attachment to his own "first dog" (95, 98), a bond which let Wharton indulge in her favorite fancy. A 1934 letter to Tyler starts off with this greeting: "Linky and I have been waiting a long time to congratulate you and Betsy on the immense privilege of having under your roof a member of the Imperial race. . . . Linky is of course less awestruck than I am . . ." (Tyler 102). In 1937, Bill Tyler writes, "I received a letter from Linky, the Pekingese, expressing a great interest in the arrival of 'IT,' i.e., our son, born in December, and concluding with the words, 'The old woman was *so* pleased that you liked *Hudson River*'" (102–3). That Wharton would find respite from her sense of herself as "Edith Agonistes" and express such intimate details and professional hopes is more than an old woman's forgivable indulgence.

Marc Shell's recent argument about family pets bears investigation precisely because he dwells on the liminality of relations between humans and animals; he meditates on the status of pets as in between "familial kin" and "species kind" (ix). Shell demonstrates how the discussion about such a seemingly innocent classification of pets is linked to a greater discourse of racial and national classifications, suggesting "that pethood derives its power from its ability to let pet owners experience a relationship ever-present in political ideology—that between the distinction of those beings who are our (familial) kin from those who are not, on the one hand, and the distinction of those beings who are our (human) kind from those who are not, on the other" (148). There is no debate that Wharton's fictions deal with the often slippery connection between self and other, but I would argue that she tested all of this out on her last pet Pekingese, Linky.

Wharton's famous love of dogs gave her occasion to contemplate such distinctions; dogs were mediating creatures between the primitive and the civilized, and she maintained no sense of species inferiority. One of her early projects with Minnie Cadwalader Jones typifies that love: they tried to persuade the SPCA to put "drinking bowls in the streets for dogs" (letters to her niece Beatrix Farrand, 26 November 1935; 14 December 1935, Beinecke Library). In fact, Wharton regularly hired a "dog-knitter," Mlle. Robinet, who would make grizzly-bear coats for Linky and for Beatrix's dog, Cublet (to Beatrix Farrand, 7 October 1936, Beinecke Library). Mlle. Robinet was one of Wharton's personal wards, with little other support than that which Wharton gave her. Cynthia Ozick's "Justice 'Again' to Edith Wharton" treats Wharton's love of dogs as a "conspicuous replacement" for other passions; in dogs, Wharton saw the "*us*ness" and the "underlying *not-us*ness" of their being (17).

But Linky, Wharton's most beloved pet, also mediates between her and an increasing alienated world. What Edmund Leach calls the taboo-loaded are animals that are like and unlike humans. Linky fit this transitional category for Wharton. Writing in the voice of the dog, Wharton would advise others about treatments of pets, but also about her novels, about her health, and about political life in general. Again, to Bill Tyler on 16 May 1937, Wharton wrote that she "understood" what dogs said "ever since I was a baby. We really communicate with each other—& no one had such wise things to say as Linky . . ." (Lilly Library). According to Leach, "The English language classification of familiar animals is by no means a simple matter; it is not just a list of names, but a complex pattern of identifications subtly discriminated not only in kind but in psychological tone. Our linguistic treatment of these categories reflects taboo or ritual value, but these are simply portmanteau terms which cover a complex of feeling and attitude, a sense perhaps that aggression, as manifested either in sex or killing, is somehow a disturbance of the natural order of things, a kind of necessary impiety" (54). Although Shell takes issue with Leach's argument, both contend that pets are "intermediating beings between animals and humans" (169) and "an especially sensitive barometer of the way human beings grouped as nations are likely to treat one another" (170). Shell concludes by showing how pets act as symbolic registers of whether nonkin, extratribal humans are reified, dehumanized, or accepted and respected.

Wharton's late fictions show that she did believe in a natural order and that her fictions center on sex and violence as transgressions (consider the Beatrice Palmato fragment in this regard).[6] For a writer devoted to presenting taboo transgressions (like incest) in her fictions, it is no wonder that she understood early her relation to dogs as the one relation protected from betrayal and transgression. For Shell, pet-owning invites questions about such taboos and transgressions: "For all its outlandishness . . . at some level, pet love traduces (or transcends) two practices we ordinarily think of as being taboo": bestiality and incest. "Pet love thus toes the line between chaste, or socially sanctioned, attraction (between a human being and a being from inside his species and outside his family) and either bestial attraction (between a human being and an 'animal' being from outside humankind) or incestuous attraction (between a human being and a being from inside the particular kinship family)" (151). Either a transitional object or totem, as Shell suggests, the pet allows an uncontroversial demonstration of familial and sexual affection, "petting." The "quest for the Beast" allows one to flee incest, which is, in anthropology, "the law of laws" (154).[7] Again, whether or not we take Barbara White's compelling interpretation of Wharton's incest victimage as the truth, we do know that Wharton's fictions keep recurring to incest and symbolic incest. The next step is to see Linky as the mediation for totems and taboo, for Freudian psychoanalysis in general. Tolerance was Wharton's answer to totalitarian politics determined to turn others into animals, things, corpses.

Whether one subscribes to Shell's "outlandishness" or not, Linky allowed Wharton's sympathies their outlet, a need that fewer and fewer humans fulfilled at the end of her life. Perhaps Bettina Tyler, Bill's wife, jocularly expressed the sense of transgression best in her letter to Wharton on 11 March 1937: "It will [be] quite alright for the Pekingeses to cohabit with the baby, but . . . in that case I must decline all responsibility in the event of the dogs getting bitten" (Lilly Library). A world where babies might bite dogs, where everything is being turned upside down by madmen, where the inner life no longer seems possible: all these help to shape Wharton's brave new politics. While her views on race regrettably never altered, and always remained conventional, her celebration of gender and class privilege did change, bravely.

Notes
References
Index

Notes

Introduction

1.   Jackson Lears's recent work, "Sherwood Anderson: Looking for the White Spot," demonstrates the cross-gender search for authenticity—for sincerity and "for unproblematic immediacy in personal as well as artistic expressions" (16). Staving off the anonymous and alienated labor of the modern work force, writers like Anderson, Crane, Norris, Hemingway, Dreiser (Lears's examples), and Wharton tried to formulate the connection between "modernism and modernization"—which only appeared to be adversarial and antagonistic (14).

2.   Whether or not she does so as an incest survivor, as has recently been intelligently argued by Barbara White, is less a concern for my work than is her focus on reproductive crises in general.

3.   In demonstrating the political rhetoric of "nature," feminist theorists—from Hélène Cixous to Carroll Smith-Rosenberg—illustrate the powerful effects of that rhetoric. In trying to define women's nature—in natural childbirth, for example, as I will show in one historical instance—various camps manipulate the rhetoric of nature and culture. Manipulation of this kind indicates that history and power circulate through rhetoric, particularly in its manifestations as patriarchal authority and language. If feminist theory has taught new historicism and ethnography anything, it has been to distrust and subvert the authoritative rhetoric of objectivity. In the chapters to follow, I will argue that Wharton's satire and social criticism do the same.

I came to this feminist political strategy because of my interest in voice and rhetoric, my rejection of what James Clifford in *Writing Culture* has called "visualism" (11). Clifford's description of the ethnographer's project recalls my own emphasis on dialogism:

> Once cultures are no longer prefigured visually—as objects, theaters, texts—it becomes possible to think of a cultural poetics, that is an interplay of voices, of positioned utterances. In a discursive rather than a visual paradigm, the dominant metaphors for ethnography shift away from the disturbing eye toward expressive speech (and gesture). (12)

Perhaps the crucial difference between the visual and vocal metaphors is that the voices of history, literature, and science are no longer privileged over and against each other. In Clifford's terms, Bakhtin (1981) shows how "dialogical processes proliferate in any complexly represented discursive space. . . . Many voices clamor for expression" (Clifford 15). This description of method comes close to a certain kind of feminist criticism—one that challenges modes of truth to show how voices gain power, flourish, and die out in cultural conversation.

Clifford argues for avoiding the monologic or the univocal, advocating a criticism that is multivocal and resonating with the objects/subjects of study. In doing so, he focuses on the "complex, often ambivalent, potentially counter-hegemonic" (9) new ethnography. In this respect, he echoes Smith-Rosenberg's appeal to Bakhtin: "By positing 'language' (and, by extension, class) as the product of an unstable balance between the forces of cohesion and of diversity, Bakhtin may have suggested a next step for our analysis both of 'discourse' as a social construction and of the interaction of class and gender" (Smith-Rosenberg 1986, 37–38). Smith-Rosenberg's stance, like Clifford's, suggests reading historical discourse as rhetoric. Bakhtin's theories provide a socio-aesthetic reading that makes possible my approach of Wharton's politics, since her politics are contradictory on the issues of gender, class, and particularly race.

4. Tuttleton, among other writers, suggests that, during Wharton's writing of *The Reef,* Fullerton "was secretly engaged to his young cousin Katherine Fullerton" (294). Tuttleton documents the "pertinence" of Wharton's affair with Fullerton to the novel. See "Mocking Fate: Romantic Idealism in Edith Wharton's *The Reef.*"

5. Both Clare Colquitt and Alan Gribben comment on the exchange of letters between Wharton and Fullerton while she was writing *The Reef.* As Gribben explains, "Her letters explicitly seek Fullerton's editorial advice, even claiming (in 1912, in Letter 24) that her close friend 'Walter Berry has never read a line of The Reef' and 'takes not the slightest interest in [her] literature'" (13). Gribben notes that Wharton offered frequent advice about Fullerton's journalistic prose, which she denounced as leaden. She wanted his book on international politics, in Wharton's words, to "be read & talked of not only by the experts but by the big 'intelligent public'" (13). See also Colquitt, 100.

6. See Jules R. Benjamin's excellent overview in "The Framework of U.S. Relations with Latin America in the Twentieth Century: An Interpretive Essay," especially pages 94–100.

7. Although Wharton invokes the Free Love advocates in ostensibly disparaging ways, she is equally critical of Anna's retreat from passion. Celibacy, to which Anna had withdrawn, proves to be as frustrating as the promiscuity Darrow enacts. In tracking down Sophy Viner to discover the truth of Sophy's passion for Darrow, Anna submits to the new sexual and social order.

Chapter 1. *Summer* and the Rhetoric of Reproduction

1. See their expression in *French Ways and Their Meaning* (1919).

2. If anything, abortion became more common during World War I, because of increased public support, despite stiffer criminal laws, and because of the suppression of information about birth control (any birth control being considered a form of abortion) (Francome 41–43; Gordon 1984, 111). Abortion went underground.

James Ashton's *The Book of Nature* (1865) was an early advice book, according to its subtitle, "Containing Information for Young People Who Think of Getting Married, On the Philosophy of Recreation and Sexual Intercourse; Showing How to Prevent Conception and to Avoid Child-Bearing; Also, Rules for Management During Labor and Child-Birth" (New York, 1865). Ashton does not moralize about abortion: "Abortions and Miscarriages being in collision with Nature's laws, should never be resorted to except in extreme cases, and then only under medical advice" (63). Immediately prior to this injunction, however, Ashton explains how abortions could be performed: through belladonna and forced passage with the hand into the vagina. These rhetorical contradictions about abortion and reproduction commonly passed into the twentieth century.

3.   One year earlier than *Summer,* the silent film *Where Are My Children?* (1916; director Lois Weber) similarly addressed issues of abortion and reproduction. As Kay Sloan writes, "the melodrama starred a flighty, upper-class woman who underwent repeated abortions rather than sacrifice her lively social life for motherhood. Her husband asks the question in the title when he learns that they are childless by choice" (Sloan 90). Regardless of its rhetoric of familialism, the film argues for the importance of birth control in a subplot about a physician who dispenses contraceptive information to his ghetto clients. The film played to audiences aware of and interested in eugenics; it kept alive a concern for "safer sex" in post-Victorian culture.

4.   While Wharton's fiction is not usually read in the context of political or social problem novels, Edith Summers Kelley's 1923 novel *Weeds* introduces the abortion and "mind cure" movements central to the debate for women's rights. *Weeds* is a novel about Judith Pippinger's life in Kentucky, a life marked by frustration, both financial and erotic. Famous for its unpublished scene (until the 1982 Feminist Press edition) of childbearing, the novel describes the birth of Judith's first child, Billy, as a scene of torture, much like Edna Pontellier's witnessing of Adèle Ratignolle's labor in *The Awakening* (1899). Later in the plot, troubled by "erotic unrest" (276), Judith has an affair with an evangelist, becomes pregnant by him, and decides—having had three children with her tenant-farmer husband—that she wants to abort this child.

Kelley also represents an abortion attempt, which remains curiously uncensored. That the childbirthing was censored—but not the abortion attempt—gives us a clue to the American scene in the twenties. Abortion was illegal, but childbirthing had not become as popular as many of the eugenicists wanted. Hence, eugenicists sought out arguments and means to persuade women to have more children. The horror or pain of childbirthing, therefore, needed to be censored; a failed abortion attempt, especially from a "dysgenic" mother like Judith Pippinger, need not be. The sexual politics of this editing are clear: dysgenic mothers should abort; however, the middle- and upper-class reading public (considered eugenically fit) must not read about painful childbirth. Judith Pippinger tries to abort by riding at breakneck speed through the countryside; when that fails, she tries a knitting needle: "at the first stab of pain she flung the instrument violently to the other end of the room. Afterward she dropped it through a wide crack in the kitchen floor so that she would not be able to find it again" (285). She also makes a "brackish liquor" from "noxious herbs." "But all that these evil brews did was to increase her sickness and lassitude. Drearily she shambled about the kitchen through the dragging days and felt too sick and weary for despair" (286). Although abortion advertisements and abortionists came under sustained attack with the passing of the Comstock Law in 1873, Kelley's novel, like Wharton's earlier one, makes clear that abortion did not become less popular in the early twentieth century.

The cultural concern with New Thought takes form in *Weeds* in the subscription to "The Farm Wife's Friend," a monthly devoted to advertisements and domestic arrangements, to which Judith's friend, Hat Wolf, appeals as her domestic guide. Along with these magazines, Hat has a book called "Old Secrets and New Discoveries," concerning the magnetic power of the personality. Consider its advice:

> When you desire to make any one "Love" you with whom you meet, although not personally acquainted with him, you can very readily reach him and make his acquaintance if you observe the following directions: Suppose you see him coming toward you in an unoccupied mood, or he is recklessly or passively walking past you, all that remains for you to do at that moment is to concentrate your thought and send it into him, and, to your astonishment, if he was passive, he will look at you, and now is your time to send a thrill to his heart by looking [sic] him carelessly, though determinately, into his eyes, and praying with all your heart, mind, soul, and strength, that he may read your thought and receive your true Love, which God designs we should bear one another. . . . (134)

This method promises a way out of women's domestic passivity through a psychological power. New Thought writers confessed an "unconquerable aversion" to housework (Parker 83), making New Thought much preferable to the domestic or Christian routine of submission offered in earlier advice to women. Again, *Weeds:* "Continue operating in this psychological manner; not losing any convenient opportunity to meet him at an appropriate place, where an unembarrassed exchange of words will open the door to the one so magnetized" (134).

5. The phrase "carbolic acid" is left blank in Wharton's handwritten manuscript at the Beinecke Library.

6. See Lev Raphael's reading of *Summer,* which emphasizes Charity's shame (290–91).

7. Wharton first met Professor Bronislaw Malinowski at the Aldous Huxleys' for lunch on 27 February 1932, where she remarked in her Line-A-Day diary that he was "charming," and later, on March 15, she made a special note that they had a "good talk" (Lilly Library). They met at least eleven times for lunch or tea throughout 1932. As Marianna Torgovnick argues in *Gone Primitive,* Malinowski's diaries are filled with references to reading novels as a temptation, to "[forsaking] the reading of novels as an inflammatory source of pleasure that provokes sensual thoughts and a longing for bodily pleasure" (229–30). No wonder, then,

his interest in Wharton's post-war novels, which so often concern the renunciation of desire. Sharing his anti-evolutionist theories (see Torgovnick 8), Wharton
sees in family life not so much the "primitive" as the key to cultural values she
would uncover in her fiction. Like Malinowski, too, Wharton was unable to
overcome her conflicted revulsion and attraction to the primitive: for Mali-
nowksi, a repressed desire for the somatic; for Wharton, an expressed revulsion
for the "primitive" Harlem culture she mistakenly associates with the horrors of
jazz, movies, modernist aesthetics, and radical politics (hazily free-associated in
Wharton's mind).

Later, Wharton would come to endorse his view that incest was "incompatible
with family life" (see Degler 249). Although Malinowski saw a "powerful urge to
incest," the taboo against it became the basis of social relations. For Wharton,
too, this taboo had less to do with instinct than with cultural prohibitions, the
stuff of Wharton's late fictions. But Wharton parted company with Malinowski
on his eugenics claims. In advocating the "mother-right" of Trobriand Islanders
in *Sex and Repression in Savage Society* (1927), Malinowski proposes that women
had social and familial power. Not only did Wharton worry about the medicalizing of the bad mother, she feared equally the celebrating of the good mother, two
extremes that were easily manipulated and misapplied in Anglo-American culture
(see Coward). Malinowski does, however, reinforce Wharton's suspicions about
"father-right" cultures. Father-right cultures (that is, patriarchies) give fathers
unearned powers, a source of family conflict and social disruption (see Malinowski 30–32). Malinowski's argument that the geographical, historical, and
social contexts of families determine the power arrangements effectively challenged the universalism of psychoanalysis (see Coward 237–39). Malinowski,
moreover, argues against the "genetic aspects of the family against the social
issues," a "'geneticism' which assumes that the biological is more important than
the social, and finally an evolutionism which assumes that Western patriarchal
forms are the highest form of society" (Coward 242–43). Coward celebrates
Malinowski's rejection of evolutionary prejudice in favor of his cultural relativism (243), rightly arguing that the universalist and culturalist polarization dominated 1920s debates. It is a debate Wharton treats in 1917 and in the decade that
follows.

8.   It is not out of ignorance of politics or of race that Wharton condemns the
Harlem Renaissance. In her last novel of the twenties, *Hudson River Bracketed,*
she returns to her denunciation of Harlem life. Certain prejudices stay with her
into the thirties, as we will see in the jokes she exchanges with her friends (see the
30 January 1924 and 26 January 1929 letters to Minnie, Beinecke Library, in
which Wharton uses the phrase "niggered").

Chapter 2. Why Gentlewomen Prefer Blondes: *The Mother's Recompense*

1.   Annette Zilversmit's (1985 MLA) perceptive reading of anti-Semitism and
Jewish characters in Wharton's fiction charts their visibility and Wharton's ambivalence about them. Zilversmit sees a link between the "stereotypical portraits

of forthright, flamboyant, status-hungry but financially astute Wall Street Jews" and Wharton's critique of the emerging phase of capitalism and financiering (1).

2.   See Leslie Fishbein's reading of moral relativism in the twenties, especially her linking of Wharton with Loos (405).

3.   The negative reception of *Nigger Heaven* among African-American literary intellectuals did not influence Wharton's opinion. She hated the book for her own reasons, sufficiently different from the review Van Vechten's novel got, for example, from W. E. B. Du Bois: "Carl Van Vechten's 'Nigger Heaven' is a blow in the face. It is an affront to the hospitality of black folk and to the intelligence of white. First, as to its title: my objection is based on no provincial dislike of the nickname. 'Nigger' is an English word of wide use and definite connotation. . . . But the phrase, 'Nigger Heaven,' as applied to Harlem, is a misnomer. 'Nigger Heaven' does not mean, as Van Vechten once or twice intimates . . . a haven for Negroes—a city of refuge for dark and tired souls; it means, in common parlance, a nasty, sordid corner into which black folk are herded, and yet a place which they in crass ignorance are fools enough to enjoy. Harlem is no such place as that, and no one knows this better than Carl Van Vechten" (vii). Interestingly, Du Bois rejects the book not as propaganda, since he does "not insist that [stories] be written solely for my point of view" (ix), but as a degradation of the depths of the majority of black life, not spent in cabarets or dives. On the contrary, Claude McKay, James Weldon Johnson, and Langston Hughes all defended the book or Van Vechten himself. In addition, Jessie Redmon Fauset acknowledged Wharton as one of her literary ancestors, as Ammons writes (1991, 140), but the sympathy seems entirely one-sided.

4.   See Ellen Dupree's "Jamming the Machinery: Mimesis in *The Custom of the Country*" for her work on Wharton's indebtedness to Robert Grant, author of *Unleavened Bread* (1900), with which *Custom of the Country* has been associated (7). Grant's heroine, Selma White, is so much like Undine that Grant wrote to Wharton, claiming that Undine "outSelma's Selma by a league" (7–9). Wharton's remark about Loos's Lorelei suggests that she similarly "outUndine's Undine."

5.   See the reviews collected in Tuttleton, Lauer, and Murray, especially the one that appeared in the New York *Sun*, 8 October 1913. Wharton is said to have created "an ideal monster" in Undine, "perfect in that at no time does she betray any human feeling, a model for other women who are pushing their way and a standard by which the people who are watching them may measure them" (202).

6.   The Protocols of Zion, according to Ford, suggested that Jewish financiers and capitalists conspired to take over all capitalist forms of business. Under pressure of a lawsuit, Ford was forced to retract his conspiracy claims and apologize for his anti-Semitism.

7.   Loos's response, however, is not as reactionary as Henry Ford's; Griffith's 1916 film *Intolerance* concerns a labor riot, and its sympathy is for the lot of the mistreated strikers, against the corporate owners.

8.   Wharton first mentions meeting Malinowski in a letter to Margaret Terry Chanler on 25 March 1932 (Lewis and Lewis 546). On several other occasions, she mentions discussing novels and anthropology with him in her five-year Line-

A-Day Diary now in the Lilly Library, Indiana University. Wharton believed that her novelistic imagination anticipated Malinowski's cross-societal perspective.

9.   See Jessica Benjamin's formulation of this struggle in *The Bonds of Love:* "The controversy about Oedipus and Narcissus, superego and ego ideal, is really a debate about sexual difference and domination. In the oedipal model, the father, in whatever form—whether as the limiting superego, the phallic barrier, or the paternal prohibition—always represents difference and enjoys a privileged position above the mother. Her power is identified with early, primitive gratifications that must be renounced, while the father's power is associated with development and growth. His authority is supposed to protect us from irrationality and submission; she lures us into transgression" (159). In Wharton's reconfiguration of this Oedipal model, Anne's narcissism allows her to reject her mother for her father's power.

10.   Laura Doyle's book on the racialized mother, *Bordering on the Body,* treats the separate development of the mother-complex in modernist and Harlem Renaissance traditions as integrated trends. By tracing the sexual-racial matrix through the racialized mother, Doyle argues that history and identity are constructed or repressed through the maternal image. From this complexly argued point emerges Doyle's theory of "kinship patriarchy." Doyle's reading of eugenics is illuminated by her attention to its racial biases. The racial differentiating of mothers—part of the eugenics movement—served as a cultural aesthetic which modern writers, like Jean Toomer, only began to underscore.

Chapter 3. Eugenics and a New Politics: *Twilight Sleep* and *The Children*

1.   Enclosed with the letter to Lapsley is another one about the threat of Jewish assimilation. The Marxian doctrine, for Riverda Jordan, is not as threatening as the breakdown of self and other that the Jewish assimilation portends. Jordan's comments are as follows:

> Naturally I am not thinking in terms of the Klan, with which I have no sympathy, but I am realizing that more and more our national attitudes are being modified by the influence of the later generations of our Jewish immigrants and other groups who have abandoned their own religious beliefs, without embracing a substitute. It is this that seems to me more insidious and dangerous than the avowed Marxian doctrine. Therefore, I should like to see some phrasing which would indicate very definitely a definition or affirmation which would line up the signer on the side of decency and fundamental morality as against the present degenerating attitude so generally prevalent. (19 June 1925, Beinecke Library)

Wharton includes a copy of this second letter to Lapsley to emphasize her point about the eugenics movement she distrusts.

2.   Such studies as Mark Haller's *Eugenics* (1963) or Robert Bannister's *Social Darwinism* (1979) are significant in their documentation of the rise of eugenics in

America; Cattell's contemporaneous work foregrounds an explicit gender argument.

3.   Jackson Lears's *No Place of Grace* explains the neuralgia and disease in antimodern life. Wharton is not so critical of "self-cures" and mind cures in her letters. She writes to Daisy Chanler on 16 February 1929 that she hopes "Mme de Ganay's electric treatment will do you . . . good" (Beinecke Library). Even so, work and activity of a more purposeful sort than Pauline Manford's are Wharton's painkillers, even though she complains of numerous attacks of grippes and pneumonia in her letters. To Max Farrand on 5 October 1922, she complains about people who "kill time": "Stopping work would probably be as impossible to Trix's [Wharton's niece and Farrand's wife] temperament as to mine" (Beinecke Library).

4.   Carol Wershoven, for instance, argues this in *The Female Intruder in the Novels of Edith Wharton*. She sees Undine's resemblance in Lita and views their functions in the novels as "nearly identical": "Like her predecessor, Lita exists as an object lesson, as the monster that her world's vices have created. Utterly self-centered, pure surface with nothing inside, Lita Wyant is Pauline Manford distorted and exaggerated" (133). Monstrous, self-centered—what makes Lita so aw(e)ful is that she corresponds neither to the maternal nor New Woman image. She is culture—jazz—rather than nature. In condemning her, critics reinforce the notion of women as having an essential nature, which Lita violates.

5.   See Judith Sensibar's "Edith Wharton Reads the Bachelor Type: Her Critique of Modernism's Representative Men" for the view that the novel is told "from a woman's view" and that it concerns one of modernism's "central and most compelling tropes: its romanticization of the erotic immaturity of the perennial bachelor and its insistence that this figure was the age's new Representative Man . . ." (575–76). Sensibar goes on to read the novel through the lens of Sedgwick's argument about homosexual panic, concluding that Prufrockian Martin finds that both Judith and Rose fail him as "screens or closets" for his homosexuality (580). Like John Marcher in James's "Beast in the Jungle," Martin Boyne has refused to confront the source of his desire.

6.   Judith does understand, even though another mother—Zinnia Lacrosse—accuses her of not understanding "a mother's feelings" (66). The film star wants to exhibit Zinnie in order to show that she can produce an heir for Lord Wrench—her new husband. Book One ends with gift of jewels from Zinnia to her daughter Blanca. As we've seen in *The Mother's Recompense,* such an exchange always marks a loaded moment. In *The Children,* Judith is left empty-handed.

7.   As Marianna Torgovnick writes in *Gone Primitive* (1990), "Freud's theories about sexuality, Malinowski's observations of male and female roles, and similar work have assured that how we conceive of the primitive helps form our conception of ourselves as sexual, gendered beings" (18).

Chapter 4. The Advance Men and Edith Wharton:
The Public Relations of Writing

1. As Tyler Anbinder argues in *Nativism and Slavery: The Northern Know Nothings and The Politics of the 1850s,* nativist sentiment galvanized the formation of the Know Nothings, or the Order of the Star Spangled Banner, over the issue of abolition: nativism was "a complex web of nationalism, xenophobia, ethnocentrism, and racism. Nineteenth-century Americans, however, used the term primarily to describe anti-immigrant sentiment" (xiv).

2. The Margaret Sanger Papers Project at New York University has published a pamphlet entitled "Margaret Sanger and the Question of Racism," prepared by Peter Engelman and Cathy Moran Hajo. They document Sanger's "unfortunate" alignment with some eugenicists with whom she had "philosophical differences"; however, they argue that "Sanger vehemently rejected eugenic definitions of the unfit based solely on race or creed" (4).

3. See John McClymer's details on E. A. Ross's ideas about social engineering in *War and Welfare* (100*n*5).

4. Ross Posnock studies Henry and William James's relation to the doctrines of scientific and social management in *The Trial of Curiosity:* "The coercive character of modernity is reflected in the ascendancy of social control as the governing concern of the social sciences in the opening decade of the twentieth century" (110). Advocating what Posnock calls "positivist sociology," a philosophy indulgent in "fetishizing fact and predictability" (111), E. A. Ross became the preeminent spokesman for social engineering.

5. Patrice Gray's dissertation, "The Lure of Romance," analyzes Kathleen Norris's fiction in the context of Robert Grant's *Unleavened Bread* (1900) and Wharton's *Custom of the Country.* Gray calls Norris's novel *Mother* (1911) "slight" but "important to the extent that Theodore Roosevelt endorsed it as an anti-dote to race suicide" (209). At first rejecting conventional marriage, the heroine Margaret "undergoes a total reversal in attitudes toward matrimony and maternity." As Gray suggests, the novel was outdated in its sentimental formula but part and parcel of a "reaction to the evils of modernity" in the teens (210).

Mary Baker Eddy's popularity increased after 1898, when she started her own publishing company. *The Christian Science Monitor* began publishing in 1908, an event which coincided with the phenomenal growth of the Christian Science membership, especially among women. With women as healers and practitioners, Mary Baker Eddy's brand of evangelism often spread through a more informal network than Billy Sunday's (see Ron Numbers and Rennie B. Schoepflin on Eddy's "religion of health").

6. See Kathleen Blee's *Women of the Klan* for a list of Indiana towns and the percentages of Klan members in them. Advance, Indiana, had a 55.8% attendance rate at Klan events for all eligible Klan members.

7. Wharton's letters are filled with anti-bolshevik sentiment, a movement which both she and Sinclair Lewis associated with fanaticism and political dogmatism (see Lewis's letter to Wharton, 20 June 1931, Lilly Library). As a popular

movement, bolshevism violated Wharton's concept of an "inner life" and private motivation. But she uses the adjective "bolchevik" as an explanation for anything from impertinence to ingratitude (16 January 1919 letter to Elisina, Lilly Library) to violence and anarchy (diary entry for 28 March 1932, Lilly Library). Bolshevism becomes a short-hand term for Wharton to mean oppositional thinking. She jokingly complains that "swindlers" and "Bolcheviks" have no barriers before them (3 May 1934 to Elisina, Lilly Library). Wharton occasionally reduces political movements to the pestering trivialities which destroy everyday life and its sweetness. When Elisina sends her "Hitler" in August of 1934, she reserves it for a quieter day when she has no guests. Her reason: "Hitler would seem a blasphemy against all this beauty" (19 August 1934, Lilly Library).

Taking Wharton's ironic tone at face value is a mistake, for her letters show that political events (like the Lindbergh baby case, fascism, Nazism) "haunt" her. At the bottom of Wharton's irony is her fear that the "world [is] at the mercy of two madmen" (16 September 1935, Lilly Library). Wharton reveals her political distress in a vision of the world disquieted and turned upside-down by the chaos of dictatorship. Her friends—especially Berenson—don't let her forget world politics. Berenson informs her about the publication of Trotski's *Literature and Revolution* (13 August 1933, Lilly Library), the "Hitler gang" (1 July 1934, Lilly Library), and her status among the bolsheviks: "Our Bolshevik weeklies speak of you with more & more respect & admiration. Remember that for a pig a bristle is a gift" (15 May 1936, Lilly Library).

8.   Perhaps Wharton gets her impetus to use Billy Sunday as a prototype for Bunty Hayes's business success from Bruce Barton's best-selling *The Man Nobody Knows,* the publishing success of 1925 and 1926. Barton uses some of the same PR strategies in his best-seller and, in fact, praised Sunday publicly for them (see McLoughlin 197). Thorstein Veblen denounced Sunday in 1922 for disseminating the "propaganda of intolerance" (qtd. in Baritz 36).

9.   But Wharton and Sunday shared more: a distrust of Christian Science and its call for spiritualism; hatred of the Huns in World War I; and abhorrence of their common enemy, the bolsheviks.

10.   Sinclair Lewis had five best-selling novels in the twenties (date indicates year of bestseller, not publication date): *Main Street* (1921), *Babbitt* (1922–23), *Arrowsmith* (1925), *Elmer Gantry* (1927), and *Dodsworth* (1929). Gertrude Atherton had *The Sisters-in-Law* (1921) and *Black Oxen* (1923). Edith Wharton had *Age of Innocence* (1921) and *Twilight Sleep* (1927).

11.   Wharton knew about modern debates about sexology from Malinowski's ethnography or from a brochure (File 224, Beinecke Library) on the new book *Sex and Public Life* by Capt. A. H. Henderson-Livesey, published by Social Services Ltd., with chapter titles like the following: "Feminism and Its Antidote," "Women in Public Life," "Organised Women," "Women in the Teaching Profession," "The Woman's Sphere," "Women and Sport," "Family Limitation," "The Thwarting of the Maternal Instinct," "The Decline of Parliamentary Authority."

12.   Shari Benstock's *Women of the Left Bank* documents Wharton's own salon life, which she claims involved Wharton in the early 1890s. Benstock writes

that "Wharton was not attracted to the fashionable salons about which Proust wrote, salons in which women of the *demi-monde* mixed with aged duchesses, in which homosexual men appeared in rouge and wigs and homosexual women wore tuxedos with monocles tucked in the pockets. Not certain enough of her social standing in European society, a shy and insecure person, Wharton sought the most conservative of drawing rooms" (40).

13. As Jessica Benjamin argues in relation to *The Story of O:* "For the slave, intense pain causes the violent rupture of the self, a profound experience of fragmentation and chaos. It's true that O now welcomes this loss of self-coherence, but only under a specific condition: that her sacrifice actually creates the master's power, produces his coherent self, in which she can take refuge. Thus in losing her own self, she is gaining access, however circumscribed, to a more powerful one" (61).

14. As Ammons writes about Wharton's last novels, they "synthesize her new endorsement of motherhood with her lifelong belief in women's right to self-determination. The synthesis is not very successful" (189).

Chapter 5. "Roman Fever": A Rune of History

1. This chapter on "Roman Fever" was first published in *College English* 50.6 (October 1988) and represents my first work on Wharton's politics. Her relation to the symbolic changes in European politics, I came to see, was etched in all of her late fictions. A subtle propagandist, Wharton never violated her sense that explicit propaganda would ruin fiction. Yet she was driven not only by financial need but also by an ever-deepening social imperative to intervene in what she saw as the madness of her culture.

2. Susan Elizabeth Sweeney has cogently argued (1993) that "Roman Fever" is a confessional tale about female transgression on a "Roman Holiday" (317), "evoking taboo sexuality and textuality simultaneously" (323).

Chapter 6. "Edith Agonistes"

1. Immigration had virtually stopped during World War I, but increased soon after the war's end.

2. For instance, on Sinclair Lewis's advice, she refused to join the Literary Council of the Authors' League of America (see letter to Minnie of 29 January 1929, Beinecke Library).

3. Adeline Tintner reads *The Buccaneers* through the scandal of Consuelo Vanderbilt, "the American heiress of the Vanderbilt millions," who married the ninth Duke of Marlborough, and, after an annulment, married "a retired officer with the French army" (15). The marital problems of one of Wharton's girlhood friends illuminate another important context for the novel, as does the existence in Wharton's library of John Esquemeling's seventeenth-century book, *The Buccaneers of America* (1678) (18). Tintner notes: "The presence in Edith Wharton's library of this volume, which in essence exposes and yet exalts the exploits of

these bandits [marauders of the New World], suggests that it may have contributed metaphorically to the exploits of the American adventuresses and their assault on English society. . . . The young American beauties exact a revenge on the seventeenth century buccaneers who invaded the Western hemisphere by repeating their conquests in reverse and invading England as their predecessors had invaded America" (19).

4. See Larry Reynolds's *European Revolutions and the American Literary Renaissance* for his treatment of the literary reaction to European radicalism.

5. Charlotte Perkins Gilman's term, in "Parasitism and Civilised Vice" (1931).

6. As Shell writes, "The taboo on bestiality thus makes unnecessary an even more repressive explicit taboo on incest. Fleeing the human for the animal and the sexual for the asexual, one comes upon the family pet with a sigh of relief. . . . The pet thus represents one solution to the incest taboo" (174).

7. Shell reads the fairy tale "Beauty and the Beast" as a dilemma between bestiality and incest, where the Beast is preferable to the incest with the Beauty's father and brothers. The conflation of the father and the beast is key, Shell argues, to the popularity of the tale and to the transcendence (not transgression) of taboo "between kin and nonkin and hence between chastity and incest" (157). Note how Linky is, for Wharton, as wise as her memories of her father in *A Backward Glance* intimate: "The tall splendid father . . . [who] was always so kind, and whose strong arms lifted one so high, and held one so safely . . ." (26). Or consider Wharton's reactions to "Little Red Riding Hood": "I was ready to affirm, there was a Wolf under my bed. This business of the Wolf was the first of other similar terrifying experiences, and since most imaginative children know these hauntings by tribal animals, I mention it only because from the moment of that adventure it became necessary, whenever I 'read' the story of Red Riding Hood (that is, looked at the pictures), to carry my little nursery stool from one room to another, in pursuit of Doyley [her nanny] or my mother, so that I should never again be exposed to meeting the family Totem when I sat down alone to my book" (28). Domesticating Linky is one way to control the terror of the family Totem.

References

Allen, Elizabeth. *A Woman's Place in the Novels of Henry James.* New York: St. Martin's, 1984.

Ammons, Elizabeth. *Conflicting Stories.* New York: Oxford UP, 1991.

Ammons, Elizabeth. *Edith Wharton's Argument with America.* Athens: U of Georgia P, 1980.

Anbinder, Tyler. *Nativism and Slavery: The Northern Know Nothings and the Politics of the 1850s.* New York: Oxford UP, 1992.

Armstrong, Nancy. "Introduction: Literature as Women's History." *Genre* 9.4 (1986): 347–69.

Aronson, Marc. "Wharton and the House of Scribner: The Novelist as Pain in the Neck." *New York Times Book Review* (2 January 1994): 7–8.

Ashton, James. *The Book of Nature.* New York: Arno Press, 1974 [1865].

Atherton, Gertrude. *Black Oxen.* New York: Boni and Liveright, 1923.

Badinter, Elisabeth. *Mother Love: Myth and Reality.* New York: Macmillan Publishing Co., 1987.

Bakhtin, M. M. *The Dialogic Imagination.* Translated by Caryl Emerson and Michael Holquist. Edited by Michael Holquist. Austin: U of Texas P, 1981.

Bakhtin, M. M. *Speech Genres and Other Late Essays.* Translated by Vern W. McGee. Edited by Caryl Emerson and Michael Holquist. Austin: U of Texas P, 1986.

Bannister, Robert C. *Social Darwinism.* Philadelphia: Temple UP, 1979.

Banta, Martha. "At Odds/In League: Brutality and Betterment in the Age of Taylor, Veblen, and Ford." *Prospects* 14 (1989): 203–72.

Banta, Martha. *Taylored Lives: Narrative Productions in the Age of Taylor, Veblen, and Ford.* Chicago: U of Chicago P, 1993.

Barker-Benfield, G. J. *The Horrors of the Half-Known Life.* New York: Harper and Row, 1976.

Barton, Bruce. *The Man Nobody Knows.* New York: Collier Books, 1987 [1925].

Bauer, Dale. "Edith Wharton's Brave New Politics." *Arizona Quarterly* 45.1 (Spring 1989): 49–71.

Bauer, Dale, and Patricia Sharpe. "Edith Wharton and the Family Romance in *Summer.*" Paper presented at the Edith Wharton at The Mount Conference, June 1987.

Bauman, Mark K. "Hitting the Sawdust Trail: Billy Sunday's Atlanta Campaign of 1917." *Southern Studies* 19.4 (1980): 385–99.

Bell, Millicent. *Edith Wharton and Henry James: A Story of Their Friendship.* New York: Braziller, 1965.

Benjamin, Jessica. *The Bonds of Love.* New York: Pantheon, 1988.

Benjamin, Jules R. "The Framework of U.S. Relations with Latin America in the Twentieth Century: An Interpretive Essay." *Diplomatic History* 11.2 (1987): 91–112.

Benjamin, Walter. "The Destructive Character." In *Reflections,* translated by Edmund Jephcott, 157–59. New York: Harcourt Brace Jovanovich, 1978.

Benstock, Shari. *Women of the Left Bank: Paris, 1900–1940.* Austin: U of Texas P, 1986.

Benstock, Shari. "Landscape of Desire: Edith Wharton and Europe." In *Wretched Exotic: Essays on Edith Wharton in Europe,* edited by Katherine Joslin and Alan Price, 19–42. New York: Peter Lang, 1993.

Blair, Karen J. *The Clubwoman as Feminist: True Womanhood Redefined, 1868–1914.* New York: Holmes and Meier, 1980.

Blee, Kathleen. *Women of the Klan: Racism and Gender in the 1920s.* Berkeley: U of California P, 1991.

Bourdieu, Pierre. *Distinction: A Social Critique of the Judgment of Taste.* Cambridge: Harvard UP, 1984.

Browder, Clifford. *The Wickedest Woman in New York: Madame Restell, The Abortionist.* Hamden, CT: Archon, 1988.

Calinescu, Matei. "Modernism and Ideology." In *Modernism: Challenges and Perspectives,* edited by Monique Chefdor, Ricardo Quinones, and Albert Wachtel, 79–93. Urbana: U of Illinois P, 1986.

Calkins, David L. "Billy Sunday's Cincinnati Crusade." *Cincinnati Historical Society Bulletin* 27.4 (1969): 292–303.

Carey, Gary. *Anita Loos.* New York: Knopf, 1988.

Carnes, Mark C. *Secret Ritual and Manhood in Victorian America.* New Haven: Yale UP, 1989.

Cattell, Raymond B. *The Fight for Our National Intelligence.* London: P. S. King and Son, 1937.

Clifford, James. "Introduction." In *Writing Culture: The Poetics and Politics of Ethnography,* edited by Clifford and George Marcus, 1–26. Berkeley and Los Angeles: U of California P, 1986.

Colquitt, Clare. "Unpacking Her Treasures: Edith Wharton's 'Mysterious Correspondence' with Morton Fullerton." *Library Chronicle of the University of Texas* 2.31 (1985): 73–107.

Conway, Helen. "We Try Trial Marriage." *The Forum* 84 (November 1930): 272–76.

Coward, Rosalind. *Patriarchal Precedents.* London: Routledge & Kegan Paul, 1983.

Cravens, Hamilton. *The Triumph of Evolution: American Scientists and the Heredity-Environment Controversy, 1900–1941.* Philadelphia: U of Pennsylvania P, 1978.

Darwin, Leonard. *The Need for Eugenic Reform.* New York: D. Appleton, 1926.

Degler, Carl. *In Search of Human Nature.* New York: Oxford UP, 1991.

De Grazia, Victoria. *How Fascism Ruled Women: Italy, 1922–1945.* Berkeley: U of California P, 1992.

Dobkowksi, Michael N. "American Anti-Semitism: A Reinterpretation." *American Quarterly* 29.2 (1977): 166–81.

Dorsett, Lyle W. *Billy Sunday and the Redemption of Urban America.* Grand Rapids: Eerdmans, 1991.

Doyle, Laura. *Bordering on the Body.* New York: Oxford UP, forthcoming.

Du Bois, W. E. B. Review of *Nigger Heaven,* by Carl Van Vechten. In *Nigger Heaven,* vii-x. New York: Harper Colophon, 1971.

Dupree, Ellen. "Jamming the Machinery: Mimesis in *The Custom of the Country.*" *American Literary Realism* 22.2 (Winter 1990): 5–16.

Eisenstein, Zillah. *The Female Body and the Law.* Berkeley: U of California P, 1988.

Ellis, William T. *Billy Sunday: The Man and His Message.* Philadelphia: Winston Publishing, 1917.

Erlich, Gloria C. *The Sexual Education of Edith Wharton.* Berkeley: U of California P, 1992.

Ewen, Stuart. *Captains of Consciousness: Advertising and the Social Roots of the Consumer Culture.* New York: McGraw-Hill, 1976.

Fass, Paula. *The Damned and the Beautiful: American Youth in the 1920s.* New York: Oxford UP, 1977.

Fishbein, Leslie. "Prostitution, Morality, and Paradox: Moral Relativism in Edith Wharton's *Old New York: New Year's Day (The 'Seventies).*" *Studies in Short Fiction* 24 (Fall 1987): 399–406.

Fox-Genovese, Elizabeth. *Feminism Without Illusions: A Critique of Individualism.* Chapel Hill: U of North Carolina P, 1991.

Francome, Colin. *Abortion Practice in Britain and the United States.* London: Allen and Unwin, 1986.

Frank, Florence Kiper. "The Presentment of the Jew in American Fiction." *Bookman* 71 (1930): 270–75.

Freud, Sigmund. *Totem and Taboo.* Translated by James Strachey. New York: Norton, 1950 [1913].

Freud, Sigmund. "Symbolism in Dreams." In *Introductory Lectures on Psycho-Analysis,* 149–69. Translated by James Strachey. London: Hogarth Press, 1963 [1915–16].

Fryer, Judith. *Felicitous Space: The Imaginative Structures of Edith Wharton and Willa Cather.* Chapel Hill: U of North Carolina P, 1986.

Fullerton, William Morton. *Patriotism and Science: Some Studies in Historic Psychology.* Boston: Roberts Brothers, 1893.

Fullerton, William Morton. *Problems of Power.* New York: Scribner's, 1913.

Furnas, J. C. *Great Times: An Informal Social History of the United States, 1914–1929.* New York: G. P. Putnam's Sons, 1974.

Gallop, Jane. *The Daughter's Seduction: Feminism and Psychoanalysis.* Ithaca: Cornell UP, 1982.

Gallop, Jane. *Reading Lacan.* Ithaca: Cornell UP, 1987.

Gibson, Mary Ellis. "Edith Wharton and the Ethnography of Old New York." *Studies in American Fiction* 13.1 (Spring 1985): 57–69.

Gilbert, Sandra M. "Life's Empty Pack: Notes toward a Literary Daughteronomy." *Critical Inquiry* 11 (March 1985): 355–84.

Gilman, Charlotte Perkins. *The Living of Charlotte Perkins Gilman.* Madison: U of Wisconsin P, 1990 [1935].

Gilman, Charlotte Perkins. "Parasitism and Civilised Vice." In *Woman's Coming of Age,* edited by Samuel D. Schmalhausen and V. F. Calverton, 110–26. New York: Horace Liveright, 1931.

Goodman, Susan. *Edith Wharton's Women: Friends and Rivals.* Hanover, NH: UP of New England, 1990.

Goodwyn, Janet. *Edith Wharton: Traveller in the Land of Letters.* New York: St. Martin's, 1990.

Gordon, Linda. "Voluntary Motherhood: The Beginnings of Feminist Birth Control Ideas in the United States." In *Women and Health in America,* edited by Judith Walzer Leavitt, 104–16. Madison: U of Wisconsin P, 1984.

Gordon, Linda. "What's New in Women's History." In *Feminist Studies/Critical Studies,* edited by Teresa de Lauretis, 20–30. Bloomington: Indiana UP, 1986.

Gordon, Linda. "Why Nineteenth-Century Feminists Did Not Support 'Birth Control' and Twentieth-Century Feminists Do: Feminism, Reproduction, and the Family." In *Rethinking the Family: Some Feminist Questions,* edited by Barrie Thorne and Marilyn Yalom, 40–53. New York: Longman, 1982.

Gramsci, Antonio. "Americanism and Fordism." In *Prison Notebooks,* edited and translated by Quintin Hoare and Geoffrey Nowell Smith, 279–318. New York: International Publishers, 1980.

Gray, Patrice K. *The Lure of Romance and the Temptation of Feminine Sensibility: Literary Heroines in Selected Popular and "Serious" American Novels, 1895–1915.* Ann Arbor: UMI P, 1985.

Gribben, Alan. "'The Heart is Insatiable': A Selection from Edith Wharton's Letters to Morton Fullerton, 1907–1915." *Library Chronicle of the University of Texas* 2.31 (1985): 7–18.

Groves, Ernest R. *The Marriage Crisis.* New York: Longmans, 1928.

Haller, Mark. *Eugenics.* New Brunswick: Rutgers UP, 1963.

Herbert, Christopher. *Culture and Anomie: Ethnographic Imagination in the Nineteenth Century.* Chicago: U of Chicago P, 1991.

Higham, John. *Strangers in the Land.* New Brunswick: Rutgers UP, 1955.

Hirsch, Marianne. *The Mother/Daughter Plot: Narrative, Psychoanalysis, Feminism.* Bloomington: Indiana UP, 1989.

Hoffman, Frederick J. *The Twenties: American Writing in the Postwar Decade.* New York: Viking, 1955.

Hofstadter, Richard. *Social Darwinism in American Thought, 1860–1915.* Philadelphia: U of Pennsylvania P, 1945.

Holmes, Arthur. "The First Law of Character-Making." In *Eugenics: Twelve University Lectures,* 177–212. New York: Dodd, Mead and Company, 1914.

Horkheimer, Max, and Theodor Adorno. "Elements of Anti-Semitism." In *Dialectic of Enlightenment,* translated by John Cumming, 168–208. New York: Continuum, 1982.

Hutchison, Percy. "Mrs. Wharton Tilts at 'Society.'" In *Edith Wharton: The Contemporary Reviews*, edited by James W. Tuttleton, Kristin O. Lauer, and Margaret P. Murray, 431–34. New York: Cambridge UP, 1992.

Jay, Martin. *Permanent Exiles: Essays on the Intellectual Migration from Germany to America*. New York: Columbia UP, 1985.

Joslin, Katherine. *Edith Wharton*. New York: St. Martin's, 1991.

Joslin, Katherine. "Reading Wharton's Letters." In *Review* no. 12, 235–47. Charlottesville: UP of Virginia, 1990.

Kaplan, Amy. *The Social Construction of American Realism*. Chicago: U of Chicago P, 1988.

Kelley, Edith Summers. *Weeds*. New York: The Feminist Press, 1982 [1923].

Kellogg, Vernon L. *Darwinism Today*. New York: Henry Holt and Company, 1907.

Kermode, Frank. *The Sense of an Ending*. New York: Oxford UP, 1967.

Kevles, Daniel J. *In the Name of Eugenics*. New York: Knopf, 1985.

Keyser, Elizabeth Lennox. "'The Ways in Which the Heart Speaks': Letters in *The Reef.*" *Studies in American Fiction* 19.1 (Spring 1991): 95–106.

Kimball, Robert, ed. *The Complete Lyrics of Cole Porter*. New York: Knopf, 1983.

Koonz, Claudia. "Genocide and Eugenics." In *Lessons and Legacies: The Meaning of the Holocaust in a Changing World*, edited by Peter Hayes, 155–77. Evanston: Northwestern UP, 1991.

Koonz, Claudia. *Mothers in the Fatherland*. New York: St. Martin's, 1987.

Kowaleski-Wallace, Beth. "The Reader as Misogynist in *The Custom of the Country.*" *Modern Language Studies* 21.1 (Winter 1991): 45–53.

Kuttner, Alfred B. "Nerves." In *Civilization in the United States*, edited by Harold E. Stearns, 427–42. New York: Harcourt, Brace, and Company, 1922.

Leach, Edmund. "Anthropological Aspects of Language: Animal Categories and Verbal Abuse." In *New Directions in the Study of Language*, edited by Eric H. Lennenberg, 23–63. Cambridge, MA: MIT Press, 1964.

Leach, William. *Land of Desire: Merchants, Power, and the Rise of a New American Culture*. New York: Pantheon, 1993.

Lears, Jackson. *No Place of Grace*. New York: Pantheon, 1981.

Lears, Jackson. "Sherwood Anderson: Looking for the White Spot." In *The Power of Culture*, edited by Richard Wightman Fox and T. J. Jackson Lears, 13–37. Chicago: U of Chicago P, 1993.

Leavis, Q. D. "Henry James's Heiress." *Scrutiny* 7.3 (December 1938): 261–76.

Leavitt, Judith Walzer. "Birthing and Anesthesia: The Debate over Twilight Sleep." *Signs* 6.1 (1980): 147–64.

Leavitt, Judith Walzer. *Brought to Bed: Childbirthing in America, 1750 to 1950*. New York: Oxford UP, 1986.

Leider, Emily. *California's Daughter: Gertrude Atherton and Her Times*. Stanford: Stanford UP, 1991.

Lerner, Elinor. "American Feminism and the Jewish Question, 1890–1940." In *Anti-Semitism in American History*, edited by David A. Gerber. Urbana: U of Illinois P, 1987.

Lewis, R. W. B. *Edith Wharton: A Biography.* New York: Harper and Row, 1975.

Lewis, R. W. B. "Introduction." In the *The Collected Short Stories of Edith Wharton.* Vol. 1, vii–xxv. New York: Scribner's, 1968.

Lewis, R. W. B. "The Letters of Edith Wharton." In *Literary Reflections: A Shoring of Images, 1960–1993,* 129–53. Boston: Northeastern UP, 1993.

Lewis, R. W. B., and Nancy Lewis, eds. *The Letters of Edith Wharton.* New York: Scribner's, 1988.

Lewis, Sinclair. *Babbitt.* New York: Signet, 1922.

Lindberg, Gary. *Edith Wharton and the Novel of Manners.* Charlottesville: UP of Virginia, 1975.

Lindsey, Judge Ben B. "The Promise and Peril of the New Freedom." In *Woman's Coming of Age: A Symposium,* edited by Samuel D. Schmalhausen and V. F. Calverton, 447–471. New York: Horace Liveright, 1931.

Lindsey, Judge Ben B., and Wainwright Evans. *The Companionate Marriage.* New York: Boni and Liveright, 1927.

Liptzin, Solomon. *The Jew in American Literature.* New York: Bloch, 1966.

Lock, Robert Heath. *Recent Progress in the Study of Variation, Heredity, and Evolution.* London: John Murray, 1906.

Loos, Anita. *Gentlemen Prefer Blondes.* New York: Boni and Liveright, 1925.

Lott, Eric. "'The Seeming Counterfeit': Racial Politics and Early Blackface Minstrelsy." *American Quarterly* 43.2 (June 1991): 223–54.

Lott, Eric. "Love and Theft: The Racial Unconscious of Blackface Minstrelsy." *Representations* 39 (Summer 1992): 23–50.

Lubbock, Percy. *Portrait of Edith Wharton.* New York: D. Appleton-Century Company, 1947.

Lutz, Tom. *American Nervousness, 1903: An Anecdotal History.* Ithaca: Cornell UP, 1991.

Luker, Kristin. *Abortion and the Politics of Motherhood.* Berkeley: U of California P, 1984.

Mailloux, Steven. *Rhetorical Power.* Ithaca: Cornell UP, 1989.

Malinowski, Bronislaw. *Sex and Repression in Savage Society.* New York: Harcourt, Brace and Company, 1927.

Malinowski, Bronislaw. *Sex, Culture, and Myth.* New York: Harcourt, Brace and World, 1962 [1930].

Marx, Karl, and Frederick Engels. *The German Ideology.* Ed. C. J. Arthur. New York: International Publishers, 1978.

McClymer, John F. *War and Welfare: Social Engineering in America, 1890–1925.* Westport, CT: Greenwood Press, 1980.

McLoughlin, William G., Jr. *Billy Sunday Was His Real Name.* Chicago: U of Chicago P, 1955.

Mencken, H. L. "The Holy State of Bliss" (rev. of *The Companionate Marriage*). *American Mercury* 13 (1928): 126–27.

Michaels, Walter Benn. "The Contracted Heart." *New Literary History* 21.3 (Spring 1990): 495–531.

Miller, Nina. "The Bonds of Free Love: Constructing the Female Bohemian Self." *Genders* 11 (Fall 1991): 37–57.

Mohr, James. *Abortion in America.* New York: Oxford UP, 1978.

Morantz-Sanchez, Regina Markell. *Sympathy and Science: Women Physicians in American Medicine.* New York: Oxford UP, 1985.

Nevius, Blake. *Edith Wharton: A Story of Her Fiction.* Berkeley: U of California P, 1953.

Norris, Kathleen. "A Laywoman Looks at 'Companionate Marriage.'" *The Catholic World* 127 (June 1928): 257–63.

Numbers, Ronald L., and Rennie B. Schoepflin. "Ministries of Healing: Mary Baker Eddy, Ellen G. White, and the Religion of Healing." In *Women and Health in America,* edited by Judith Walzer Leavitt, 376–89. Madison: U of Wisconsin P, 1984.

Ohmann, Richard. *Politics of Letters.* Middletown, CT: Wesleyan UP, 1987.

Ozick, Cynthia. *Art & Ardor.* New York: Dutton, 1984.

Papke, Mary. *Verging on the Abyss: The Social Fiction of Kate Chopin and Edith Wharton.* Westport, CT: Greenwood Press, 1990.

Parker, Gail Thain. *Mind Cure in New England.* Hanover, NH: UP of New England, 1973.

Peterson, M. Jeanne. "The Victorian Governess: Status Incongruence in Family and Society." In *Suffer and Be Still: Women in the Victorian Age,* edited by Martha Vicinus, 3–19. Bloomington: Indiana UP, 1972.

Porter, Carolyn. "Are We Being Historical Yet?" *South Atlantic Quarterly* 87.4 (Fall 1988): 743–86.

Posnock, Ross. *The Trial of Curiosity: Henry James, William James, and the Challenge of Modernity.* New York: Oxford UP, 1991.

Price, Alan. "The Composition of Edith Wharton's *Age of Innocence.*" *The Yale University Library Gazette* 55 (1981): 23–28.

Proceedings of First National Conference on Race Betterment. Battle Creek: Gage Printing Company, 1914.

Rafter, Nicole Hahn. *White Trash: The Eugenic Family Studies.* Boston: Northeastern UP, 1988.

Raphael, Lev. *Edith Wharton's Prisoners of Shame.* New York: St. Martin's, 1991.

Reynolds, Larry J. *European Revolutions and the American Literary Renaissance.* New Haven: Yale UP, 1988.

Rich, Adrienne. *Of Woman Born.* New York: Norton, 1976.

Ross, Dorothy. *The Origins of American Social Science.* New York: Cambridge UP, 1991.

Ross, E[dward] A[lsworth]. Wisconsin State Historical Society Archives, Holdings on Microfilm.

Ross, Edward A. *Social Control and the Foundations of Sociology.* Edited by Edgar F. Borgatta and Henry J. Meyer. Boston: Beacon Press, 1959 [1901–1905].

Royde-Smith, Naomi. "New Novels." In *Edith Wharton: The Contemporary Reviews,* edited by James W. Tuttleton, Kristin O. Lauer, and Margaret P. Murray, 440–42. New York: Cambridge UP, 1992.

Rubin, Herman H. *Eugenics and Sex Harmony.* New York: Pioneer Publications, 1943.

Russell, Bertrand. "The Ostrich Code of Morals." *The Forum* 80 (1928): 7–14.

Sacher-Masoch, Leopold von. *Venus in Furs.* Rahnghild Edition. New York: William Faro, 1932 [1870].

Sandelowski, Margarete. *Pain, Pleasure, and American Childbirth: From the Twilight Sleep to the Read Method, 1914–1960.* Westport, CT: Greenwood Press, 1984.

Margaret Sanger Papers Project. Pamphlet prepared by Peter C. Engelman and Cathy Moran Hajo. Department of History. New York University.

Sarti, Roland. *The Ax Within: Italian Fascism in Action.* New York: New Viewpoints, 1974.

Schmalhausen, Sam. "The Twilight Sleep for Women." *International Socialist Review* 15 (1914): 232–35.

Schriber, Mary Suzanne. *Gender and the Writer's Imagination.* Lexington: UP of Kentucky, 1987.

Sensibar, Judith. "Edith Wharton Reads the Bachelor Type: Her Critique of Modernism's Representative Man." *American Literature* 60.4 (December 1988): 575–90.

Sharpe, Patricia. "Twilight Sleep and the Dream of Female Modernism." Unpublished paper.

Shell, Marc. *Children of the Earth: Literature, Politics and Nationhood.* New York: Oxford UP, 1993.

Shields, Stephanie. "Functionalism, Darwinism, and the Psychology of Women: A Study in Social Myth." *American Psychologist* (July 1975): 739–54.

Showalter, Elaine. "The Death of the Lady (Novelist): Wharton's *House of Mirth.*" *Representations* 9 (Winter 1985): 133–49.

Singer, Linda. "Bodies—Pleasures—Powers." *Differences* 1.1 (Winter 1989): 45–65.

Sklar, Robert. Introduction to *The Plastic Age, 1917–1930,* 1–24. New York: George Braziller, 1970.

Sloan, Kay. *The Loud Silents.* Urbana: U of Illinois P, 1988.

Smith, Paul. *Clint Eastwood.* Minneapolis: U of Minnesota P, 1993.

Smith-Rosenberg, Carroll. *Disorderly Conduct.* New York: Oxford UP, 1985.

Smith-Rosenberg, Carroll. "Writing History." In *Feminist Studies/Critical Studies,* edited by Teresa de Lauretis, 31–54. Bloomington: Indiana UP, 1986.

Snyder, Carl. *The World Machine.* New York: Longmans, 1907.

Stallybrass, Peter, and Allon White. *The Politics and Poetics of Transgression.* Ithaca: Cornell UP, 1986.

Stepan, Nancy Leys, and Sander Gilman. "Appropriating the Idioms of Science: The Rejection of Scientific Racism." In *The Bounds of Race,* edited by Dominick LaCapra, 72–103. Ithaca: Cornell UP, 1991.

Suleiman, Susan. "Writing and Motherhood." In *The (M)Other Tongue,* edited by Shirley Nelson Garner, Claire Kahane, and Madelon Sprengnether, 352–77. Ithaca: Cornell UP, 1985.

Sundquist, Eric. *Home as Found: Authority and Genealogy in Nineteenth-Century American Literature.* Baltimore: Johns Hopkins UP, 1979.

Sweeney, Susan Elizabeth. "Edith Wharton's Case of *Roman* Fever." In *Wretched Exotic: Essays on Edith Wharton in Europe,* edited by Katherine Joslin and Alan Price, 313–31. New York: Peter Lang, 1993.

Taylor, Frederick Winslow. *The Principles of Scientific Management.* New York: Norton, 1967 [1911].

Tintner, Adeline. "Consuelo Vanderbilt and *The Buccaneers.*" *Edith Wharton Review* 10.2 (Fall 1993): 15–19.

Tompkins, Jane. *Sensational Designs.* Oxford UP, 1985.

Torgovnick, Marianna. *Gone Primitive: Savage Intellects, Modern Lives.* Chicago: U of Chicago P, 1990.

Tracy, Marguerite, and Constance Leupp. "Painless Childbirth." *McClure's Magazine* 43.2 (June 1914): 37–51.

Tracy, Marguerite, and Mary Boyd. "More about Painless Childbirth." *McClure's Magazine* 43.2 (October 1914): 56–69.

Trumpener, Katie, and James M. Nyce. "The Recovered Fragments: Archeological and Anthropological Perspectives in Edith Wharton's *The Age of Innocence.*" In *Literary Anthropology,* edited by Fernando Poyatos, 161–69. Amsterdam: John Benjamins, 1988.

Tuttleton, James. "The Feminist Takeover of Edith Wharton." *The New Criterion* 7.7 (March 1989): 6–14.

Tuttleton, James. "Mocking Fate: Romantic Idealism in Edith Wharton's *The Reef.*" In *The Magic Circle of Henry James,* edited by Amritjit Singh and K. Ayyappa Paniker, 294–312. New York: Envoy Press, 1989.

Tuttleton, James W., Kristin O. Lauer, and Margaret P. Murray. *Edith Wharton: The Contemporary Reviews.* New York: Cambridge UP, 1992.

Tyler, William R. "Personal Memories of Edith Wharton." *Proceedings of the Massachusetts Historical Society* 85 (1973): 91–104.

Van Vechten, Carl. "A Lady Who Defies Time." *The Nation* 116.3006 (14 February 1923): 195–96.

Van Vechten, Carl. *Nigger Heaven.* New York: Grosset and Dunlap, 1926.

Vita-Finzi, Penelope. *Edith Wharton and the Art of Fiction.* New York: St. Martin's, 1990.

Waid, Candace. *Edith Wharton's Letters from the Underworld.* Chapel Hill: U of North Carolina P, 1991.

Walker, Nancy. "Mothers and Lovers: Edith Wharton's *The Reef* and *The Mother's Recompense.*" In *The Anna Book: Searching for Anna in Literary History,* edited by Mickey Pearlman, 91–97. Westport, CT: Greenwood Press, 1992.

Warren, Kenneth W. *Black and White Strangers: Race and American Literary Realism.* Chicago: U of Chicago P, 1993.

Weeks, Howard B. "Billy Sunday, the Promotor." *Public Relations Journal* 21 (September 1965): 28–32.

Wershoven, Carol. *The Female Intruder in the Novels of Edith Wharton.* New Brunswick: Associated UP, 1982.

Wertz, Richard W., and Dorothy C. Wertz. *Lying In.* New York: The Free Press, 1977.

Wharton, Edith. *The Age of Innocence.* New York: Scribner's, 1970 [1920].

Wharton, Edith. *A Backward Glance.* New York: Scribner's, 1964 [1933].

Wharton, Edith. *The Buccaneers.* New York: D. Appleton-Century Company, 1938.

Wharton, Edith. *The Children.* New York: Appleton, 1928.

Wharton, Edith. *The Custom of the Country.* New York: Penguin, 1984 [1913].

Wharton, Edith. *French Ways and Their Meaning.* New York: Appleton, 1919.

Wharton, Edith. *The Glimpses of the Moon.* New York: Appleton, 1922.

Wharton, Edith. *The Gods Arrive.* New York: Appleton, 1932.

Wharton, Edith. *The House of Mirth.* New York: Berkley, 1981 [1905].

Wharton, Edith. *Hudson River Bracketed.* New York: Scribner's, 1929.

Wharton, Edith. Manuscript and letter collection, Yale Collection of American Literature, Beinecke Rare Book and Manuscript Library, Yale University.

Wharton, Edith. Manuscript and letter collection, Lilly Library, Indiana University, Bloomington, IN.

Wharton, Edith. *The Marne.* New York: D. Appleton, 1918.

Wharton, Edith. *The Mother's Recompense.* New York: Scribner's, 1925.

Wharton, Edith. *The Old Maid.* New York: Berkley, 1981 [1924].

Wharton, Edith. *The Reef.* New York: Scribner's, 1912.

Wharton, Edith. *Roman Fever and Other Stories.* New York: Scribner's, 1964.

Wharton, Edith. *A Son at the Front.* New York: Scribner's, 1923.

Wharton, Edith. *Summer.* New York: Perennial Library, 1980 [1917].

Wharton, Edith. *Twilight Sleep.* New York: D. Appleton and Company, 1927.

White, Barbara. "Neglected Areas: Wharton's Short Stories and Incest." *Edith Wharton Review* (Spring 1991): 3–12.

Williams, Henry Smith. *Twilight Sleep.* New York: Harper, 1914.

Wilson, Edmund. "The All-Star Literary Vaudeville." Reprinted in *The Culture of the Twenties,* edited by Loren Baritz, 310–27. New York: Bobbs-Merrill, 1970.

Wilson, Edmund. "Review of *Twilight Sleep.*" *The New Republic* 51 (8 June 1927): 78.

Wolff, Cynthia Griffin. *A Feast of Words.* New York: Oxford UP, 1977.

Wolff, Cynthia Griffin. Introduction to *Summer,* by Edith Wharton, v–xxvii. New York: Perennial, 1979.

Zilversmit, Annette. "Edith Wharton, Jews, and Capitalism." Paper presented at the annual meeting of the Modern Language Association, Special Session on Female Perception of the Capitalist Hero in American Society, Chicago 1985.

Index

Abortion: in *Summer*, 28–43 *passim*; portrayed in mass culture, 33, 195*n2*, 195*n3*, 195–96*n4*; and women's power, 33–34, 36–37; legality of, 41–42, 194*n2*; attitudes toward, 42, 127, 133, 134, 194–95*n2*; and the idealization of motherhood, 47; as potential cause of death, 49–50; in companionate marriage, 111, 133, 134, 136; condoned by the Ku Klux Klan, 133. *See also* Reproductive regulation

Adler, Alfred, 118

Abundance theory, 55, 56, 65–66. *See also* Christian Science

Adorno, Theodor, 6; his "Elements of Anti-Semitism," 162, 163

Advance men: Wharton's discomfort with, 113–14; defined, 128, 129. *See also* Sunday, Billy

Advertising: Wharton's attitude toward, xiii, 54, 111, 124, 126, 129–30; as antidote to Bolshevism, 66, 66–67; as threat to "inner life," 67; roots of, 113; and individual genius, 120–21, 124–26, 141; effect of, on Wharton's writing, 124; and the "religion of commodities," 129; and fascism, 130; mentioned, 6, 104, 132, 144

Age of Innocence, The: Pulitzer Prize for, xi, xiii; anthropology in, 11, 12, 173; critical discussion of, 13–14; and companionate marriage, 131, 133; social exclusion of immigrants in, 166, 167, 171–76; racial purity in, 171–73; Bohemianism in, 173–75; antimodernism in, 177; mentioned, 15, 64, 75, 77, 115, 121, 171, 179, 184, 186, 202*n10*

Allen, Elizabeth, 159

Ambivalence: in Wharton texts, xiv, xiv–xv, 36, 47, 49, 102, 104, 121, 136, 139, 166–67, 175, 183, 185; cultural sources

of, 3, 4–5, 9, 15–16, 25, 53, 62, 81, 119–20, 125, 178, 198*n1*; within Free Love movement, 25; Wharton's, toward propaganda novels, 59; defined, 81; as awareness of cultural contradictions, 82, 178; as Wharton's political position, 85; Wharton's, about race, 166–67; and cultural dialogics, 194*n3*; mentioned, 36

"Americanism, 100%", 28, 170

American Mercury, The, 127

Ammons, Elizabeth: on motherhood, xiv, 167–68, 170, 203*n14*; on *The Reef,* 26; on *Summer,* 34–35; on *The Mother's Recompense,* 80; on *Twilight Sleep* 101–2; on *The Buccaneers,* 186; mentioned, 4, 18, 19, 20, 74, 124, 198*n3*

—*Edith Wharton's Argument With America,* 4, 101–2

Anbinder, Tyler: on nativism, 201*n1*

Anderson, Sherwood, 193*n1*

Anthropology: of social customs, 11–12, 15, 173; degenerationalist, 16; popularity of, 171–73; Wharton's interest in, 178, 199*n8*; and pet love, 189. *See also* Boas, Franz; Lévi-Strauss, Claude; Malinowski, Bronislaw; Mead, Margaret; "Primitive"

Antimodernism: Wharton's attitude toward, xii, 4–5, 97, 143–44, 147, 177–78, 200*n3*; defined, 4; effect of, on Wharton's popularity, 5. *See also* Modernity

Anti-Semitism: and cultural fears, 60, 66, 67, 163; and "The Protocols of Zion," 67, 198*n6*; in Wharton's thinking, 111, 147, 150–52, 162–64; in Wharton texts, 147, 150, 198*n1*; mentioned, 52, 54, 145, 151, 152. *See also* Assimilation; Racialism

Armstrong, Nancy, 85

Aronson, Marc, xiii

Artistry. *See* Genius